I Remember
When MEMORIES OF BRITAIN

FROM THE FRANCIS FRITH COLLECTION

Dedication

This book has been compiled from a selection of the thousands of personal memories added by visitors to the Frith website and could not have happened without these contributions. We are very grateful to everyone who has taken the time to share their memories in this way. The combination of all these personal stories provides a wonderful insight into British life and this book is therefore dedicated to everyone who has taken the time to participate in the Frith Memories project.

Each memory is personal to the writer yet the pictures painted are part of a shared inheritance, reminders of a life that so many people still cherish in their memories. For others, these memories will provide an insight into a way of life that has now vanished.

In the current uncertain times it is comforting to find so many stories full of human warmth which bring back happy memories of 'the good old days'. We hope that everyone reading this book will find stories that amuse and fascinate whilst at the same time be reminded of why we feel affection for Britain and what makes us all British.

Francis Frith always expressed the wish that his photographs be made available to as wide an audience as possible and so it is particularly pleasing to me that by creating the Frith website we have been able to make this nationally important photographic record of Britain available to a worldwide audience. Now, by providing the Share Your Memories feature on the website we are delighted to offer an opportunity for members of the public to record their own stories and to see them published (both on the website and in this book), ensuring that they are shared and not lost or forgotten.

We hope that you too will be motivated to visit our website and add your own memories to this growing treasure trove – helping us to make it an even more comprehensive record of the changes that have taken place in Britain in the last 100 years and a resource that will be valued by generations to come.

John M Buck
Managing Director
The Francis Frith Collection

I Remember When

When MEMORIES OF BRITAIN

Compiled from personal memories contributed by visitors
to The Francis Frith Collection website.

Mablethorpe, Lincolnshire, Donkey Rides c1955 M1053p

Folkestone, Kent, Cockles and Whelks Stall c1965 F35154p

Filey, Yorkshire, Primrose Valley c1935 F23099p

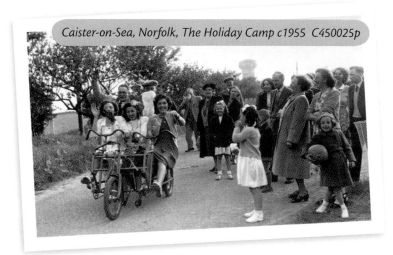
Caister-on-Sea, Norfolk, The Holiday Camp c1955 C450025p

Contents

FRANCIS FRITH, founder of the world-famous photographic archive, was a complex and multi-talented man. A devout Quaker and a highly successful Victorian businessman, he was philosophical by nature and pioneering in outlook.

By 1855 he had already established a wholesale grocery business in Liverpool, and sold it for the astonishing sum of £200,000, which is the equivalent today of over £15,000,000. Now a very rich man, he was able to indulge his passion for travel. As a child he had pored over travel books written by early explorers, and his fancy and imagination had been stirred by family holidays to the sublime mountain regions of Wales and Scotland. 'What lands of spirit-stirring and enriching scenes and places!' he had written. He was to return to these scenes of grandeur in later years to 'recapture the thousands of vivid and tender memories', but with a different purpose. Now in his thirties, and captivated by the new science of photography, Frith set out on a series of pioneering journeys up the Nile and to the Near East that occupied him from 1856 until 1860.

INTRIGUE AND EXPLORATION

These far-flung journeys were packed with intrigue and adventure. In his life story, written when he was sixty-three, Frith tells of being held captive by bandits, and of fighting 'an awful midnight battle to the very point of surrender with a deadly pack of hungry, wild dogs'. Wearing flowing Arab costume, Frith arrived at Akaba by camel sixty years before Lawrence of Arabia, where he encountered 'desert princes and rival sheikhs, blazing with jewel-hilted swords'.

He was the first photographer to venture beyond the sixth cataract of the Nile. Africa was still the mysterious 'Dark Continent', and Stanley and Livingstone's historic meeting was a decade into the future. The conditions for picture taking confound belief. He laboured for hours in his wicker dark-room in the sweltering heat of the desert, while the volatile chemicals fizzed dangerously in their trays. Back in London he exhibited his photographs and was 'rapturously cheered' by members of the Royal Society. His reputation as a photographer was made overnight.

THE RISE OF FRITH & CO

Characteristically, Frith quickly spotted the opportunity to create a new business as a specialist publisher of photographs. He lived in an era of immense and sometimes violent change. For the poor in the early part of Victoria's reign work was exhausting and the hours long, and people had precious little free time to enjoy themselves. Most had no transport other than a cart or gig at their disposal, and rarely travelled far beyond the boundaries of their own town or village. However, by the 1870s the railways had threaded their way across the country, and Bank Holidays and half-day Saturdays had been made obligatory by Act of Parliament. All of a sudden the working man and his family were able to enjoy days out and see a little more of the world.

With typical business acumen, Francis Frith foresaw that these new tourists would enjoy having souvenirs to commemorate their days out. Frith's studio was soon supplying retail shops all over the country. To meet the demand he gathered together a team of photographers, and published the work of independent artist-photographers of the calibre of Roger Fenton and Francis Bedford.

In order to gain some understanding of the scale of Frith's business one only has to look at the catalogue issued by Frith & Co in 1886: it runs to some 670 pages, listing not only many thousands of views of the British Isles but also many photographs of most European countries, and China, Japan, the USA and Canada. By 1890 Frith had created the greatest specialist photographic publishing company in the world, with over 2,000 sales outlets.

POSTCARD BONANZA

The ever-popular holiday postcard we know today took many years to develop. The Post Office issued the first plain cards in 1870, with a pre-printed stamp on one face. In 1894 they allowed other publishers' cards to be sent through the mail with an attached adhesive halfpenny stamp. Demand grew rapidly, and in 1895 a new size of postcard was permitted called the court card, but there was little room for illustration. In 1899, a year after Frith's death, a new card measuring 5.5 x 3.5 inches became the standard format, but it was not until 1902 that the divided back came into being, so that the address and message could be on one face and a full-size illustration on the other. Frith & Co were in the vanguard of postcard development: Frith's sons Eustace and Cyril continued their father's monumental task, expanding the number of views offered to the public and recording more and more places in Britain.

Francis Frith had died in 1898 at his villa in Cannes, his great project still growing. The archive he created continued in business for another seventy years. By 1970 it contained over a third of a million pictures showing 7,000 British towns and villages.

FRANCIS FRITH'S LEGACY

Frith's legacy to us today is of immense significance and value, for the magnificent archive of evocative photographs he created provides a unique record of change in the cities, towns and villages throughout Britain over a century and more. Frith and his fellow studio photographers revisited locations many times down the years to update their views, compiling for us an enthralling and colourful pageant of British life and character.

We are fortunate that Frith was dedicated to recording the minutiae of everyday life, for it is this sheer wealth of visual data, the painstaking chronicle of changes in dress, transport, street layouts, buildings, housing and landscape that captivates us so much today. His images offer us a powerful link with the past and with the lives of our ancestors.

THE VALUE OF THE ARCHIVE TODAY

Historians consider The Francis Frith Collection to be of prime national importance. It is the only archive of its kind remaining in private ownership. The archive's future is both bright and exciting.

Francis Frith, with his unshakeable belief in making photographs available to the greatest number of people, would undoubtedly approve of the computer technology that allows his work to be rapidly transmitted to people all over the world by way of the internet. His photographs depicting our shared past are now bringing pleasure and enlightenment to millions around the world a century and more after his death.

Goyt Valley, Derbyshire, Stepping Stones 1914 67587t

Introduction

Nostalgia is a powerful emotion. Its power is all the stronger today. On average we move house every five years, and most of us no longer experience the continuity of life within a single community that our grandparents enjoyed. As a result, our memories grow ever more remote, yet correspondingly more vital to us.

So nostalgia can affect us profoundly. We all know that suddenly hearing a line or two of a favourite song can evoke the past. Looking at old photographs can be an even more powerful springboard to recovering forgotten memories. Taking time to enjoy old photographs can help us keep our bearings in a rapidly-changing world by encouraging us to recall the places, buildings and people that were once vital parts of our lives and those of our parents and grandparents.

The Frith photo archive is a unique treasure house of memories. It is an exciting thought that every single one of its third of a million photographs is special to someone, for each depicts someone's house and someone's neighbourhood – a place intimately known, and rich in personal association and significance.

Looking at the Frith photographs in this book, mostly taken in the mid 20th century, inevitably makes us feel nostalgic. They seem to depict a slower, more innocent world than our own, one where there was always time to stand and stare. Yet we must remember that they record the details of daily life in times of war or great change. Life was not easy, rationing was a continuing reality of daily living, and 'make do and mend' was the watchword for every family. When the Frith photographer pressed the shutter on his camera he was not recording nostalgia but life as it was being lived. The people who look out at us from these old photographs conjure a poignant reality.

This book is unapologetically nostalgic. It's about looking back into the past and revisiting our memories. However, it has only been made possible because of cutting edge technology – it is paradoxical that we are now able to look back as a result of the internet. The Frith website (www.francisfrith.com) holds 120,000 photographs of the towns and villages of Britain in years gone by, and they can be seen by anyone from anywhere in the world at the touch of a button. It is only through modern computer technology that so many people can now see so many images from the archive. Indeed, how else could they write about their feelings about Frith photographs of their favourite places and share them with so many other people?

The 'Share Your Memories' feature of the Frith website began in a modest way. But now, two years on, it is a busy meeting place with people browsing the archive every day to revisit the many places where they have lived and worked during their lives. What's more, new photographs are being added all the time, so increasing numbers of Frith 'regulars' return time and again, revisiting more and more of the places in their lives, and sparking new memories to enjoy and share with their families and with the worldwide Frith Memories community. It is not surprising that the Frith website maintains its position as one of the top ten giftware sites in the United Kingdom. It offers visitors so much: it is a national treasure house of British life and character, a source of memories waiting to be tapped by every visitor.

At Frith we find it heartwarming and compelling to browse through the daily posts on the 'Share Your Memories' section of the website. Clearly we have created a very special place – albeit virtual! – where every one of us can recall the places, people and events in our lives and share our unique experiences with thousands of others.

Reading this book is a moving – and very often hilarious – experience. Many contributors may think their entries are humdrum and unremarkable, yet it is the minutiae of daily life that combine to make a complete picture of an already remote-seeming past.

There is nothing stuffy about this book. It is an irresistible and heady mix of stories and recollections that reveal an unwavering zest for life. Funny, warm, and sometimes tragic, they offer us a colourful panorama of life during the 1940s, 50s and 60s. We hope you will enjoy reading this book as much as we did compiling it. So dip in and enjoy this extraordinary anthology! We are sure that when you leaf through its pages you will jog memories of your own.

And then why not visit the Frith website yourself and add your own stories to this growing treasure house? You could well find yourself in print – we're hoping to make this book an annual publication. By contributing, you will be helping to build a vital national memory bank. The 'Share Your Memories' feature of the Frith website is fast becoming an institution, a rich and expanding record of daily life in Britain during the middle years of the 20th century and beyond. It is Britain's history told not by historians but by the people who were there at the time – making it.

Throwing the Milk Jug

I lived in a cottage by the pond some 20 odd years ago. My neighbour, well into her nineties, was Mac May (a version of her true name garbled by other neighbours' kids) who, every day, was out in her wellies digging in the garden. We had a copy of this photo and, knowing Mac May had lived in the cottage all her life, asked if she knew the children. She did, and she also remembered the photo being taken.

The boy and the girl in the middle are Mac May's elder brother and sister; the little girl is Mac May herself, and her brother has just thrown the milk jug at her (the small white object in the middle foreground).

James Moodie

Ashtead, Surrey, The Fish Pond 1904 52587p

They'll come home when they're hungry

MEMORIES OF CHILDHOOD

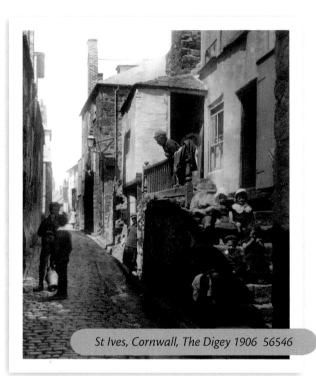

St Ives, Cornwall, The Digey 1906 56546

Ready for a Fight!

The young man on the outside of the pavement is me. The two on my right are demanding to know where I am going – as it happened I was going to see my gran.

I did not know who the kids were, and still don't, but if you look at the picture my fists are clenched. I was ready for a fight, but they backed off. I still walk with clenched fists to this day!

If you took a picture in the same place today it would look very much the same.

David Bailey

> ❝ If you look at the picture my fists are clenched.
> I was ready for a fight ❞

Biddulph, Staffordshire, Children c1955 B611015x

Sea Pinks for the Seabirds

St Ives born and bred, my family had lived in a couple of houses upalong before moving to 22 The Digey (the middle door) sometime in 1967 … I remember the 'Torrey Canyon' disaster: my brother was on the news because he was playing on the beach while they were filming it, but we all missed it on the telly, of course. A gang of us Digey children picked hundreds of sea pinks and sold them in the Meadow Square to raise money for the disaster fund, and I remember crying over dead and dying seabirds that we couldn't help.

Carolyn Abbott

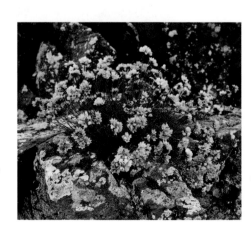

Biddulph, Staffordshire, High Street c1965 B611057

A North Devon Fishing Village

I have a copy of this Meeting Street photo, because the girl standing in the road (with the black sleeve) is my grandmother Sarah Powe (née Lesley). The family house was at 29 Meeting Street just out of view. Grandmother also ran the Bell Inn in Appledore for a number of years, and on retirement moved back into Number 29. Sarah and Grandad Bill Powe had two daughters, Louise, my mother, and Ruby.

Sarah passed away in 1977. Ruby now lives in Bideford, and I often visit and then take a trip to Appledore, where some memories return. I remember the three docks, the quay, Hockings ice-cream, and the ships, in particular the 'Kathleen and May' and the 'Irene'. I also remember a tug-boat, the 'Roma', which would often moor up off the Bell slipway by the lower dock.

The man on the footpath to the right of my grandmother was the local postman, and the pub at the bottom of the hill is Ye Champion of Wales, with the Seagate Hotel on the opposite side. The Bell Inn is no longer a pub, but has been converted to apartments.

Michael Ewings

Appledore, Devon, Meeting Street 1906 55968p

Appledore, Devon, The Quay 1923 75145

The schooner 'Kathleen and May' arriving at Bideford, three miles up the River Torridge from Appledore

Out All Day

It is strange now to remember that we used to take ourselves to school and go out all day without our parents getting in a panic. 'They'll come home when they're hungry' was a sure thing then.

Peter Butterwort

Salcombe, Devon, the Quayside 1896 38483

Lerryn, Cornwall, The Bridge 1893 32568

Playing in Salford's Streets

I was born and bred in Newall Street in Salford in 1960. It was a small street just off Eccles New Road near to Cross Lane. I often sit and remember the tight, cobbled streets where we played Rallyheaveho, football and Kick Ball Hide. All the kids, all the time, we just loved playing Robbers Knock, a game that would get us a clip round the lughole if we were caught! 'The Purse Trick' was our favourite. An old purse would have cotton tied round the clasp and be placed outside the door of the corner shop at night. We would hide and be in stitches as people bent down to pick it up only to have it tugged away when they were within an inch of grabbing it! Some of the embarrassed faces we saw were priceless.

The rag and bone man, the coalman and even the ice cream man – we never see them any more. Kids played out on bikes, scooters and pogo sticks and even shared roller skates with somebody else, flippin' one each.

We would run to the shop for a neighbour, knowing the prize was a dip in the penny tray for going – we'd get Mojos, Black Jacks and Fruit Salad chews. We collected Bazooka Joe comics and sent off for a torch.

Wilf Veevers

Can You Believe Your Eyes?

This view (above) shows Customs Quay, just out of sight on the right is the Customs House. Mrs Florrie Gasson and her husband lived there, and she would make a great show to the visitors of feeding the swans. A flock of 20 or so would swim in the water looking for her, and she called each one by a different name.

I can remember sitting here with my friend Michael Hodder when film makers arrived to shoot a washing powder commercial. I never saw the finished ad, but a friend told me that the happy family descended the steps to the foreground of the photo to soft golden sand! Such artistic licence! In reality, it was more like shingle and mud. And the film crew used large silver discs to reflect the sun on to the towels to make them appear snowy white. I have never trusted commercial advertising since.

William Lapthorn

 The film crew used large silver discs to reflect the sun on to the towels to make them appear snowy white.

Daventry, Northamptonshire, The Recreation Ground c1965   D83085

Our Favourite Old Chuffer

I remember the day that this engine arrived in the rec. It was a source of great entertainment for us, as originally every part of it was accessible. I remember climbing up on the footplate and seeing a little lad emerging from the firebox. It was rumoured that it was possible to get into the boiler and exit up the funnel, but I never saw it done! It was great for playing hide and seek – I found one hiding place that no-one ever found. Sadly, even back then, steel plates were soon welded over the more interesting points of access, but it remained a popular attraction on every visit to the rec. Notice the railings around the roof? They are more recent. One proof of male bravado amongst the 9 to 12 year olds was to jump off the roof onto the grass below. Can you imagine that happening nowadays?
Dave Cairns

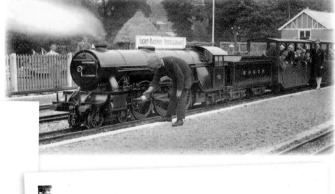

The Hiding Place

When I was ten years old this old tree was a delight. It was ancient and hollow inside, so we children were able to crawl inside while Mother did her shopping. We watched people pass on their way to and from the blacksmith, the grocer or the butcher, firmly believing that they had no idea we were there. If we were lucky we would be given an ice lolly or a sweet to eat in the tree. It was often thought by visitors that it was an oak because of the eponymous pub in the Square. It was, I think, an elm. Now the tree is long gone, replaced by something small but with nice seats around on a paved area where villagers can rest in the shade.

Maggi Stamp-Loshak

Yattendon, Berkshire, The Royal Oak c1965   Y32026

Yattendon, Berkshire, The Old Elm Tree c1965   Y32003

Back to Windsor

I've been here, on this very spot, with the precious women of my life – my Mom when I was a child, and with my children when they were women. How can it be that it looks exactly the same in 1890, 1971 and 2001? I can feel the cool brick under my hand, and see the flowers over the edge. I wanted to jump down and walk there when I was a child and later with my girls. How can it be that the air and the sky is the same? When I want to remember, to feel, to grieve, to rejoice – I go back – back to where memories and feelings are connected – back to Windsor.

Kelly Mitchell

Hopwas, Staffordshire, The Canal c1965 H413002

Windsor, Berkshire, The Norman Tower c1890 W111504

A Canal Childhood

Watford, Hertfordshire, The Canal 1921 70492t

This photograph (above) shows me and my brother David fishing from the bottom of the garden of 4 Nursery Lane. I was born in 1955 in Tamworth and we moved to Hopwas in April 1961 when I was just 6 years old and my brother 5 years old.

Our bungalow was built in part of the house next door's garden, which was owned by Len Harper. Mum was disabled and Dad, Leonard Jones, bought the land from the Harpers and had the shell of a bungalow built as Mum couldn't manage the stairs in our house in Tamworth. His brothers Bob and Peter Jones and brothers-in-law Harry Harper and George Collins were responsible for the plumbing and the electrics. My aunt and uncle, Myra and Harry Harper, lived at the end of the drive in 10 Nursery Lane, and tracks were worn with the comings and goings between the two bungalows.

Many an afternoon was spent at the bottom of the garden fishing or watching the boats going along the canal. Christmas was particularly exciting as the boats met up at Fradley to celebrate Christmas, and the boats would be decorated with a Christmas tree and fairy lights. I seem to remember that Father Christmas used to arrive by narrow boat and had a little present for

every one of us. In many ways our childhood in Hopwas was idyllic, with wonderful walks in the woods or up Hints Lane to see the flamingos in the pond at Molly Badham's bungalow at the top of the lane.

Thomas Barnes Primary School was a small village school with just two classes. My brother started off in the infant class ruled by Miss Podmore, who always wore her hair up on top of her head. I started off in the junior class taught by the Headteacher, Mr Hawkins, who once played football for Bristol Rovers. The day started off with ten mental maths questions on the blackboard, and our science lessons often led to a walk along the towpath to Hopwas Woods. The toilets were outdoors in single brick building that were very cold in the winter. They have given me a life-long fear of daddy-long-legs, which seemed to frequent every dark nook.

Ann Meade

Three Kings Piece

I don't know why we called it Three Kings Piece, but in the mid 50s to the early 60s when I was growing up, that was what it was known as. I lived in the flats in Armfield Crescent, and when we went to Three Kings Piece we went the back way, down St Mark's Road to Baker Lane (on the corner was St Mark's Church), and on to Hilary Avenue. At the end of the avenue was an alleyway. It had a high wall on one side with broken glass embedded on the top and the blank sides of houses on the other. I don't know what was on the other side of this long wall, as there was broken glass on the top of the wall. At the end of the alleyway was Commonside East and the Three Kings Inn.

Mitcham, Greater London, The Pond and Three Kings 1959

Over the road, opposite the inn was Three Kings Piece with its pond and island. I don't think it was very deep, maybe a foot or two, with a lot of gooey mud on the bottom. It's been there for at least 300 years, according to local history. I used to go to the pond at different times of the year – something was always happening there. In autumn it was at its most colourful with the trees on the island at the end of the pond changing its mantle and colours. The swans that lived on the pond usually disappeared around this time. We would use our home-made nets of long thin bamboo sticks with one of Mum's old stockings threaded through a loop of wire stuck in the end of the bamboo. We would try to catch tiddlers. If we caught any we would take them home in a jam jar that had a string tied around the ribbed top and looped over the jar to form a handle. It was very rare that we did. We had more success in the spring, when we mostly caught frogspawn. We would take the frogspawn home, so we could watch it hatch into tadpoles. When it got to the stage of the tadpoles growing legs, we would be told in no uncertain terms to take them back to the pond where they would turn into frogs.

Winter came, and we would go down to see if the pond would freeze over. More times than not it only had little bits of thin ice floating on the top, but a few times it froze over completely. Then we would hope that it would get thick enough for us to walk on to get to the island. This never seemed to happen, so I never got to see what was on it.

In spring we went to the pond with our stale bread. We knew that the swans had their nests there, as in the spring we would see the cygnets following their parents about on the island and swimming on the pond. We enjoyed breaking up the bread into small pieces to feed the swans. Now and again we would pop a piece into our own mouths. The swan population never seemed to increase, even though they had young ones every year, so I assumed that the young ones must have gone off to other areas in the autumn when they were bigger.

Carole Baldwin

Enfield, Middlesex, Hilly Fields c1955   E179015

Something Quite Magical

Situated at the top of our road, Hilly Fields was quite magical to us as young children. In winter we would trek our home-made sledges over to the toboggan hill and hurtle down to the brook at the bottom of the hill at breakneck speeds. Summertime meant climbing trees, and fishing for sticklebacks in the brook. We played the game known to us as 'jumping dogs' which

entailed jumping over the brook without getting your feet wet, but often falling in and getting soaked. There was a park keeper's hut next to the putting green where you could play 18 holes for 3d, followed by an ice lolly for 1d from Gaylers, the shop attached to the Rose and Crown. On glorious long summer evenings we would play over at Hilly Fields until it was too dark to see. There was never anything to be afraid of in those days. When the grass cutter mowed the huge expanses of grass, we would collect huge piles of grass and dive headlong into them. Autumn meant conkers and throwing sticks up into the branches to dislodge the waiting conkers, and piles of gold and brown leaves piled up to play in. Spring meant catkins and sticky buds. And I remember the walk up to Fourteen Arches and shouting under the arches to hear the echoes, the steam trains that went over the arches between Gordon Hill and Crewes Hill stations, and the bandstand where in summer we could enter talent competitions.

Roger Davis

Bonfire Night Bangers

Guy Fawkes Night at Whixley in Yorkshire could be quite hazardous. Although I don't remember anyone ever being seriously hurt, it was certainly a close run thing.

Keith Bradley, although not from farming parents, had many relations who were involved in farming, and so he had ready access to certain farming apparatus like binder twine. One particular Bonfire Night in the late 50s or early 60s he had got hold of a long string of small explosive charges used for bird scaring. These were nothing more than a large number of bangers joined by varying lengths of fuse so as to make the bangs occur at irregular intervals once the fuse was lit. These turned out to be very disappointing – the fuses were far too long to be used as bangers, and the final bang was not very loud – so in disgust he throw the whole string, 30 or more charges, on the fire.

But a small bang multiplied 30 times is quite impressive, especially if it's in the middle of a bonfire, making ash, cinder and assorted burning rubbish fly everywhere! Fortunately for him and for us no one was hurt, and no one had seen who had thrown what on the fire.

When a little older I had the job of lighting the fire. At that time my best friend was Brian Carling, whose father owned the local garage. It had been a wet day, and so Brian suggested he get a little something to make the fire start easily – a half-gallon tin of waste sump oil, diesel and petrol mixed. To my credit I knew enough to stand well clear and throw a match from a great distance. It worked wonderfully. Unfortunately Brian didn't want his tin back, so not knowing what to do with it I threw it on the now roaring fire. As luck would have it I hadn't put the top back on, so the exploding vapour and dregs left in the can caused a sheet of flame to shoot ten or more feet upwards, neatly separating myself and Brian. I still shudder to think what would have happened if the can had been sealed. We would also experiment with bangers, then readily available. We made guns by sealing the banger in a copper tube before lighting it, or we dropped a lighted one into a milk bottle. It's a wonder any of us are still alive to tell the tale.   Nigel Ward

Girly Giggles at the Town Paddling Pool

This picture reminds me of my dear childhood friend, Peta Fenner. Peta celebrates her 50th birthday soon and it is quite possible that both she and I are in the photo. We spent many days of our summer holidays playing in the paddling pool. The big pool was always cold and swamped with older children and we would have to build up our courage to venture there. Our childhood was filled with laughter. We giggled at anything and everything, from peering through the holes in the wood partitions separating the cubicles at the end of the pool to laughing at how courting teenagers behaved. We once dared each other to wear our swimming hats through the town on our homeward journey from the park. Not a good idea, as we both had long hair, and removing the rubber hats later was very painful – but oh, so hilarious.

> ❝ We spent many days of our summer holidays playing in the paddling pool ❞

Warminster, Wiltshire, Lake Pleasure Ground c1965　W261062p

Even now all these years later I think of Peta when I walk down Weymouth Street, and I can still hear the noise coming through the hedge where the pool used to be. The pool has been turned into a sunken garden and is a delightful place to have a picnic, surrounded by plants and waterfalls, and so peaceful until you let your memories reappear. The paddling pool has been revamped and is surrounded by rubber matting, and there is a huge blue dolphin that fills the pool.

Children of my generation would queue up to sit astride the water jet that used to trickle into the pool. The bottom of the pool was concrete and worn in places, so slipping over was all too easy to do, and many bottoms got bruised sliding on the slabs surrounding the pool. One of our friends even fell from the top of the slide on to the concrete. Thankfully she escaped with just a broken arm. The park had a resident keeper and many full-time staff back then. Flower borders were planted up twice or three times a year. On either side of the lake there were borders all beautifully kept. Not any more. Most have been grassed over, which is a great shame.

Christine Mabbett

Warminster, Wiltshire, The Pleasure Ground c1950　W261004

Saffron Walden, Essex, The Hospital 1912 65094

A Village Church in the 1960s

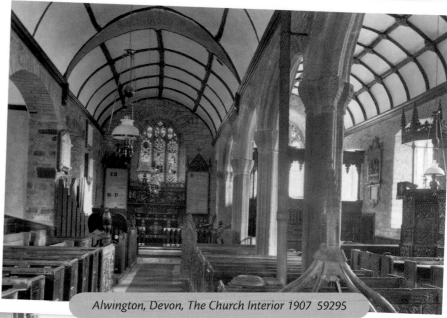
Alwington, Devon, The Church Interior 1907 59295

A Patient's View

When I was eight I was admitted to Saffron Walden General Hospital for surgery. My parents were told that I would be discharged home at the end of the week. I vividly remember the feeling that I was suffocating when the pad of chloroform was put over my face to anaesthetise me.

But during the week a young girl was admitted to the ward with suspected polio. She was encased in a glass cubicle, and the next day she was transferred to the isolation hospital. It was decided that all the children in the ward should be put into quarantine for three weeks, so my week turned into four. Visiting hours were restricted to a short time in the afternoon on Tuesdays, Thursdays and at the weekends, as it was considered unsettling for children to see their parents more frequently. The weeks seemed very long. However, it obviously didn't affect me too adversely, as ten years later I trained to be a SRN (State Registered Nurse).

Helen Sharpe

As children we used to walk from Fairy Cross to Alwington. We would wind our way through the narrow lane, sometimes picking wild strawberries in summer, until we arrived at St Andrew's Church. We always sat up in the choir stalls with Mrs Elston, who was my first teacher at Abbotsham school. I remember that at special services, at Christmas for example, some children would read from the Bible to the congregation. When I did this I was always very nervous, and once I lost my place and it seemed like ages before I found it again. Old Colonel and Mrs Pine-Coffin were always in the Portledge pew, and when the sermon went on a bit too long I think the old Colonel used to doze off – he certainly had his eyes closed regularly!

On Sundays the children stayed for half of the service and then we filed out of the church to the old schoolrooms next to the church for Sunday School. In winter the schoolrooms were freezing, and a few times we stayed in the church and had Sunday School in the old minstrels' gallery that came originally from Portledge House. After Sunday School we walked home again, ready for our Sunday roast dinner, which we always looked forward to. This was just a normal way of life for us then. Looking back, I think we were very lucky to have experienced childhood this way – no computers, no fast food and only limited television, but we were healthy, we entertained ourselves, and we were very happy with simple things.

Derek England

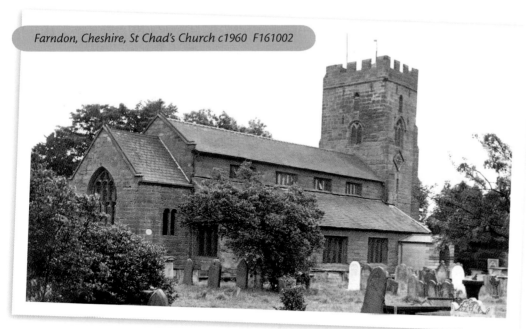

Farndon, Cheshire, St Chad's Church c1960 F161002

Where's the Sea?

I always remember going here with my Mum, my Aunt Edith and my cousin Dick when I was a little girl. Mum would say: 'We are going to Burnham Beeches today'. I could never quite understand when we got there why there was no sand and sea … and I realise now that 'Beeches' meant 'trees' … and not the seaside!
Lorna Lewis

Burnham, Buckinghamshire, Burnham Beeches 1929 81697

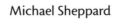

❝ I could never quite understand … why there was no sand or sea ! ❞

Churchyard Terrors

This is the church (left) where my 17-year-old son was christened. It is also the place where I spent most of my childhood. From about the age of 10, my friends and I went grave rubbing. We actually spent more time cleaning the old graves with an old twig and reading about who was in there. As we got older, around the age of 13, we would go into the graveyard for a sneaky puff of our cigarettes, and hide any spare ones we had in the big old tree at the entrance of the church.

Around the same time, I did the paper round for Mr Jones near the church and the estate where I lived. I did that same round until I was 17, and I was in full-time work then too. My wage was £3.90 in 1986 – that was for 7 days delivering ruddy heavy newspapers.

Anyway, in the winter it was always pitch dark around the church area. I had one paper for the vicar and one for the major who lived over the road. Both houses were directly outside the church gates. I used to be scared to death every morning, and I really mean that. I would run as fast as I could, which was always hard with a sack full of papers. My other option was to leave the bag at the gate, run up the path as quickly as I could, then run straight over to the major's and go back and get my bag. To me this was always too much hassle, so I just ran with my bag knocking against my leg and digging into my shoulder. Goodness knows what I was scared of, but I nearly wet my knickers nearly every morning.
Tracey Nevitt

Ritual Initiation

Seeing this photograph of the font in St Mary's brought back memories of my time as a choirboy there, a tradition in our family. Our choirmaster Mr Sellers taught at Geneva School, and was known as 'Jumbo' because of his large ears!

New boys (including me) were initiated into the choir with a ritual in which you had to run around the outside of the church, were hit on the head with bell rope, and finally thrown into the holly bush. It sounds cruel, but it was done and taken in good humour by all, and I enjoyed my time in the choir immensely.
Michael Sheppard

Bideford, Devon, St Mary's Church Font 1906 55945

Newby Bridge, Cumbria, The Swan Hotel 1914 67414p

Boating

The children in the boat are Leslie (the little boy), Harry (his brother), and Noel (his sister) Wren. His other sister Millie Wren is sitting on the riverbank. The other child is a neighbour. For many years Millie Wren was a teacher at Lightburn School, Ulverston.

Jean Wren

Moving Up in the World

In 1947 my parents, my sister aged 4 and myself aged 10 moved from two rooms in a shared house in Pricetown to a run-down three-storey house in Llewellyn Street, Nantymoel. Llewellyn Street is the third row of houses in the foreground of the picture (top right). It had three bedrooms on the top floor, two living rooms and a pantry on the middle floor which was accessed by the front door from street level. Below ground under the pavement was a coal cellar and another pantry which opened onto a further unusable living room with a back door to the garden.

Immediately outside the back door was a toilet, a wooden bench 2ft 6ins wide with a hole. It emptied into a sewer but had no flush – you just emptied a bucket of water down after it was used. The only water tap in the house was a standpipe just inside the back door, so at least you didn't have far to carry the heavy bucket. A zinc bath hung on the outside wall. It was carried up to the first floor every Friday evening – and then began the filling of it. The hot water was supplied from the reservoir at the side of the fire. Cold water was carried up via ladder-type stairs. After my mother, my sister and I had had our bath (Dad bathed at the colliery) the water was carried out one bucketful at a time and thrown down the gutter drain outside the front door.

Yet we thought we were in heaven because we had the whole house to ourselves. The front and back doors had latches and no locks, so the only time the house was secured was at night when you shot the bolts before going to bed.

Margaret Davies

Nantymoel, Mid Glamorgan c1955 N121014

Ynyshir, Mid Glamorgan, The Pit c1965 Y33001a

Loughton, Essex, High Road 1948 L106006

Saturday Morning Pictures

I went to Saturday morning pictures in Loughton every week. We were members of a club with a badge that said 'Grenadier' as it was a Grenada cinema, though the actual building said Century above it.

There was a confectionery shop next door that sold packets of fake cigarettes – they were hollow tubes with foil at one end to look like glowing ash. We filled them with talcum powder and blew it over the kids in front of us. The seats must have been very dusty!

At Christmas we had a competition to make the best decoration. I won it one year, but for some reason they thought I was a boy and my prize was a kit to make a toy tank!

I don't really remember any films – it was a social event as much as anything else. But there was always a serial; I never quite worked out that if the hero died there wouldn't be anything on next week – was I daft, or what?

Susan Capes

‘ We filled them with talcum powder and blew it over the kids in front of us ’

Artists at the Feathers

Groups of artists used to visit Ludlow in summer and stay at the Feathers Hotel. After breakfast they chose their locations, some at the church, some at the castle, while others went to the middle of Broad Street. They would set up their stools and easels and stay there all day. There was very little traffic in 1955.

One afternoon, I was invited to join them and I drew the mud and wattle buildings with charcoal. At the age of 13, it was a great honour to be included in this wonderful group of people.

Those were great days. I lived at the Feathers Hotel where my parents were managers for a couple of years. My best friend at school was Judith Hollings who said her sister was learning Swahili! I had never heard of such a language. But at 18, I was hired by a family to be nanny to their two children in Tanganyika, East Africa and I learned Swahili within six months!

Charlotte Gatling

Ludlow, Shropshire, Broad Street c1955 L111040

Lemonade Pop at Nine Springs

I played at Nine Springs with my two brothers every Sunday. We always stopped at the old cottage where you could buy a glass of home-made lemonade for an old halfpenny, and if you had a penny sometimes two biscuits as well.

The old couple who lived there were very friendly and we would sit on their small veranda, and pet their old black dog, and listen to the noise of the springs as we chatted and had our rest break. I went inside the cottage to use their small bathroom, and it was very old with little steep stairs, and I used to find it a bit dark and scary.

Sadly the cottage was demolished many years later. I would often see the old couple and their dog wandering the streets of Yeovil town. I once went up to them and thanked them for the lovely memories they gave me, and their hospitality. Nine Springs was our 'back garden' and we had fun racing to see who could find all nine of the springs the fastest. In springtime we took frogspawn home, and would take great delight in watching the frogs hatch and grow. Then we returned them back to Nine Springs in big plastic buckets, and stopped at the cottage to tell the old couple.

Jacqui Morton

Yeovil, Somerset, Nine Springs 1912 64531a

Minehead, Somerset, Church Steps 1903 49646

Grandmother's Christening

My great-grandparents Thomas and Louisa Sparkes and their children moved from Minehead to Cardiff. Their youngest child Hilda, my grandmother, told stories to my mother. One of them was that she could remember running up Church Steps to her christening in 1900, when she would have been four years old.

Kay Baker

The cottage at the foot of Church Steps in Minehead (just out of sight) was our corner shop. On Saturday afternoon I would call in at the shop for a bar of chocolate, and post letters in the box set into the wall outside the shop. More often than not the chocolate I bought was either Cadbury's Turkish Delight or mint flavoured Aero, then a new innovation. And the 'letters' always included competition entries. I was a competition geek and entered many of the contests in magazines such as 'Girls Crystal', 'School Friend' and 'Girl'. Sometimes I even won!

Pam Gotham

Ipswich, Suffolk, The Docks 1893   32208t

A Deserved Dunking

This is a family story about a dunking. Once upon a time there was a naughty little boy (later to be known by me as Pop). He and his friends decided they fancied the Bibles and candles from the local church. They took them and decided to run for it, then the boy and his mates decided to finish the day by pushing out an old coal barge just for a laugh. But the powers above had him fall straight into the docks … followed by a good beating from the ladies in his neighbourhood once he returned home wet and cold. That would teach him to take something that wasn't his!
Tami Cross-Halls

Mini Fishing

We went fishing here with our mini bottles. We caught minnows with wine bottles with the bottom knocked out. I remember once being trapped under the arches of the bridge when the river was rising and being surrounded by cows that had come down from the field. They are very fond memories.
Michael Bailey

Shipston-on-Stour, Warwickshire, The Bridge c1960 S296023

Bagshot, Surrey, The Church 1906 57176

A Big Hedge to Clip

My dad, Eric Berry, used to clip this hedge – by hand.

When we are little, things always seem bigger than they really are, but my recollections of watching my dad clip this hedge on the days he did the gardening at St Anne's Church were pretty accurate. It really is as big as I remember.

I also went to St Anne's Hall with my mum to collect our ration books. At the bottom of the hill was Fortuna's Ice Cream Parlour – I can still remember the luscious creamy taste.
Liz Schultz

Sunderland, Tyne and Wear, Fawcett Street 1890 S263001

Lost in Binns

One day, when I was about five years old, Mother took me to Binns, which was a big store in Fawcett Street. While I was standing by one of the counters, lost in a daydream, Mother went to another counter a few feet away. I woke from my dream when the shop assistant leaned over and asked me what I wanted, and because I couldn't see Mother, I thought she had gone away and left me there. I rushed out into the street crying, and a small crowd collected around me. A lady asked me where I lived, and I was able to tell her. She gave me money for my tram fare, and I travelled home on the top deck, happily singing to myself, for I'd got over my fright. By the time I reached Seaburn, where I lived, I was happy again, and couldn't imagine why Mother was in tears.

Diana Dioszeghy

Clapham, Yorkshire, the Old Footbridge c1955   C109037p

Firm Friends

Of the two girls crossing the Brokken Bridge – one is certainly my friend who lived opposite, the other is perhaps myself. Our families moved, but we still go back to visit, and have recently met up again after 50 years!

Jean Potts

Tring, Hertfordshire, St Peter and St Paul's Church c1960   T81033

Grampy Rodwell and My Grandmother

My grandmother was born in Tring in the late 1800s and like many of her family was married in Tring church, on Christmas Day 1909. Her grandfather was a very peculiar character who had to be taken to the village pump for his weekly wash, and he used to sit on the wall to jeer at the churchgoers. He was known as Grampy Rodwell. Once a week free bread was given out, and he was always the first in the queue. He used to bag his loaf by poking the bread with his filthy hands. I loved hearing stories about him.

My grandmother was in service and worked for the Rothschilds as a cook. She was, apparently, the first woman in Tring to ride a bike. I have recently read 'Lark Rise to Candleford', and it takes me back to sitting round my Aunt Em's table and hearing her daughters call her 'Our Mum' and listening to them proudly chanting a childhood rhyme: 'Tring, Wing and Ivanhoe, saw three churches all in a row, take my shoes and stockings off, and jump over them.'

Christine Beddows

My Beloved Grandmother

I grew up in and around London as a young girl. When my parents divorced it was the hardest thing for me to get over. But I had the best nan in the world – and she lived in Six Acre Cottages at Fawkham. This house and the surrounding area was a haven for any child. She worked in the school and at the big house on the hill, and when I stayed with her we went to the big house to see Mrs Lemet. She was so friendly, and so were her children.

I remember walking down the path to the village in the summer and was enthralled at the wild life you could see there. It started just opposite the school and carried on to the village, where my nan took me to the shops to buy daily provisions – and of course sweets. My grandad had an old farm building at the bottom of the garden where he kept his old banger, and I played in the field behind that with my nan's dog Dukey-Boy when he wasn't knocking me over. He was a St Bernard – big in size and big in nature. My nan would nurse my knees when they were bleeding, and would love me for all to see.

The woods going up by the side of the school were the best place to play because then there was no fear of being hurt by anyone, and I had a freedom that you couldn't have in London. My nan would be in the kitchen cooking puddings I still like, while I was playing and pretending to be a princess

or Snow White. Winters were bitter, but Nan wrapped me up well so I could play in the barn. I remember being really scared one time when I heard something knocking on my bedroom window, but it was only the ivy that was growing around the house. The open fire in the lounge was lovely, especially when it was cold and wind was howling through the windows and doors.

There was a family that I visited with my dad who had chickens in a shed, and we used to go egg collecting. They had pigs as well, and we used to mother the piglets. I had no brothers or sisters at the time, and was the only grandchild for a few years, and so I was pretty spoilt. Nan and Grandad didn't have lots of money, and both had several jobs so they could make ends meet, but they had so much love for me.

For a day trip me and my nan used to walk to Longfield. We walked across the fields as it was quicker. I stayed with my nan for a few weeks in the summer,

and I dreaded the end of it, as I knew that I would have to go back to the old smokey which I hated.

My nan died in 1977, and I still miss her dearly. I returned a few years ago in the early 80s to see where my nan is buried, and to walk the routes that we did from the station along the fields to the house. Then I walked into the village – oh, how it has changed. My nan's grave is the only thing that was left in Fawkham that has any significance to me now. I miss the tranquillity, the peace and the people of Fawkham. So much of my life is there even now. I wasn't born there, and I wasn't a resident, but I was made so, so welcome by the people who were. If anyone does get the chance to place a flower on my beloved grandmother's grave, please do so. She would have done the same for you.

Her name was Mabel Edwards.

Belinda Barton (née Edwards)

Egg in the Window at my Nan and Grandad's

As a young girl I visited my grandparents' house in Monega Road, Manor Park, East Ham, London. They lived in a three-up, two-down with a funny kind of coal shed under the stairs. They lived a few doors away from the Monega Road School, which both my mum and uncle went to as little 'uns.

I remember walking down the tree-lined street with my grandad. I must have been about three or four. He knew everyone we met.

I still remember the smell of my grandparents' house: stale cigarettes and Old Spice. I remember my grandad using a cut-throat razor with his face lathered in special soap!

My grandparents had upright wooden chairs with tapestry seats that you sat on in the back room, because the front room with the sofa was for special occasions! You had to put the television set on 10 minutes before your programme started so it could warm up. I remember sitting at my nan's butterfly table for lunch, which was usually egg in the window (fried egg on a plate under a piece of fried bread with a hole cut out so you could see the egg). Nan always cut the white off because she said that part was the chicken's feathers!

Jenny Watts

My Family had the Whole Town Covered

This photograph brings back so many memories to me. All my childhood memories are of the wonderfully happy times I spent at 3 Chain Road with my Grandma and Granda Love. Hugh Love (old Ped) was at various times milkman for Skimmings, drove Palmers tippers, worked at the precast, and ran the caravan site for the council and then Willie McMillan. Grandma Love was equally industrious, having many wee jobs including cleaning at the Ellangowan. Great-granny Hughes lived on Harbour Street. Auntie Eck and Uncle Willie (Hughes) lived in Loudon Place. I think my family had just about the whole town covered – Great-uncle Ernest Wilson had the hardware shop and was church organist, Granny and Granda Parker were up in Chain Terrace, and then the boathouse, and Uncle David worked the nets for Captain Caird. Wherever I went to the village I could always get a jelly piece. And I can't forget the king of the ice cream makers, Marina Sisi – her ice cream still the best I've ever had, anywhere in the world.

Raymond Parker

Creetown, Dumfries & Galloway, Chain Road c1955 C608001

Arundel, Sussex, Park Avenue 1908 60166

Groom to the Duke of Norfolk

This is my grandfather, Joseph Smith, and my two great-aunts, Kathleen and Josephine. He was about 12 in this picture. They lived yards from where it was taken, in the lodge at Arundel Park gates. My great-grandfather, William, was a groom to the then Duke of Norfolk (Henry) and my great-grandmother, Kate, was a domestic.

Nicholas Seward

The Mercers of Cranleigh

The low building to the right was the shop of George Mercer, boot maker. The building to its right was the home of my great-grandfather, Henry Mercer, who expanded into two and then three of the cottages as his family grew (he had 10 children). Henry worked on the opposite side of the common at the wood yard.

   The man in foreground with the horse is probably Mr Stemp who was the groundsman for both Cranleigh School and Cranleigh Cricket Club. My grandfather Albert (Jack) Mercer later took over his job, and moved from the common to a tied cottage, Barnside, near Cranleigh School lower fields. The war memorial in Cranleigh includes the name E A Mercer (Edward Allan Mercer, son of Henry Mercer) who was killed aged 17 in the Royal Navy in what was known as the Live Bait Squadron. He was on one of four ships sunk the same morning by a German U-boat.

Alan Mercer

Cranleigh, Surrey, The Common 1904 51313

Cranleigh, Surrey, The War Memorial 1925 78102

Whitby, Yorkshire, A Group of Fisher Children 1891 28866p

The Whitby Pearts

These are some of the children of the Peart family of Whitby. Their mother and father were Jane (née Leadley) and David Peart who lived on the Tate Hill. David and Jane Peart took in summer visitors (as they said then). Amelia, the eldest aged 17, holds her baby brother George. Next to her on the rock is Robert Leadley Peart, and at her side is Robert's twin Matthew. Next to Matthew is Jane (known as Ginny) and then Tom. Jane (Ginny) was born on 18 September 1884 and was six years old in this photograph.

Robert (sitting on the rock) was drowned aged 20 on 19 July 1908 after being swept overboard at St Petersburg. George was also drowned, in the sinking of HMS 'Hogue' on 22 September 1914, during the First World War. He was 23.

There were also two other brothers who are not shown in the photo – David, who died aged 53 years on 11 July 1925, and William, who died aged 39 years on 7 June 1918.

Ginny married Ernest Swales, a ship's carpenter, when she was 25, in 1909. They lived in the warehouses under Ginny's parents' pub, the Duke of York. Ginny had three daughters and four sons and stillborn twins. She died aged 92 years on 5 January 1977.

Susan Storr

Old John Barleycorn

The children shown were known as the John Barleycorn children. They got the name because at the staithe where they used to play there is an inlet, and in the 1920s, when boats came past, the children would sing 'Old John Barleycorn, if you throw us a penny we will sing you a song'. Sometimes handfuls of pennies would be thrown. The people on one boat, the 'Nelson', were always quite generous. It was quite a scramble for each child to get a couple of pennies.

The Frith Memory Archivist

Belaugh, Norfolk, The John Barleycorn Children c1930 B495003

Axmouth, Devon, The Bridge c1955 A83024

My Dad was a Fisherman

I believe that the girl sitting on the grass looking towards the sea in the photograph below is me. My name then was Susan Groves, and my dad was a fisherman. We owned a shop down the bank called the Shell Shop where dad sold many things, including crabs and lobsters. He made me a boat in which I rowed him out to his coble to empty his crab pots or to collect urchins. I loved the Bay as a child, it is truly a wonderful place, and even though I left when I was fourteen I still return as often as possible and consider it to be home.
Susan Cooper

Robin Hood's Bay, Yorkshire, Looking South c1960 R41077

A Slower Pace of Life

I am the little girl standing by the boat in the photograph on the left – Pauline Reel (now Morgan), and my brother Cliff is wading through the water. The cabin cruiser on the opposite side of the river is the 'Silver Swan', owned by Gilbert Hazel of Castle Cary and looked after by my father, Rock Real. Our family spent many happy hours on and in our beloved River Axe. Now in my mid 60s I still love to row or outboard up the river and enjoy the solitude still on offer there – with just the birds for company and the river gently slapping the hull of my boat.

This wonderful photograph reminds me of a time when the pace of life was much slower and carefree. Most of the children of Axmouth learned to swim in the Axe at the harbour and later took their first dives from the wall.
Pauline Morgan (née Real)

Fun and Romance on the Parrog

I was born in 1968, and lived in a small two-bedroom house in Maes Morfa, Newport, Pembrokeshire with my elder brother and sister and mother and father. Although life seemed to be quite difficult in those days, for money was short, I feel we had a wealth of beauty living in Newport. From my parents' window we overlooked the local playing fields and Newport Estuary and as far as Berry Hill Farm. The river was home to many different birds, and their songs and cries are all a part of my memories of home.

From the time I was very young, the Parrog was a place we visited regularly with our mother. During the summer holidays, her basket was always full of picnic treats. The rocks we sat on to eat our lunch are still there and I always remember the warmth of the stones – the rising sun had heated them up. When the tide was fully out, we crossed The Chain, the shallowest part of the river, and ran onto the big beach. We had so much fun running and jumping into the river. The Parrog was a very stony beach, so it was always nice to feel the soft sand between our toes. My sister and I spent hours looking under rocks and in rock pools for crabs and fishing for shrimps in the river. We had quite a collection in our bucket of seawater

Newport, Dyfed, The Parrog c1955 P201021

at the end of the day but we would always return the creatures back to the water before heading for home.

One of my fondest memories is of the rowing races. Crowds of locals and holidaymakers gathered and we all stood on the quay wall waiting to see the boats coming down the estuary. The buzz was incredible. Afterwards families would gather for drinks and refreshments in the Boat Club.

Every August Bank Holiday we had a firework display and disco on the Parrog. Hundreds of people lined the whole of the Parrog and the marsh to wait for what was always a wonderful display. Every year the regatta committee spent more and more on the fireworks.

During the summer holidays when I was a teenager, my friends and I spent hours on the Parrog, playing on

Bank y Rhodyn, and swimming at Betws and the Cwm, small beaches a little further along the coast – all within walking distance. Many of us experienced a holiday romance and that first kiss upon Bank y Rhodyn was an experience never to be forgotten, a summer love made all the more romantic by the beauty around us.

There was a little beach café on the Parrog. We used to call it 'George and Millie's Caff'. We would spend a couple of hours on the beach, and then go to the café for a hot sausage roll, a drink and then a lemon sparkle lollypop. What a treat!

Linda

Childhood in a Mining Village

I was born and brought up in Goldthorpe and I have many happy memories of playing on the market stalls. They could be anything in our imaginations, a house, a bus, a pirate ship, or whatever we wanted them to be.

Another special place was the Empire picture house on a Saturday, where we used to pay 1d (one old penny) to go to the matinee. The local policeman was always on hand to keep an eye on us (I think we called him Bobby Dick). Most weeks the film would be Roy Rogers with Trigger his horse, and I remember that it always used to get to the most exciting bit before the programme ended – 'to be continued next week'.

My dad was a miner until he was injured in a pit fall. I remember the sound of the clogs: they sounded like an army as the men walked to work on day shift (at about 5am in the morning), and also the knocker-upper tapping on the bedroom window with a long wooden pole (or clothes prop) to make sure that they were up in time. I think he got a penny a day for this service from each miner.

Pauline Seddon

Goldthorpe, South Yorkshire, Doncaster Road c1965 G110011

Mitcham, Greater London, Upper Green East c1955 M296043

Winkles and Shrimps for Tea

Opposite the Majestic Cinema, you can just see the Tudor brickwork of the Bucks Head Inn on the London Road corner. A seafood stall, parked beside the pub on a Sunday, sold cockles, whelks, winkles, mussels, shrimps and jellied eels. My dad would give my sister and I, or my brother Robert, some money to buy half a pint of winkles and a quarter pint of shrimps for tea.

When we got home it was our job to take the eyes out of the winkles with a needle, and then stick the needle in its 'head' and slowly unwind it from its shell. Mum would put them in a dish and add vinegar. Woe betide us if we broke the winkles as we were getting them out of the shell. They were a special treat, and we missed out on them if we did not do it right. The shrimps were for Mum and Dad. We took off the shell casings, and then got the little black vein out, once again being very careful, as there were not many of them. They were just the best Sunday teatimes, as we had real butter on our bread with the winkles. We finished with a slice of bread and jam, or sometimes, if we were lucky, Mum had bought a small piece of walnut butter cake from Marks & Spencers if she had gone to Tooting on Saturday.

Carole Baldwin

My Parents – and a Poltergeist

In the early 1990s my parents bought an old railway carriage bungalow at 66, East Front Road on Pagham Beach. The place was a total dump, so they burned it down on the beach! (This was allowed by the council back then, if the fire was below the tide line.) It now seems a terrible waste of the antique railway carriages that were hidden inside layers of plywood and plaster boards. We did save some of the old fittings, but they are since lost.

They built an ugly brick L-shaped modern bungalow with too many steps. It was always damp on one side, even though the footings were massively deep and the damp course was fine. I know, because I helped build that house.

My dad found a whole heap of Molotov cocktail-type bombs buried under the old footings which were left over from the Second World War. The Army Bomb Squad had to come in and blow them all up.

Dad was Peter Tayman, plumber and builder extraordinaire, and Mum was Elizabeth. They were pretty well known around Pagham. Dad was a total flirt, very handsome and he loved the ladies, which was heartbreaking for Mum. No wonder she tried to drink her pain away.

He passed away in his new house at 5am on 6 July 1994 aged 52 years and our lives were never as good or rich again. He was a larrikin, jovial and generous, and the most capable, inventive man I have ever met. He was also prone to getting into trouble with the local undesirables – Pagham attracted all sorts of petty crooks.

Pagham, Sussex, East Beach c1955　P251047

Exploring the Tombs

The church always seemed so huge and scary with its giant red doors, but my brother and I had such fun in the churchyard, climbing the trees and exploring the broken tombs and crypts. I always expected a monster to grab me and take me down inside, never to be seen again! I think the horror movie of the time was about zombies and the living dead. We also used to pick the daffodils and sell them in bunches for a tanner a bunch, till one day the vicar caught us and gave us a right telling off!

Denise Masters

Camberwell, London, St Giles's Church c1955　C516013

Mum also passed away youngish, as she couldn't live without him. Dad left behind three children – me, my brother Dave and our half-sister Tracy, who never even got to meet him.

I rented a railway carriage bungalow called Aramanches, also in East Front Road, and my new husband Steve and I had a dreadful time there as it was haunted by a poltergeist. It was really bad, and my father had to come down to see what all the fuss was about. The haunting went on for the entire time we rented there, and then followed me to our first house in Mons Avenue, Bognor.

I think I can see the house in the photo – possibly the second one in on the left. That's what got me started writing all this! We always had to turn the power off at the mains because the ghost loved turning everything on when we were at work, especially heaters and the stove hotplates. It used to move things around, open all the cupboards up, and bang on the doors all night long. We would see it (or her) looking at us through an internal glass door from the kitchen area, to the old lounge room. It always walked from the old laundry room into the bathroom, so it would pass us by. It would start fires in the hearth in the middle of the night, and slam doors.

It drove us mad, but I was never afraid, just keen to help it find peace if I could. It led to a lifelong study of 'things that go bump in the night', and now I am a parapsychologist and writer on the topic, so it was helpful after all. I wonder if any other owners or tenants had any ghostly encounters there too, or was it just us?

Zaryn Hammersley

The Flats, Bearmans, Lyons Café, and Pie and Mash

I often think how lucky we post-war Leytonstone kids were to be born in the East End of London, yet have the whole of Wanstead Park, the flats and what we called the forest at the end of our street, Browning Road, to get lost in. I also remember the mysterious Quakers Meeting House surrounded by the massive and famous 'Red Wall', where we all scratched our names in the soft red bricks.

Lyons Corner House was a treat. You lined up with your tray after shopping with your mum and had pie and chips with gravy, and I'll never forget those lovely trifles in little cups. However, as far as real authentic East End gourmet food is concerned, what could compare with pie and mash from Cowleys at the Harrow Green, or fish and chips from one of Lukover's shops that dominated Leytonstone's take-away trade in those days. Other food memories include Israel's greengrocery shops selling exotic Brazil nuts or mandarins in gold and silver paper at Christmas time, and the pease pudding van outside the Red Lion or the whelk stall outside the Green Man.

What else do I remember? That terrific scrap yard by the railway arch where you could get a 'still running' old Ford or Morris for about £10. The build-up to Guy Fawkes night saw

Leytonstone, Greater London, High Road c1950 L374001

us lads with home-made guys in prams outside the banks and various prime sites in the High Road. It was not uncommon to make as much as five quid on a Saturday and you could get an awful lot of fireworks for five quid! For a serious adventure there was the boating lake at Whipps Cross. The lovely old wooden rowing boats had ropes that you pulled to steer while the other bloke rowed.

Ray Murray

Cheating the Scrap Merchant in Camberwell

I forget the name of the road, but Mum got us to drag bags of rags weighted with stones to make them heavier to the scrap yard up the road from the church. One time the bloke opened the bundle (I think we might have overdone the rocks a bit). He was furious, and bellowed at us, and tried to clip us round the ear. We were really scared, and told him that Mum didn't have any money – so he gave us some anyway, but told us never to come back again. I don't think we ever did.

Denise Masters

Nelson, Lancashire, Leeds Road c1955 N146052

Pop and Crisps outside the Borough Hotel

In 1971, as a kid aged five, me and my older brother spent three hours on a Saturday afternoon playing outside the pub (the Borough Hotel) and on the steps of Woolworth's (a bit further up the street). We waited for one of our parents to come out of the pub every hour or so with bottles of pop and bags of crisps for us, only to say 'Just another 10 minutes'. An hour later it would be the same again – but we didn't mind too much, as we enjoyed pop and crisps!

I know it's a strange one to remember, but every time I look at this photo that's what pops into my head.

Andrew Duerden

Ironbridge, Shropshire, The Bridge from the River 1892   30891

Carnivals and Coracles

I was born in 1924 and I lived with my family just downstream of the bridge. I attended the 'Blue School' and St Luke's Church. Twice a day we climbed the 100 or more steps past the church to go to school, belting home at midday for something to eat. I remember Rector Roberts and Mr Wragg, the headmaster at the school, with great affection.

Every year we all attended the church anniversary. All the girls were dressed in frilly dresses made by my mother. We had white socks, black patent shoes, and straw bonnets. In the summer we all entered the Carnival in which we won prizes every year. I still have some of the photos of it, including one of the Carnival King and Queen with my sister and me on the stage as attendants, dressed in our fancy dress costumes.

My father owned a punt (a flat-bottomed boat) in which he took us all out on the river. He made little paddles for us and off we would go, paddling like idiots upstream towards Buildwas with no thought of the danger – none of us could swim. Sometimes we stopped at a little island nearby.

Living on the riverbank was exciting at flood time. We also had to climb over my auntie's garden wall and through the gardens of neighbours, and sometimes through the old cottage belonging to Mr and Mrs Wright. We also had great fun making paper boats. We set them off at the bottom of the back yard, then we tore through the house to catch the boats at the front door – my mother used to go mad with all the wet footsteps trailing through.

As well as his punt, my father had a coracle which he took out on the river, sometimes to fish, but usually to catch tree trunks washed down with the flood water. He would show off, spinning his coracle round like a whirling dervish. This was a mad thing to do, because he couldn't swim either.

Ethel Jones

Ironbridge, Shropshire c1960 I20055

Penn, West Midlands, The Village 1968 P157022

Sixpenceworth of Batter Bits

This photograph revived my memories of the Fox and Goose pub on Penn Road. My mum was the cleaner there for a few years when my sisters and I were young, and I can remember sitting on the steps outside the pub collecting car numbers in an old exercise book and drinking a bottle of Vimto and eating Smiths crisps while I waited for mum to finish cleaning, and then we'd walk all the way back home to Warstones estate where we lived. It was such a long way, but we never minded.

We didn't have a car, and money was very tight, so we couldn't catch the bus. Sometimes if it was near lunchtime mum would stop and buy sixpenceworth of batter bits from the fish and chip shop that we passed on the way home – and we'd think it was such a treat if a little bit of fish had somehow made its way in to the batter bits. Now I have grown up 'children' of my own, and often tell them stories of when I was growing up. I think they find it difficult to imagine that a bottle of soft drink and packet of crisps plus the fact that we had bits of batter for lunch was such a treat.

Kathleen Adams

When Snow Stopped Play

I remember Aston Terrace, Aston, Yorkshire, and sliding down Outcrop and sitting on wooden steps leading to Brookhouse pit. On pay day miners used to give us some coppers and we would share them out.

I can remember when a cage accident happened at the pit, and all the women went running down to see if their loved ones had survived. I was only about seven at the time.

I also remember having to be dug out of the house one winter as it was feet deep with snow, and my mum had bought me a hula hoop for Christmas and I couldn't go outside because it was that deep.

There was only one house in Aston that had electric, and the owner was called Albert Silkstone. He used to charge us a penny to watch TV – we were mesmerised.

Christine Ryczek

the Park

It was a long w   ve lived as children. We   est Ham. Weekends an   a picnic for the six of us,   Mum had some, and a   ad our jam jars and nets for   ‹s, a bat and ball, and also a f   e day, as most East End c‹

We woul   ²ark side. It was a short walk through a small woo   s seemed so tall, and the ground was soft. I can remember the smell of the soil – it was always damp. Sometimes we would see a squirrel or a small mouse, and I can remember the sound of small birds, which in the streets where we lived you didn't see or hear. Then came the open space of green grass – the grass would tickle your legs as you ran through it. It was then just a short walk to the pond, and by the side of the pond was an ice cream and tea shop. Sometimes if Mum had given us a penny each we would put it together and buy one ice cream and share it. I can also remember the sound of children playing, and the shouting when one of them had caught a stickleback.

The six of us would always stay together, making sure that we were all in sight of each other as Mum had instructed for safety. We would fish and paddle in the pond and, after catching our little fish to take home for Mum to see, we would have our picnic. It was then time for a game of cricket or football. Susan, my sister, and I would be put out as fielders, as our brothers knew it would take us time to find the ball, allowing them more time for runs.

Then after a few whinges I would be allowed to have a go at batting. It was my brother Daniel who taught me how to hold the bat, and I soon got the hang of it. When the game of football began, it was not long before there were more than the six of us. We would get a full team, maybe more – what fun it was. We would always have a few scratches by the time the game was over.

Daniel would then check the time, as we had to be home by 4 o'clock. How quickly the time would go. We would change the water in the jars with hopes that the fish would still be alive when we got home for Mum to see. Then came the long walk home. There Mum would be waiting for us with dinner ready. After dinner, it was time for a strip wash – we had no bathroom in those days – and then off to bed. Susan and I shared the same room. We would talk about what we had done and seen that day and what we had enjoyed most about Wanstead Park. Susan, being two years younger than myself, would always fall asleep before I did. The next day we would have done it all again.

Joan Doble

Big Toe Stuck in the Drain

I remember this paddling pool (right) so well. When I was about eight years old I would be there with my nana (in fact it looks like me in the photograph). She would sit on the bench and eat her rich tea biscuits. I begged her to let me swim every time we were there, but I would mostly paddle. One day the pool was empty. I was playing around the drain when I got my big toe stuck in it. I was really scared and started to cry, and then to my horror the pool started to fill up – I was sure that I was going to drown. I remember screaming so loudly that the man that tended the park came over and shut the water off ... Whew!

There were swings on the other side of the pool, and a water fountain. The park also had crazy golf that was so much fun to play.

Vicki Bowman

Newmarket, Suffolk, The Paddling Pool and St Mary's Church c1960 N23057

Manchester, Greater Manchester, Latchford Locks and Manchester Ship Canal 1894 33697

Gifts from the Crew

Sadly we see very few ships passing down the Manchester Ship Canal these days. When I was a kid I lived in Latchford, not far from the locks. We used to spend many hours watching the ships pass through the locks on their way to Liverpool or Manchester. We were occasionally rewarded by a pack of cigarettes or sweets thrown by the crew to us kids.

Ian Miller

Glued to the Set

Most weekday evenings would find my mum, dad and I sitting around the fire, Dad intermittently reading the paper and dozing off, Mum sewing or knitting, and me doing my homework. Mum and I would get blotchy red mottled marks that resembled the moon's craters on our legs from sitting too close to the fire. Our big arc-shaped Marconi wireless brought the outside world into our living room, and we sat glued to the set as Dick Barton performed his daring deeds with the aid of his cohorts, Jock and Snowy. 'The Archers' – 'an everyday story of country folk' – was another 'mustn't miss', but the best of all was 'Journey into Space' which, for effect, we'd listen to with the lights off. Dad added his own effects. He could make me jump out of my skin by suddenly whispering 'Whassat?' during this programme. And, as we sat rooted to the spot, nothing ever tasted so good as toast done on a fork held before the coals of the fire, with lashings of butter.

Combe Martin, Devon c1960 C145113

Combe Martin, Devon, Rest on the way to Hangman Hill c1955 C145031

Speaking of butter: it was possible during rationing to get an extra butter ration if a member of the family was declared a vegetarian. I was our family's appointee. Mum and I would take three buses to Harrow and back, every week, to get my supplemental ration of nuts and peanut butter at the 'nut shop'. Though I was our token vegetarian, I still ate meat at home, but school lunches were something else. The concoctions Mum devised were admirable, considering what she had to work with. Egg sandwiches, tomato sandwiches, lettuce sandwiches, lettuce and tomato sandwiches all finally ran their limit, so she tried pickled herring sandwiches and, when all else failed, there were sugar sandwiches and the ensuing teeth cavities.

Dad was a frugal Scot, and controlled the purse-strings. Certain house rules prevailed, unless there was company, and only then were they lifted. For example, the electric lights were not turned on until you could barely make out the presence of another

person across the room, and heaven forbid you should ever leave a room without turning a light off. Often as not, if we had company for tea, Mum would whisper 'FHB' to Dad and me. This meant there wasn't enough to go around, so 'family hold back'.

Tap dancing classes were par for the course for almost every little girl growing up in the forties, and as one of Beryl Jewell's 'little gems', I tapped and sang my way through such timeless classics as 'Ashby de la Zouche Castle Abbey', 'Hey Little Hen', 'Slow Boat to China' and 'Mairsy Doats and Dozy Doats', all decked out in tulle and sequins lovingly sewn by Mum in the sure knowledge that her pride and joy would one day be strutting her stuff at the Windmill (we-never-close) Theatre, if not the Palladium.

> " Dad was a frugal Scot ... electric lights were not turned on until you could barely make out the presence of another person across the room "

Summer holidays were usually spent in Combe Martin, which was an unspoiled hamlet near Ilfracombe in North Devon. If Mrs Darch's B & B was fully booked, we stayed at the Dolphin Inn, opposite the harbour. On a fine day, we would climb to the top of the hills, Little Hangman and Big Hangman, overlooking the harbour, or while Mum sunned herself in a deckchair, Dad and I went rock-climbing or fishing in a rock-pool with a limpet on a bent pin and a length of cotton. We never caught anything, but I did drive a few sea-anemones crazy. If it rained, and when didn't it, there was a skittle alley and a little cinema that showed Charlie Chaplin and Laurel & Hardy films.

Heather Rohrer

Cricket by the River

Cricket was a very popular game with all the neighbourhood kids at Bishopstoke. There was a permanent set of stumps painted on the brick wall of the hardware store shed, and if you hit the ball in the river, you were out. Johnnie Butt, one of my best mates, would rescue the ball when it came round in the current by hanging by his feet upside down from the railings, something I was never game to do. If the ball got washed downstream, we all made a dash for Scotter Road bridge and waited on the rim of the iron girder bridge to grab it. If we missed, it was gone forever.

John Sibson

Bishopstoke, Hampshire, Montague Terrace c1955 B693006

Chatting Up the Girls

When my friends and I were about 10 or 12, we used to sail our model yachts on the pond in Rosebery Park, and in our teens we spent a lot of evenings in the park chatting up the girls! Happy, happy days. I must admit there was a tear or two in my eyes when I saw all those lovely trees felled by the great storm.

Brian Robinson

Epsom, Surrey, Rosebery Park 2005 E37707k

Sledging in Sacks

We knew this spot as Brown's Fields. Farmer Brown had the dairy in Broad Street and used to drive his cows down the lane by the Lynch. In summertime we used to go down to the river to play and have picnics. In the wintertime it was a great place to use your sledge. We often used to sit inside big sacks and slide down the hill (hopefully missing the cow pats). In the summer we used to pick little wild strawberries off the viaduct. I'm sure we weren't supposed to go there, but we never came to any harm.

Denise Lazenby

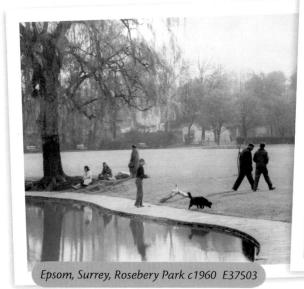

Epsom, Surrey, Rosebery Park c1960 E37503

Somerton, Somerset, The Viaduct 1906 55819

Enfield, Middlesex, White Webbs Park, the Pond c1955 E179020

Ducks, Swans, and Ranger the Dog

Little children with their mothers clutched bags of bread to feed the ducks and swans on the lake in White Webbs Park – an adventure for any small child. One winter the lake froze over completely and we were able to skate on the lake and also feed the hungry ducks and swans. Unfortunately, in the late 1950s one of the swans died. Although many attempts were made to introduce another swan, it would not be accepted, as swans mate for life.

Across Flash Lane lay 'second woods'. Here we as children used to pick blackberries, and find our way to the centre where Ranger's Tomb was situated. Ranger was the much-loved dog of the gamekeeper some time during the late 19th century.

Roger Davis

Enfield, Middlesex, White Webbs Park, the Pond c1955 E179018

Sunshine Corner

I used to live in tree-lined Lister Street at Rotherham. All I had to do was climb over the back wall to the rear of my house to get into Clifton Park. I remember Sunday School held at the Bandstand:
'Sunshine Corner, always jolly fine,
Is for children under 99.
All are welcome and it's all free,
Clifton Sunshine Corner is the place for me!'

I can remember the kids' play area and the paddling pool. I can also remember the Remembrance Gardens being built, and prisoners of war sitting on the grass there.

John Wigglesworth

Rotherham, Yorkshire, Clifton Park, Children's Paddling Pool c1955 R60014

At Peace with All Creation

It was 1955. We lived at Southbourne in a new bungalow. One of my cherished memories as a child is of walking down to the cliff steps (then very steep) and standing halfway down in a thick mist – I couldn't see a hand in front of my face – feeling almost totally isolated except for the sound of the waves crashing below. Yet I was totally at peace and one with all creation at the same time. It was a great stress-releaser.

Now I begin to understand why I loved it so much, being a poet, dreamer, musician, photographer and artist of sorts. I've never managed to take my son there, and I haven't been back myself for 50 years. I've just realised this is the 50th anniversary year, as we left with Mum in November 1957 to move to Toronto. Dad had been working with De Havilland's at Christchurch, and moved to the Canadian company the previous January.

I remember walking down the lane nearby which led to the sand dunes on the top of the cliffs behind the row of shops. Strangely enough, I ended up living in Castle Matrix, Rathkeale, County Limerick, Ireland, in 1981 only to discover that our nearest neighbour, Doreen Guiry, had worked for those same years in one of the Victorian bed and breakfasts along St Catherine's Road where I used to walk past!

I still miss the sand dunes – even though the wind shared them with our front lawn, much to my mother's chagrin – and those misty weather walks down the road to the cliff top with only the sound of the birds and waves for company. Everybody else was much too sensible to be out on those days!

Liz Forrest O'Driscoll

Southbourne, Dorset, The Beach 1908 61202

Diving Champions

I lived in Gloucester during the war years. At weekends, when the weather was great, my friends and I would take the bus to Cheltenham and spend the day at the Lido. I thought it was a wonderful place. There were masses of American servicemen stationed in the area at that time, awaiting the start of the D-day landings. Well, they would love to show off on the high diving boards, and we girls in turn loved to watch them. I suppose to us they were the equivalent of today's superstars. *June Jackson*

In 1943 the American servicemen June Jackson saw on the diving boards were top American diving champions who were stationed here. They used the pool at the Lido to keep up their diving skills.
Joyce Cummings

I can't remember the 5 metre diving boards in this photo of the Lido at Cheltenham, but I certainly can remember the 3 metre ones that replaced these, which have also now gone. I spent many an afternoon diving and jumping off these boards, first starting on the 1 metre, then the 2 metre, and finally getting the courage for the 3 metre. I can't imagine jumping off the 5 metre board, as the water depth hasn't changed – you could certainly do some damage to yourself if you made a mistake. Obviously that is why it is no longer there.   *George Tarte*

Cheltenham, Gloucestershire, The Lido 1937 87927a

Barnstorming Scouts

This view (left) is exactly as I remember this lovely village where the Scouts from Hatch End spent a two week summer camp in 1957.

Although I no longer recall the name of the particular farm where we set up camp, I do remember our troop carrying out a good turn for the farmer. We were asked to demolish one of the ruined outbuildings, and a month or so later we received an impressive scroll from him giving us the 'right to call ourselves barnstormers and to march over his land forever with flags flying and knives unsheathed'. A great thrill for this 11 year old! The farmer's scroll was displayed in the Scout Hut back in Hatch End for many years as we all had such lovely memories of our two weeks in Piddletrenthide!

John Howard Norfolk

Piddletrenthide, Dorset, The Village c1955 P231016

Games on the Green

Growing up in a cul-de-sac (in Melrose Gardens, Edgeware in Middlesex) was like having a huge family where all your siblings are farmed out to the adjacent homes. We were a close-knit bunch of more than twenty kids ranging in age from three to sixteen, and we were never short of things to do. Someone could always bring their mum's clothesline with which we would skip by the hour. 'Under the stars and over the moon' could accommodate as many as ten skippers at one time. And when we doubled up the rope, one or two extremely agile girls, whom we'd dubbed 'double-jointed', could skip 'Double Dutch' while the two ropes were turned in opposite directions at the same time. Anyone who could do anything that the majority of us couldn't was said to be double-jointed. Oh, how I wished I was double-jointed. As it was, they said I had a strong arm, so they let me be rope-turner much of the time.

Whip and top, marbles or 'migs', five stones or 'jacks', and balls were our constant companions. A very large green with seven elm trees formed the centre of our little community, so as long as you could get enough kids together, a game of rounders could always be counted on to pass the time. Once 'rounders' was called, each team did its best to recruit Eric Treemane or Terry Frewin who no longer came out to play at the drop of a hat, but could be depended on to slog the ball over the rooftops. At seventeen, they didn't mind the opportunity to show off for the girls and flex their batting arms, but that was the extent of their involvement with us 'little kids'.

Heather Rohrer

Polzeath, Cornwall c1960 P705029

Special Days at Polzeath

My family lived at Trelights. My Uncle Reg was a Trelights boy although he was a school teacher in London, and when he came home in the summer holidays in his old Austin 6 he would often take us to Polzeath. They were special days.

Off we would go loaded up with sandwiches and apples, not forgetting the little primus stove to boil the kettle for cups of tea and the wooden boards for riding the waves. The beach even on hot days was never crowded and no one sat in the middle, only around the edges in the rocks, mainly for shelter from the sea breezes.

We made huge sand castles and sand boats, and would sit in them when the tide was fast approaching, to see how long the walls would hold out. Oh, the screams from the children when the sea breached the sides!

Jan Cowling

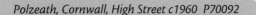

Polzeath, Cornwall, High Street c1960 P70092

Polzeath, Cornwall, St Enodoc's Church 1903 49953

Box, Wiltshire, Glovers Lane c1965 B374033

Memories of Box

This is a picture of myself with my sister and brother and my sister's friend (left). I was 13 years old. My sister Theo is the girl with the handbag, she was 9 years old and my brother John was 3 years old. We had been to the local store, Bences, and are standing outside the smallest pub in the county, The Chequers Inn. Our family home was at the top of Glovers Lane. The garden with Dad's apple and cherry trees can be seen in the photograph running the full length of the lane (right).

Ann Blake

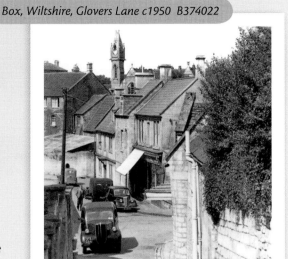

An Evacuee's Best Friend

I was evacuated to Devizes in 1940 from Tilbury, Essex. I was 11 years old. I can remember where we all assembled, in what I think was the Catholic school, which I believe was St Joseph's. There were about 40 of us, and I was the last to be picked for accommodation with a local family. The lady who picked me was Phyllis Hillier, and she was very kind to me, as were the rest of the family. I remember going down a big hill towards the canal and crossing a small bridge and turning left down into a building which was originally a prison, but had been converted into flats. It was a ground floor flat, and it was very nice and comfortable. After settling into my new home, I started school. To reach it we had to walk along the canal or back up the hill to the town. This was where I met up with all of my friends and my sister, Kitty. We all chatted and found out where everyone was living. My friend Billy Watts was about 10 minutes walk from where I was, so we saw each other every day, going to school and playing together at weekends.

I recall that Phyllis had a sheepdog whose name was Biddy, and we were great friends. After a time I used to go regularly to a wood yard that was about two miles away on the other side of the town – I recall going about twice a week. I used to push a wooden cart and fill it with logs for the fire, and Biddy came with me every time. He would sit in the cart going and walk beside it coming home. One day a couple of boys I met on the way got a bit rough with me, but Biddy soon cleared them off, so he became very protective of me.

I was evacuated to Devizes for about 12 months and enjoyed every moment of it, even though I used to go and get wood and also clean around the house. Phyllis would clean and polish every day, and I helped sometimes.

Devizes, Wiltshire, Quakers Walk 1898 42315

During the latter part of my stay in Devizes most of my friends had returned home, even my sister, but I was not keen on returning. One day, however, my mother arrived in Devizes to fetch me back home, which was a shock as I was not expecting it. I did not want to go, but I had to because all my friends had returned home. I was most upset, because I was very happy there – and I did not want to leave Biddy.

John Ryan.

Duffle bags, wooden desks and inkwells

MEMORIES OF SCHOOLDAYS

Scared of the Gargoyles

Before it was bought by George Harrison of the Beatles, Friar Park was run as a school by sisters of the St John Bosco order. It was my first school, and I had to walk all the way to the main door along the winding drive each morning, passing by the huge rhododendron bushes which lined each side. As I approached the large arched entrance door shown in the photograph, I could see the gargoyles dotted around the building – they seemed so frightening, and I would hold my head down and wait for one of the sisters to come and welcome me in for the day. The first step took me into the porch, which then opened into the great hall. There were many doors, and a set of grand stairs leading to the balconied upper floor where the classrooms were.

One door led to the chapel. In the opposite corner was my favourite place, the Holy Shop, a small cabinet hung on the wall with rosaries, hymn books, book markers and other items on sale to children during morning break.

The dining room was behind the main building. It resembled a large greenhouse with glass panes. It was very important to eat everything on our plates, as nobody was allowed to leave the table until the meal was completely finished. The sisters worked hard in the huge kitchen gardens and grew all the vegetables that we ate. There were tennis courts and playing fields and gardens, with a stunning fountain and landscaped gardens where Sports Day was held. On Saints' Days there were candlelit processions with all the children walking in line along the front terrace.

On sunny days the sisters took us for walks around the amazing gardens and through the trees to the Matterhorn, a miniature version of the real thing. There were the Japanese gardens, which one of my ancestors was involved in building. I was too scared to cross the slatted bridge over the water garden and got a good telling off for being a coward.

Just once or twice we walked to the edge of the estate all the way to 'roly poly' hill. We were allowed to roll down and climb back up the steep grass bank.

I told Sister Ella I was allergic to milk, and she excused me from drinking the half pint we were given at morning break time. One day she caught me drinking a bottle and I got into so much trouble, not for drinking the milk, but for lying to her about my 'allergy'.

There were about six or seven classes in all, from kindergarten onwards. I was bell monitor and had to ring the bell for break time. It was a good old-fashioned heavy hand bell. When it was our turn, we would walk up and down the long balconies overlooking the grand hall ringing for all we were worth.

The interior architecture of Friar Park was as Gothic as the outside, and I was never quite brave enough to look upwards for fear of seeing another gargoyle face peering down. Sometimes I would meet a novice nun scurrying along with brush and pan or mop and bucket, but they never talked to the children, as if they were not allowed to, but I was always pleased to see a friendly face as I performed my lonely bell-ringing duty.

Mandy Lester

Henley-on-Thames, Oxfordshire, Friar Park, The Drive c1900 H73303

Kind and Compassionate Nuns

I was also a pupil at Friar Park from 1955 to 1962 (see the photograph on the opposite page). I have nothing but wonderful memories of this amazing school. The endless drive with rhododendron bushes opening into the huge circle where an Edwardian Gothic mansion stood will always be etched in my memory. The incredible sweep of the lawns on the West Terrace leading down to carefully contrived pools and bridges which hid amazing caves and tunnels that led back into the school itself were like a Gothic fairytale. At the Christmas Fair the nuns used to open these faintly lit caves, and around each corner you always expected to see at least a goblin sitting with his legs crossed!

The nuns made all the costumes for the Christmas plays which were performed in Henley Town Hall. My memory is of classical music drifting through the doors of their large workrooms as they sewed before opening night. If you had to have a fitting, a novice would come to your class and spirit you down. You had to stand very still, otherwise the pins would stick into you.

I was good at tennis and encouraged to play in matches. Even as a little girl they were quite competitive but a lot of fun, with the nuns cheering you on. I won a small cup which I still have.

I had a wonderful education at Friar Park. If you were weak in a subject, the nuns would tutor you after school. But everything had to end by 5 o'clock for evening prayer. I still remember the nuns silently moving around the perimeter of the great hall towards the chapel. Like the little bronze cross I was given before I left, I have carried the compassion and kindness I learned from this period of my life with me always. There was something very magical about this school, and I am sure that many former pupils feel the same as I do.

Angela Hamblin

My Days at the Ormerod

Lytham, Lancashire, Abraham Ormerod Convalescent Home 1929 82647

I went to the Ormerod Home, at the age of about eight or nine, as the Local Authority (Blackpool) had a number of reserved places there. Homes such as this were built along the sand dunes near Blackpool to provide a healthy environment where youngsters from the north west could spend their holidays away from the smoke and grime of the Lancashire cotton towns.

I was the youngest of four children whose father had died five years earlier. My mother worked both day and night to make ends meet. These days you might say that I was sent for a period of respite. My stay here seemed to last for about three or four months and stretched over the Christmas period. I had two parts in the Christmas plays. The first was as John the Baptist in the nativity play, and then the second was as one of Cinderella's horses in the panto. The days were spent either going for long walks on the beach or playing in the huge indoor playroom. Another vivid memory of Christmas was having Christmas pud straight after Christmas lunch, it was far too rich for some of us, and made us ill.

The staff were Anglican nuns from an order known as the Sisters of the Church. The regular Sunday services in the home's own chapel gave me my early grounding in the Christian faith. All in all, my stay here was a good, safe opportunity to stand on my own feet.

Roy Haskett

Some Memorable Teachers

On my first days at school I was taken in my little blue coat and cap by the girls next door. I seemed to cling to them for ages.

I finally graduated to playing with the boys, sliding in the school yard in black boots with 'segs' in. It was all boys, because the yard was divided by a wall and the red brick toilets, and you just didn't venture into the girls' half. What is now the school field was still 'Carter's' field, where Alf kept his pigs.

Others of my generation will recall the huge thermometer on the wall, dinners in the WI, sitting on the pipes in the winter, 'Tommy's Pantry', and maybe the old oak desks with wooden pens and ink-wells. Surely, though, the most lasting impression must be of a certain Miss Elizabeth Heslop. 'Lizzie', with her imposing figure, grey moustache, specs stuck on the top of her head and her booming voice, could strike terror into the hearts of your mam and dad, while the mere mention of Long Tom or Little Willie was enough to make any seven-year-old wet himself! This woman would have had most present-day teachers for breakfast, while a confrontation between her and Margaret Thatcher would have surely been no contest. However, I remember her with great warmth and respect, and I am convinced that if every school had one or two Lizzies we would now be living in a much more civilised society.

A couple of years on, and it was nature walks with Gladys Gardiner, or 'Polly', as she was known. Polly also took us for drill.

On to the top class, and although we must have been given great tuition for so many of us to do well in the eleven-plus, all I can really remember Jimmy Savage teaching us was sport. We called him 'Cromwell' for his apparent sternness and discipline, but his

enthusiasm and commitment to making a football team out of resources so limited that even I was an automatic choice, must have rivalled that of Brian Clough. His efforts were justly rewarded, and I'll never forget how proud he was to present us with our medals for winning the Bishop Auckland District League.

David Quinn (a memory of schooldays at Howden Le Wear, County Durham)

Bad Beer and Manure

What a dump Iwerne Minster seemed to a London schoolboy of the 60s sent to that boarding school in the middle of nowhere. The locals spoke in a strange unintelligible dialect, the air was sometimes thick with the stink of manure, and you had to be 14 to buy beer from the off-licence at Tarrant Hinton! Now, 50 and more years on, it doesn't seem such a bad place at all. In fact, it's quite nice down there. The beer is not so bad either.

Stewart Henley

Iwerne Minster, Dorset, Clayesmore School c1960   I65015

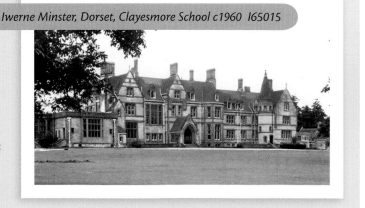

‘ the huge thermometer ... sitting on the pipes in the winter ... the old oak desks with wooden pens and ink-wells ’

Hadleigh, Essex, Central Broadway c1955 H167002

Hiding in the Bus Shelter

As I live in Canada now, I'm not sure if the bus shelter in this photograph (above) is still there. In the early 60s I and my brother and sister caught the bus from this stop to our school, Holy Family RC Primary, in Benfleet. We'd have our pink bus passes at the ready and join a host of other kids on their way to their respective schools. It's a sign of the times that I don't think anyone now lets their primary school-aged kids travel by themselves on public transport.

One winter the weather was really bad with lots of snow, and some of the public buses didn't run. We had a couple of days off school and were disappointed when we heard that our school – and only our school – had arranged for a special bus. Trudging to the bus stop that morning, one or all of us hatched a plan to have one more day at home. As the bus approached we hid behind the circular seat in the shelter and waited for the bus to leave without us. We then skipped back through the snow and told our angry mother that the bus hadn't arrived. I'd like to think the bus driver didn't spot us hiding, that the head nun, Sister Frances, didn't know what we were about, and that our mum believed that the bus really hadn't come. Now I have kids I know how unlikely that is.

Chris Gahan

School Milk

The Red Lion Building in Somerton used to be a post office run by Mr and Mrs Salter. The boys' school was next door. Boys and girls went to separate schools in those days – the girls were taught by Miss Bibby at Monteclefe, and the boys by Miss Lacy at the boys' school. I'd been at Monteclefe for a year when they moved us all up to the boys' school. We were crammed in together while they modernised Monteclefe. When we eventually moved back, Monteclefe became co-ed, and we were taught by Mr Davis and Miss Swain – Miss Lacy was our head mistress. She was very creative, and I loved our art classes.

I loved going to school, but my worst memory is of school milk. We used to be given a third of a pint every day. In winter the frozen milk was brought in and placed near the big stoves in the classrooms to thaw out. I had allergies and wasn't supposed to have milk – I used to try and sit next to someone who loved milk so that I could swap my full bottle for their empty one, but I often got caught and was made to drink it and it always made me sick!

Denise Lazenby

Somerton, Somerset, Broad Street c1960 S147059

> ❛ I was one of those strange children who had allergies and wasn't supposed to have milk ❜

Unusual Punishment

Somerton, Somerset, Langport Road c1960 S147048

On the corner you can see the Infants' School run by Mrs Williams. The school became a bit crowded, so the little ones were sent around to the Drill Hall behind Berry where Mrs Lareham was our teacher. We had to walk round the corner to the school two by two holding hands. If you were naughty Mrs Lareham hung a notice around your neck with things like 'Keep away from me, I bite' or 'Keep away from me, I tell lies' written on a board on strings. After lunch we had to get out the mats and have a rest. Then we were allowed out in the playground where there was a big wooden jungle gym.

Denise Lazenby

Arithmetic and Frogspawn

The village school had only about 50 children, and only two classes; the elder children were taught by Mr Jackson the headmaster, and the younger ones by 'Miss'. Mr Jackson sat on a very high lectern-like wooden desk, so he could see everything that was going on. He terrified me. So did arithmetic, which he taught. In every annual report he commented that 'Rosemarie must learn to overcome her fear of arithmetic'. I never have.

As children we had plenty to keep us entertained. There were wonderful playing fields below the church, where I spent hours on the swings and took many a tumble from the slide onto the gravel. There was no supervision, and scabby knees were the norm – we simply cried, then started again. My friend John Dunkley and I loved to go to the stream where we collected frogspawn and watched the tadpoles develop, and caught minnows and sticklebacks, caterpillars, butterflies and ladybirds. Now I shudder to think how many of these creatures we destroyed in our attempts to understand how their anatomy worked.

Rosemarie Delaney (a memory of schooldays at Byfield, Northamptonshire)

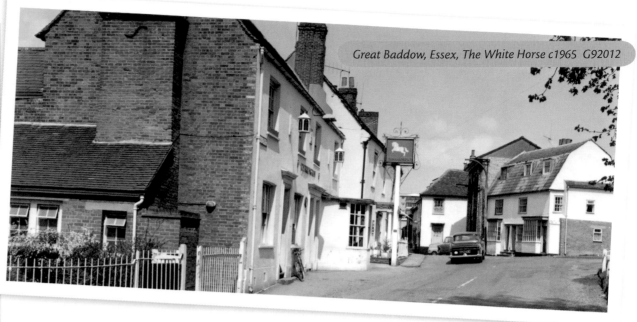

Great Baddow, Essex, The White Horse c1965 G92012

Straw Hats every Sunday

I was sent to a children's home in Great Baddow when I was about twelve. My memories are both sad and happy ones. Miss May and Miss Abbs ran the home. Miss May had a boxer dog, and many years later I bought one too in memory of Great Baddow children's home. We went to the local church dressed in our uniforms with little straw hats.

I told everyone I was an orphan. It sounded better than not being wanted from the age of 3 and having many foster parents. But I have no regrets. I have had, and continue to have, a happy life. My only sad memories are of not being able ever to say these two words: Mum and Dad. I remember running away from the home when I first went there, as I needed to find Mum and Dad. I never did.

Vicky (née Morrisson)

Shock Makes your Hair Fall Out

While at Bearsted school I got into trouble with a teacher called Mrs Edwards, and she grabbed a handful of my hair and shook my head to and fro. A lump of hair came out as big as half a crown. When I went home my dad was cutting up meat, and as I was very young and small, he could see the top of my head.

He called out to my mum and they decided to take me to the doctor's. After he had had a look, he said 'Because he had his tonsils out a few weeks ago, it is the shock coming out', and he gave my parents a bottle of Metho in a blue fluted bottle to dab on my head. My dad never knew the truth.

Ian Simmons

Mr Madden's Cane Cupboard

Seeing this photograph of Hugh Bell School conjures all sorts of memories. I remember two headmasters, 'Taffy' Evans, the cane-toting, foot-stamping disciplinarian, and

Charles Harmer, a gentle man with a persuasive manner. Mr Evans sometimes took us for music, and he always pushed 'Sweet Lass of Richmond Hill', to the point where we got fed up with it. Once the class sang 'Sweet Lass of Richmon Dill', and we thought he was going to blow a gasket!

My favourite subject was maths with 'Buller' Madden. His teaching methods would certainly be outlawed today, but in most cases he got results. Ex-pupils will remember how he entered a classroom filled with silence, marked the register, and then went to his cane cupboard. Having selected his favourite for the day, he would hit his desk top a few times and then start going around the class. 'Area of a square? You don't know, get out. Circumference of a circle? You don't know, get out', and so on until everyone in the class had been asked a question on formulae. The 'get out' instructed those who hadn't answered correctly to go to the front of the class, where they would be caned and sent back to their seats. I was never caned, and can still remember all the formulae some 60 years on. Unfortunately there were some who were caned quite a lot.

When I started at the school I was small for my age, and I know my parents worried that I might be bullied. They need not have been concerned as two of the tallest lads in the class kept an eye out for me: 'Polly' Wharton and 'Dicky' Purvis. My best pal was Fred Kirby until his family emigrated to Australia.

Clifford Wilson

Middlesbrough, North Yorkshire, Hugh Bell School 1896 37557

Middlesbrough, North Yorkshire, Linthorpe Road 1951 M71004

Hysteria in Church

My first and last visit to Eaglesham church was as a schoolboy at Lawmuir Agricultural School in nearby Jackton. Lawmuir was a boarding school then, and pupils went on a voluntary basis, paid for by Glasgow Corporation Education Department. The idea was that we would spend half a day in school and the other half working on the farm. The school was split into two different groups, giving the farm work a full day's cover. We boarded for a fortnight at a time, and went home every second weekend, leaving one group of lads to help milk the cows and feed the pigs and so on over the weekend.

Our headmaster thought that our spiritual needs required some attention, so he decided that those of us not required on the farm should scrub up, put away our copies of the News of the World, and pay our respects to the vicar and his parishioners during their mid-morning service. We were a bunch of Glasgow lads from all areas of the city, who only ever went to church to be christened, married or buried, and even under these circumstances very reluctantly.

It was a nice spring morning, as we walked from Jackton to Eaglesham. There were about 20 of us walking in double file. The teacher in charge of us was a Mr Macindoer, a no-nonsense Islay man. The nearer we got to the church, the more

Eaglesham, Strathclyde, The Church c1955   E118302

Eaglesham, Strathclyde, Main Street c1955   E118301

nervous we got, for most of us had never seen the inside of a church, let alone been to a service. We arrived at the entrance, and Mr Macindoer lined us up and warned us of the dire consequences if we misbehaved. But he did not want to be there any more than we did. No doubt a God-fearing man and churchgoer, he certainly did not want to be in charge of a group of Glasgow riff-raff.

We were led into the church by Mr Macindoer. Eaglesham being the God-fearing place it is, the church was full, all except for two rows of pews reserved for us. To a man all eyes were on us, and we felt as though we had invaded their holy place. Almost immediately we sat down, there were a few giggles, but even Mr Macindoer could not contain our hysteria when during one of the psalms a large lady began to sing with a voice so shrill and off-key that we all went into uncontrollable fits of giggles. The more our teacher tried to stop us the worse it got. The infection spread through all of us. Somehow we got to the end of the service, and Mr Macindoer could not get us out of there fast enough. We were all of the same mind – escape.

The strange thing was that he never said a word to us all the way back to the school. Perhaps he was afraid of what he might do to us if he vented his anger. Needless to say, church was never again mentioned after that, and it was back to the good old News of the World on a Sunday morning.

Angus Brennan

Convent School Life

During the 1940s I lived in Weymouth, but from May 1942, when I was five, until July 1947 I was a boarder at the convent school in Bridport. I was happy there, and still remember the names of my teachers, Sister Anne, Sister Edith and Sister Magdalene. We went for a walk every Tuesday and Saturday afternoon. We walked in twos, with one nun leading the column and another bringing up the rear. Sometimes we just went to West Bay, at other times we would go to Loders (which seemed very far) or Allington, Symondsbury Copse or Eype.

Meals were taken in silence and we had to attend Mass every morning at 7.45 before breakfast. On Tuesday and Saturday evenings we attended Benediction. I was an altar server and choirboy.

On VE Day 1945 Union Jacks and Belgian flags were hung from the top windows of the convent and we had a game of cricket in our convent field opposite.

We had spiked iron railings around our playground and one morning in 1947 I happened to look out of one of the top windows of the convent building (before it was time to get up) and saw what seemed to be a grey shape draped over these railings. A cow or bull had tried to jump them and killed itself in the attempt.

The school closed down about 1970, and the whole convent building was demolished in 2000. Houses have now been built on the site.

James McGuinness

Bridport, Dorset, The Convent 1903 50486

Eype, Dorset, The Beach 1930 83371

West Bay, Dorset, The Rocks 1922 72800

I was born in 1950 and attended the convent school at Bridport as a boarder, leaving in 1958. I travelled by train with my mother from New Street Station, Birmingham, to Paddington Station, London, where the convent nuns met us and the other schoolchildren to accompany us for the rest of the journey to Bridport. We used to have long country walks during the summer, and I remember going to a place covered in long ferns, where we played. The regime at the convent was very strict, and the educational standard extremely high. French and Latin were taught well before the 11+ stage. I still have a couple of the bills for my upkeep that were sent to my mother. I also have some photos of myself taken during my time at the convent. One of them shows my classmates and me in the classroom being taught by Sister Edith, I believe. Our clothes had to be marked with our name and number. Mine had Cash's name tapes, and my number was 4. I still have my teddy bear with my name and number attached to his ear! I returned to see the convent in 1982 during a holiday in the area, and met Sister Anne. Her first words on seeing me again after many years were 'Good God, it's Alan Yardley'!

I have mixed feelings concerning my time at the convent. Whilst the standard of education was extremely high, I personally experienced treatment that these days could be considered little short of abuse. I remember standing in front of a stone sink in an unlit ground floor room washing my underwear with a large bar of soap whilst a nun stood behind me telling me how wicked I was for having soiled myself. I have every respect for some of the nuns who taught me. The young novices were especially kind. Some of the older nuns, however, were little short of sadistic bullies. Alan Yardley

Good Teachers, Good Friends – and 'the Stimulator'

I was born in Ilford in 1933 – and lived in Elstree Gardens near Loxford Park. After attending Woodlands Road Primary School I went to Cleveland Road School, off Ilford Lane. Although we were very well behaved, at the end of lessons we hurried to get out into the playground. This involved descending the many granite stairs to the ground floor at breakneck speed. The roar of this exodus as kids sped to freedom is something I will never forget. The headmaster was a very kind man called Mr Edwards and our teacher was Mrs Strachan (pronouned Strawn). They made our school years happy.

They also taught us something, because I passed the 11+ exam and was sent to the best school in the borough, Ilford County High School. We went to ICHS during the war years, and the corridors were still reinforced with brick blast barriers to protect pupils against bomb blast. The barriers were removed shortly after the war ended. The headmaster of the school was Mr Harry S Kenward, a stern disciplinarian, although gentle when you got to know him. The head teacher was Mr MacPherson, a very likeable man who taught economics. Every morning we had assembly when Mr Kenward gave announcements and led most of the boys in hymns and prayers. Music was provided by Mr Selwyn Lowe on the grand piano – he used to turn bright red if the boys substituted a rude version for the words of the hymns. We attempted to learn French, but it was difficult as none of us then could see the point of it. The French teacher was Dr Bryant. In the back of his cupboard he kept a small cane that he called 'the stimulator'.

We had a good education at ICHS and I owe much to it, having now retired after a successful career in journalism. I still see some of my old school friends monthly at a pub in Epping, Essex. Considering that we left ICHS in 1949, this says something for the strength of friendships made at school.

Alan Massam

Ilford, Greater London c1967 I34020

Ilford, Greater London, Ilford Lane, The Market 1948 I34002

Ilford, Greater London, Valentine's Park 1949 I34012

Escape from the Cane

Almost from the moment I took my seat in Miss Gow's class at Roe Green Primary School in London, I had this sinking feeling in the pit of my stomach. School and I were not a match made in heaven. The terrible tales of the cane as administered to non-conformists by the head mistress, Miss Hopkins, should have been enough to keep me in line. But before I knew it, the words were out – I had committed the unforgiveable. I had talked in class. Then came the sentence: 'Down to Miss Hopkins' office' – oh please let me die right here and now, thought I. By the time I knocked on Miss Hopkins' door, I was sobbing my heart out. She called me in and must have seen the utter fear that convulsed me, because she said, 'If you don't tell anyone that I didn't cane you, I won't, but you must pretend I did. It'll be our little secret'. How do YOU spell relief?

Petersfield, Hampshire, The Market Place c1955 P48039

By the time I was nine, Mum realized that her daughter's potential was not being tapped at Roe Green School, so she sent me to Henrietta Barnett Junior School, a girls' school in Hampstead, where I quickly crossed swords with drill teacher, Miss Wells. Compared to Miss Wells, a Marine Drill Sergeant would be like Mary Poppins. She seemed to derive the utmost pleasure in making us perform tortuous contortions on the various apparatus.

As if to add insult to injury for my long-suffering mother, I failed the eleven-plus exam better than anyone else in the history of the school. Without missing a beat, Mum promptly enrolled me in a boarding school, far away from anyone who knew me, in the sleepy little town of Petersfield, Hampshire. For the first time, teachers started to make sense. Our geography teacher, Miss Humphries, with plaited hair wound like snail-shells around each ear, and wearing thick brown stockings, brogues and tweed, managed to get it into my head that Hobart is the capital of Tasmania. We all developed kinks in our necks from reading her writing on the board, which went from top left and dropped dramatically, like a stock market graph, to finish at bottom right.

Mr Marks, our English teacher, made an indelible impression on me. If he spotted you looking indolent, he caught your attention by shooting his propelling pencil at your head with deadly aim. Miraculously, at the age of thirteen, mostly to the credit of Mr Marks, I found myself top of the class – not at all to my mum's surprise.

Heather Rohrer

Petersfield, Hampshire, The Pond c1960 P48032

Dancing round the handbags

TEENAGE MEMORIES

My First Guitar

I was a 13-year-old rocker, a 14-year-old mod and a 15-year-old hippy. My weekends were spent hanging about on Figges Marsh with my reefer jacket, tiger's tail or cow bell (depending on the current trend), as my cousins all lived in Mitcham. We used to go to 'band practice' at the church hall just off Gorringe Park Avenue on the border of Figges Marsh to see The Oddz 'n' Enz and do the Memphis dance.

I spent a lot of time in Tooting Broadway. I was a Grenadier child and went to Saturday morning pictures at the Grenada, and from 1963 onwards I went to as many concerts at the Grenada as my Saturday job could pay for! I saw the Rolling Stones, the Beatles and Helen Shapiro, to name but a few, with my little sister and my cousin in tow. The Beatles lodged in a house in Trevelyan Road, as I'm sure many Tooting-ites will remember.

Tooting, Greater London, The Police Station 1951 T201019

I bought my first guitar from the Broadway music shop for £52, which I saved from my wages. My dad used to take £1 10s housekeeping money, and I would have about four quid left for myself. That lasted all week, and I had a good time on it. I used to walk the whole length of Garratt Lane, and turn off at Earlsfield and along Penwith Road to Merton to save the bus fares to buy that guitar. It was a 12-string jumbo and would cost a small fortune now.

Then there was the Lots o' Fun arcade at Tooting Broadway. I was forbidden to go, as 'the boys there all smoke' as my mum used to say. Of course I took no notice, and went anyway, and smoked as many fags as I could blag. If I had a spare shilling, I would play pinball and try to get as many free balls as possible.

Then there was the wonderful Harringtons pie and mash shop. I went there on Saturday nights with my glass jar for 'licker'. It didn't seem to matter what size jar you had, they filled it up anyway. Lovely grub. Sundays in the Summer of Love of 1967 were spent on Tooting, Mitcham or Wimbledon common (or Hyde Park if we could afford the tube fare), with a guitar or portable record player in hand, cow bells round our necks. I had the time of my life!

Jackie Rice

One of those Everlasting Summers of Youth

In June 1964 a group of us – all Belfast grammar school boys – crossed the sea to Liverpool and took a long coach journey south to spend the school summer vacation working in the Bournemouth beach cafés.

Three of us shared a bedroom at Pat and Alvin's, a short bus ride from the town centre. Our 'digs' cost just £1 10s a week each, out of a wage of £5 at the beach cafés. The café provided lunch, and in the evening we ate at the Golden Griddle in the Square. We were able to buy clothes out of our pay packets: the fashions that summer were bell-bottom jeans, pink shirts and grey crewnecks and we grew our school regulation short-back-and sides down to our shoulders.

In the two months we stayed in Bournemouth it rained on just one afternoon. We were incarcerated in the dark steamy wash-ups of the café during the blazing daytime hours. But the evenings were mellow and divine; we seemed to float in the softness, between the pier and the gardens. Bournemouth had a continental feeling about it. We sang Irish folk songs sitting on the grass as the light slowly failed. We went to the bowling alley and ate chips before getting back to bed by about half-past-ten.

Later there was light-hearted flirtation and romance with a group of local girls. Whatever became of little blonde Carol, I wonder? It was one of those youthful summers to last forever as a glow of enchantment in the memory. I was 16 then, and will be 60 next year.

When we got home to Belfast, our long hair and pink shirts caused heads to turn along Royal Avenue. We felt like a pop group.

John McMillan

Bournemouth, Dorset, The Arcade c1955 B163153p

Bournemouth, Dorset, Pavilion Gardens c1955 B163154

Great Acts and Frothy Coffee

When I left school in 1962 my pal Chris Marks and I used to go to the Lyndale in Eccles, over Burton's the tailor's. We saw some great acts – Herman and the Hermits, the Rockin' Berries, Brian Page and the Chapters, the Stylos, and loads of local groups that didn't make it.

Then we graduated to the Jungfrau in Manchester where you could dance the night away without the need for alcohol – instead it was coffee (frothy), Coca Cola or Pepsi. Or we went to the Twisted Wheel, where we saw acts like Long John Baldry, the Rolling Stones, or the Hollies. It was a fantastic time to be a teenager. I actually saw the Beatles at the Ardwick Apollo – live! I worked opposite Granada TV, and met the Kinks, Karl Denver, Gerry and the Pacemakers, the Stones and the Beatles in the early 60s. What wonderful memories – if only we could go back. If we missed the bus home we would take off our shoes and walk, with no fear at all.

Moira Edge

A Californian Flower Child in Chester

I am an American who went to school in Chester in 1966/67. Rather, I should say that I was registered for school at Chester College. However, I can't say I was actually in the building very often. There just always seemed to be somewhere else to go, and something more interesting to see instead.

I arrived in Chester just as the hippies were raising their flowered heads back home in the beach areas of southern California where I came from. I remember my new English friend Tristin, wearing very, very long hair (for 1966), a burlap caftan, and sandals, riding a donkey from the college across the Dee bridge to the cathedral while the rest of us followed, chanting and waving branches that were supposed to resemble palm fronds of some sort. I think we were the first hippies in Chester, but then I also seem to recall that the very next day we went right back to being Mods. The donkey had been extremely disagreeable, and the caftans were quite breezy for November, as well as scratchy.

I remember throwing bits of cotton candy (candy floss) to the swans on the River Dee because we didn't have bread with us, but the cotton candy immediately dissolved upon hitting the water, and we had to run for our lives when the angry swans came up out of the water and chased us around the bandstand. I would now like to sincerely apologise to the very slow little old couple with the walking canes who tried to hide behind a tree.

On one of the rare occasions when I was inside the college building I played

Chester, Cheshire 1906 55280

my Motown soul albums in the common room. My new English friends wanted me to teach them how to dance the 'Soul Strut'. I had never been to a dance in my life, but had I not watched 'American Bandstand' every week? It did not seem necessary to explain such a small detail to any of them. I may not have been a good student in that building, but I must have been a dazzling teacher.   *Linda Ashworth*

Redhill, Surrey, The Market Hall 1899 43148

Saturday Nights

What memories this building holds. It gave a lot of teenagers the opportunity to have their first Saturday nights out. The entrance price was 1s 6d unless there was a known group appearing, and then it was 2s 6d. I went to Redhill Tech and worked on a Saturday at Woolies on the sweet counter. Most of the day was spent chatting to various friends who came in, and there was great excitement in waiting for the evening to arrive.

I would rush home, wolf down some tea, and then spend about two hours trying on outfits, usually wearing the first dress that I had put on. Minis were just coming in, and there were clothes that were actually designed for teenagers, rather than trying to make them look like mini adults. One of my favourite outfits

was a mustard-coloured dress with black buttons and mock drop collars – I thought I was the bee's knees!

I would meet up with friends and we'd all troop off together.

We cottoned on to the fact that the groups would stay in the old South Eastern Hotel. I vividly remember when the Hollies came to town and my mate Liz and I just sat there looking and trying to sound cool when answering any of their questions. Liz came away that night with a chicken bone that Graham Nash had nibbled on. I wonder how many years she kept it.

And the handbags! A great pile on the floor with all the girls dancing round them, while all the boys sat around the outside of the dance floor eyeing up the girls and trying to look big.   Sue Hoyland

Oh to be Sweet 16 Again!

I think the girl in the photo (right) with the shopping bag is myself at the age of 16 or 17, judging by my hairstyle at that time. I recognise the skirt as one I made myself, and my walk as well. I had just walked past a cake shop where my sister worked, and I am looking in a jeweller's window. I would have been very interested in the rings, as I was due to be engaged on my 18th birthday in January 1965. The Wynd is pretty much the same as it was then – very quaint and olde worlde – it was always a favourite place to saunter and window shop.

Margaret Batey

Darlington, County Durham, Post House Wynd c1965 D2032p

Missing the Last Bus Home

So I missed the last bus home, in my case to Castlemilk from St Enoch's Square, after a night at the Locarno. It was winter, cold, wet and windy, and I knew I had to do it. I had to stand and wait for the number 2 bus to get me into Castlemilk, but never near to where I lived. Oh, the thought of waiting for the stupid bus at the Square and the dreaded walk home, which was about two miles from the nearest bus stop.

If that wasn't bad enough, the wrath of my mother awaited me on the other side of the door. She was ready with her lecture about the importance of never again missing the 10 o'clock bus.

Come Christmas, waiting seemed a treat, as the lights in George Square in Glasgow were gleaming and somehow all was well with the world. Even my mother's words didn't seem as harsh.

But did I ever miss the bus again? You bet. I couldn't miss that last dance. Miss the bus, yes, but never that dance.

I have wonderful memories of George Square. On each visit home from Texas I seem to end up every day around the Square, but the old post office phone boxes are no longer there to shield me from the rain. That is the sad part. But the change in the area is incredible. No longer empty after midnight, it is jumping with excitement, and lots of memories are still being made. How I love it.

Helen Clark

Glasgow, Strathclyde, George Square 1897 39759

I Still Miss Northwich

I was born in Northwich in 1966 and I still remember my time here as the best days of my life. I lived in Greenhall Road, and my best friend Tracey lived on Victoria Road. We were great friends then, and are still friends now, even though we have both moved away from the area.

Most of my best memories are about boys, probably the only thing you think of when you're 13 and 14. Tracey and I would finish school on Friday nights, get dressed up, and go straight to the Rudheath youth club. On Saturdays we'd go down the town. Off to the chippy first, then downtown, where we'd buy a few records, then go for a drink in Popormbies (cream soda was great), then to Woolworth's to look at more records, and then we messed about in the phone box for a while. Then home, usually round to my Auntie Nonie's to watch wrestling – well, more to laugh at my Uncle Tommy watching it. He used to get so worked up, and it was hilarious.

On Saturday nights we went up Greenbank or Leftwich to sit on the benches there, but we had to be home by 9. We didn't dare to be late. We went through the arches and past Roker Park, it never bothered us then, but we would never do it now. Or sometimes we'd go through the graveyard where my Nana is now buried. She used to tell us 'it's not the dead that will hurt you, it is the living'. I will remember her saying that forever.

I went to Victoria Road Primary School, and had some great friends and good times there. Then I went to Rudheath High School, one of the best schools around. Sadly my Nana died when I was 13, and Mum and Dad decided to move away and buy a shop in Padiham, Lancashire. I was devastated to leave, and cried all the way. I missed Tracey and all my friends. My mum found it hard to settle too, and kept going back all the time. We got used to living here, but I will never forget my roots, and I still have happy memories of Northwich.
Vicky Wood

Northwich, Cheshire, Witton Street c1950   N43005

Leicester, Leicestershire, De Montfort Hall c1955 L144126

De Montfort Rocked!

It is good to see De Montfort Hall as it used to be. It was a great venue to see bands. Once the small blues clubs had ran their course, bands needed larger venues to ply their trade, and De Montfort was one of the first.

Groups I saw here were Rory Gallagher, John Hiseman's Colosseum, Yes, Sutherland Brothers/Quiver, and Free when they reformed briefly. The last band I saw before the modernisation of the hall was Uriah Heep, with a rather drunk David Byron fronting the band. Other major bands to visit De Montfort were Genesis, Supertramp and The Sensational Alex Harvey Band.

Today, De Montfort is an all-seater venue – no more standing on the dance floor! Although it needed a make-over for many years, in doing so it has lost its soul. The only similarity to those 70s years is the rush for the bar in the interval, although now it appears to be well dressed men and women thrusting their money under the barmen's noses – God! maybe one of those well dressed men could be me ... I take it all back!

Mick Austin

> 6 I recall we saw cut-away graves near the top of the cliff with several leg bones protruding 9

Dunwich, Suffolk, The Church Ruins 1891 28359

Graves, Bones and a Skull

I spent my teenage years in Dunwich, and I had freedom, long walks, the beach and sea, cliffs, marshes and the old tank defences from the Second World War. My best friend Justin North and I spent hours roaming, swimming, canoeing, making carts to career down the hill from the monastery, and resurrecting a storm-damaged painter's punt washed ashore to row to Walberswick on the irrigation rivers behind the dunes.

Although All Saint's Church had fallen off the cliff long before we were born, some of the cemetery remained on the cliff top, including numerous unmarked paupers' graves. Pieces of masonry and rubble still lay at the foot of the cliff, now covered frequently by the tides and the pebbles, but occasionally washed clean for brief periods, allowing us to scramble over them. Our most interesting times were after the neap tides in the spring, when high seas would wash away more of the sandy cliffs, causing minor falls and the exposure of more graves. On one occasion we saw cut-away graves near the top of the cliff with several leg bones protruding one above the other, clearly mass graves where a number of bodies had been buried in the same grave. The local vicar used to come along with a plastic sack and collect the skulls and bones that had been revealed, and would re-inter them in the graveyard at St James's, the more modern church at the bottom of the main street.

Justin was about to attend Art School, and was very interested in photography. On one occasion we found a complete skull that had been embedded in a lump of sandy cliff that had slid down from the graveyard. We liberated it, and Justin took it home, cleaned it, and photographed it in various lights, including with a lighted candle inside. I can't remember what eventually happened to it, but if anyone digs the garden at Marshside and finds human remains, they probably came from the clifftop cemetery.

James Ritchie

Those carefree summer days

HOLIDAY AND LEISURE MEMORIES

The Gypsy Horse Fair

I lived on Long Street in Topcliffe from 1958 to 1972, opposite the old school, on the other side of the road from this photo. I was excited by the fair: horses trotting along the road, smells, sights and sounds different from usual, and lots of people, including photographers who wanted to take pictures from our upstairs windows and the occasional visitor who would ask to use our loo.

Gypsy children attended Topcliffe school in the period before the fair. But village people and the Gypsies didn't seem to mix, although a generation earlier, Gypsies came to give condolences on the death of my grandfather, who was a butcher in the village, so there must have been some channels of communication. And for the generation before my grandfather's, I believe that the fair lasted three days or more, and there were fairground rides.

In 1969 or early 1970, I spotted a notice on the door of the village shop saying that the next fair would be the last. The reason given for stopping the fair was that it caused traffic problems on the A168, the road shown here. Topcliffe didn't get a by-pass until the mid 1970s. Unofficially, the stoppage may have been connected with a degree of ill feeling. The last fair was a bit of a damp squib, with fewer Gypsies and horses.

Topcliffe, North Yorkshire, The Annual Gypsy Fair 1962   T138022

The fair left such a strong impression on me. I now regularly visit Appleby in Westmorland Fair, the largest Gypsy/traveller event of its kind in Europe. But I think that 'visit' is the key word – just as in the days of Topcliffe fair, there seems to be a glass wall between the Gypsies and the spectators.

Jan Dickenson

London, Nomads 1885 L130212p

Posing and Preening at Congleton Open Air Baths

It had an entrance worthy of a theatre, two steps up with an overhanging portico and glass doors that opened up to a foyer. At the point of payment there was a turnstile that was painted council silver and a lady who collected 6d for swimmers and 2d for spectators. Some people had a season ticket that cost 7/6d and there was a competition amongst the kids to have the lowest-numbered season ticket, number 1 or 2 being the prize. The lowest I got was number 6.

When you went through the turnstile you turned right. Swimmers turned right again, but spectators went straight ahead into the surrounding area of the pool. There were wooden stepped seats all down the left-hand side, which was more than enough for the amount of speccys. The diving boards were terrific. They were at the deep end, shadowed by the gas bags at the gas works.

> ‘ Sunburnt, no Brylcreem, socks inside out, but clean, we went home ’

The changing rooms were cold, wet, wooden chicken huts. And why do men sing when they are put into an environment where they have to undress and there are other people around? They would sing 'Hang Down your Head Tom Dooley', 'What Do Ya Want if Ya Don't Want Money', 'Does Your Chewing Gum Lose Its Flavour on the Bed Post Overnight'!

The bloomin' footbath was so damn cold that we tried all kinds of ways to avoid it, from doing a trapeze act on the overhanging water pipes to trying to jump it completely. It was there to prevent the spread of athlete's foot, but there were more athletes who avoided the footbath with their feet than went through it.

The pool was absolutely great. Blue, clean and inviting. After the first dive, the immediate thought was, 'What the blinkin' heck did I do that for?' It soon got rid of the Brylcreem in your hair and shrunk the parts that only Heineken could reach.

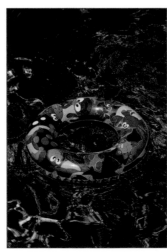

The fountain at the shallow end was a marvel, a cascading waterfall that was a part of the filtration process after the water was heated in the boiler house, which was all pipes, valves, knobs and had a smell of chlorine. The superintendant was always busy. He had a broom connected to a 30 or 40ft pole for brushing the bottom of the pool and he doubled up as the lifeguard.

I think the biggest emergency I saw was when an elderly man lost his false teeth and the 'super' dived in (fully clothed) and retrieved them, to much applause from the crowd.

Car inner tubes were always a favourite as floats. The trouble was that the metal valve used to inflate the tube would dig into your flesh. It left your back looking as though you had been a galley slave on a Viking ship who had been whipped. Someone tried to bring in a tractor tube, but it got stuck in the turnstile at the point of entry.

Congleton, Cheshire, The Baths c1950 C151006

On many a good summer day the pool was packed. It became impossible to jump or dive into the water, and those who had the courage to do so would either land on the torso of a hostile swimmer, or would make a good friend.

When the super/ lifeguard blew the whistle, the pool would fill up with all the posers who had spent the afternoon sunbathing and wanted to cool down, while other swimmers who had been in the water all afternoon made a quick exit to ensure that they had a cubicle to change in private.

> ‘ The changing rooms were cold, wet, wooden chicken huts with cages ’

It's still here in my head: 'Hang Down Your Head Tom Dooley', 'Li'l White Bull', 'My Boomerang Won't Come Back' – sunburnt, no Brylcreem, socks inside out, but clean, we went home.

Alec Coles

Giving the Girls a Fright at the Pool

On carefree summer days we would cycle from Myland to the pool, leave our bikes, unlocked, in a heap outside, pay our 6d and go to the dank, cold, changing room under the bridge. The girls had to cross the end of the pool by a boardwalk to their changing room on the other side. There were high diving boards, so the pool was about ten feet deep at the deep end. We discovered that there was a hole in the underwater wire netting beneath the boardwalk where we could dive down to come up under the boardwalk to bang on the boards as the girls walked over.

Peter Gant

Colchester, Essex, The Swimming Pool c1960   C136042

The Ballad of Davy Crockett

When we went to 'Dick's' for lunch, there would be me, my kid sister, my parents and my maternal grandparents, plus Mum's youngest sister. She was only five years older than me – 'Auntie Betsy' – and more like a big sister. She was the prodigy of the family, learning to play the piano, and Grandma used to pressure a reluctant Betsy to play something on the pub piano. This was at the time when Fess Parker was hitting the screens as Davy Crockett, and the theme tune was one of Betsy's special pieces. Unfortunately, one particular key on the pub piano was way out of tune. For those who remember the tune, the intro was sort of 'da dum di dum dum dum, dum di dum dum …' The bum note was on the fourth dum – it must have been an octave out – and the bar was crowded. It brought the house down, much to Auntie Betsy's mortification!

Pete Widdows

Eldwick, West Yorkshire, Dick Hudson's Pub 1921   71288

Ripped Off by a Millionaire

Summer. Our first car, our first boat, our first meetings with the young ladies of Llangefni. It could have been 1969, when a group of mates from St Helens set out on holiday in a grey Triumph Courier van, registration number 837 EDM. On top was a white polystyrene boat, and inside a top-of-the-range tent. The weather then was always glorious in summer, and we were on our first adventure.

We met some ladies from Llangefni and we all spent the days and evenings together. They then walked home and we walked around to the pub (the Ship). What we didn't realise was that pubs were shut on Sundays. The first Sunday, because we didn't have enough money to join St David's Club, we drove all the way home to St Anne's Club in Sutton. We then drove all the way back to go to sleep and prepare for another day of heaven. During the next week we got friendly with the steward in charge of St David's Club. It was an oasis in the desert, and he allowed us in without paying a fee.

It was in the club that we met a very old, down-at-heel man. We had very little, but he was counting his pennies. So every time we got a pint, we would buy him one. This went on for a few days, and it made us feel good that he could get out each day because of our charity. On one of our last days at the camp the steward said 'Why do you keep buying drinks for someone you don't know?'. I said 'He's old and he ain't got much and he's quite good company, we'll be like that one day'. The old man didn't come in that day, so it was a cheaper day.

The next morning the three girls from Llangefni were at the tent cooking a beautiful breakfast. It was our last day. We had had the best holiday that anyone could have. We met locals, we met tourists. We spent our last few hours in the club, and who should come in but the old man.

He wouldn't have a drink, but he said 'Any time you come to St David's, everything is yours, you have all made an old man happy'. Wow. He then left, and the steward said 'Go and look out of the window, he'll wave to you'. I then saw this RED ROLLS ROYCE with a chauffeur opening the door. Our old man waved, and then disappeared. I said to the steward 'Who was that?'. He laughed. 'He is the owner of the camp site and all of the land you can see for miles around'. We had been ripped off by a millionaire.

All I want to know now is – who was that old man? I would love to retrace my steps and stay at St David's Head and buy that man another drink and tell him my stories.

Dennis A Mee

Red Wharf Bay, Gwynedd c1950 R338034

> ❝ All I want to know now is – who was that old man? ❞

Weather Glorious, Lovely Time

It was the year before I married that my husband-to-be and I went on holiday to Weymouth. We had a lovely time and the weather was just glorious for us. We always said that when we married we would revisit Weymouth. Well, we did in the year 1968 with our first-born. She was 4 years old at that time. I remember so well enjoying a day on the beach, and my little daughter had such fun watching Punch & Judy shows. I will visit Weymouth again one of these days to relive all those memories of bygone days.   Brenda Vanderwert

Weymouth, Dorset, The Beach c1955   W76098t

Avoncliff, Wiltshire, The Aqueduct c1950 A329012

Canter across the Canal

It must have been around the late 1960s and early 1970s when my sister and I used to ride our ponies down to Avoncliff. We lived a short distance away in Upper Westwood and our mother liked us to ride along the towpath, as it kept us away from the roads and any traffic that might spook our ponies. Avoncliff

was a favourite place – at that time the aqueduct was dry, and instead of going down and under the bridge we used to take our nimble ponies down the bank, canter across the bottom, and leap up the other side! I'm sure our ponies enjoyed it as much as we did, as they would start prancing around in anticipation as we came round the last corner and approached the canal.

The towpath was very overgrown and a haven for wildlife. We pretty much had it to ourselves. Once across, we would canter all the way to Bradford on Avon, only slowing down for a rest when we got to the tithe barn, also overgrown, where we would stop for a while and let the ponies eat some grass. Then we would jump back on and continue our ride along Frome Road over the canal bridge and back towards home up Jones Lane. Mum's dog Yogi would hear our ponies clip-clopping along the road long before anybody else could, and would sit out in the road waiting for us to return.

Frances Nelson

Sanctuary on a Long Journey

Savernake Forest is significant to me because this was the chosen halfway point on our family's mid 1950s journey from Hereford to Portsmouth for our annual summer holidays.

Here, my stepfather would pull the old Hillman off the road amongst the huge oaks of this ancient historic forest. We would take out the sandwiches and lemonade we had packed for the trip and wolf them down (I was always hungry). This was followed by stretching our legs in the cool of the forest before resuming our journey.

Dylan Rivis

Savernake Forest, Wiltshire, Long Harry Walk 1908   60945

Merched Y Bryniau: Memorable Performances by the Choir

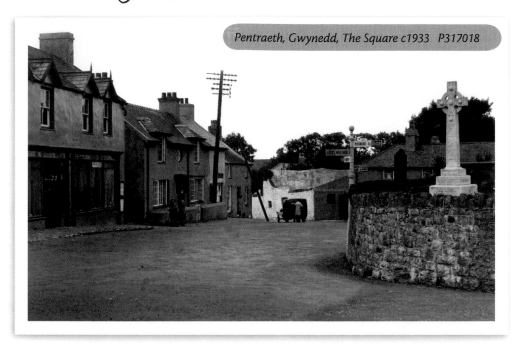

Pentraeth, Gwynedd, The Square c1933 P317018

About 38 years ago, I was approached by some of my former pupils, now mostly married and with children of their own, with the idea of forming a Pentraeth-based entertainment group. The village had always had an excellent reputation for choral singing and they wanted to revive the tradition, but on more modern lines.

They wanted me to weld them into an acceptable group. My protests about not being able to play an instrument, read music, or act as choirmaster went unheeded. Most of them had good voices and an ear for harmony, so they would monitor themselves, and learn as they went along. All they wanted from me was the ability to discipline and organise. So Merched Y Bryniau was born. At the final count, the group had over 40 ladies aged from 30 to over 60, a mixture of mums, daughters, and a couple of grans, all eager to make a success of the whole project.

The programme was ambitious, stretching from Welsh traditional songs to Welsh pop, English favourites ancient and modern, South American collections and sea shanties. The choral pieces were interspersed by solos, duets and comedy spots. At one stage they even experimented with a skiffle band, complete with washboards.

Invitations to perform at various venues began to roll in. Most were enjoyable, but some places presented certain hazards. One such was at Llanddona Village Hall. The hall was full. Merched Y Bryniau opened the evening with a

collection of South American and West Indian songs, starting with the Banana Boat Song. The ladies looked as authentic as possible, and each member carried a basket of bananas on her head. No sooner had they reached the first chorus, when the lights went out and plunged everyone into darkness.

A panic-stricken whisper reached me at the side of the stage: 'What shall we do, Mrs Davies?'. 'Stay exactly where you are', I ordered. 'Put your baskets on the stage beside you. The lights will be back, oh, in no time'. Half an hour passed before they did, and in the meantime we heard strange scuffles, wafts of moving air, and stifled giggles around us in the darkness. When the lights finally came on, they showed empty baskets on the stage, and the children in the first two rows of the audience polishing off the last of the bananas.

Another time, at the old hall in Newborough, just as the group launched into a lively Welsh chorus, the whole stage dropped by two inches under their feet. Everyone kept their nerve and no one screamed, but the whole evening had to be abruptly terminated. Old age and woodworm in the hall had won the day.

The newly formed skiffle band had a brief moment of glory headed by a baton-wielding bandmaster, well known as a joker in Pentraeth. Merched Y Bryniau were invited to entertain at a social evening in a large chapel room in Upper Bangor. The final item on the programme was the skiffle band.

Unknown to the rest of us, the bandmaster had dressed up in a full clown regalia, with a bushy red wig, 2ft-long shoes, a red nose, and a pair of baggy check trousers held up by red braces. She was an instant hit with the audience. As the band reached a final crashing crescendo, under the waving baton the bandmaster purposely dropped the baggy pants around her ankles and revealed a pair of red and white striped boxer shorts underneath. The cheers from the audience hit the roof.

Later, at supper, I was approached by a grim-looking gentleman who wanted to know if I was responsible for this dreadful group. When I replied that I was, he launched into a tirade about the amount of smut shown in television these days – now he was having to put up with it in his own chapel hall as well. We should be thoroughly ashamed of ourselves. Looking around, I could not see a single person who shared his sentiment, but I did go home that night suitably chastened.

Ross Davies

From the Majestic Cinema to the South Pacific

Between the tree and the cinema you can see the roof and top floor of one of the blocks of flats in Armfield Crescent, where we lived, so we did not live far from the cinema. When we were small we were given a shilling to go to the Saturday morning pictures – the ABC Minors we were called. We even had a song we sang before the films began.

It cost sixpence to get into the cinema, and we had sixpence to spend on lollies or ice cream. There you would meet up with other kids you knew and see where they were going to sit. I remember the westerns with Hopalong Cassidy, the Cisco Kid, and the Lone Ranger with Silver, his horse, and his sidekick Tonto. I also remember the cartoons – Bugs Bunny, Popeye, Donald Duck and all those Warner Bros characters. I now have them on DVD, and my grandchildren watch them.

As I grew up we went to the pictures at night. One of my most memorable films was 'South Pacific' with Mitzi Gaynor. I saw it a few times and was determined to go to the South Pacific. I finally did that by getting a one-way ticket on a slow boat to the South Pacific on my 20th birthday in 1966, and I set sail in March 1967. I am still roaming the islands of the South Pacific, be they large or small, and I have still not made up my mind where to put down my roots in the evening of my life.

Just across the road from the Majestic was a music shop where I bought my first record. It was a 45rpm and one of many that I purchased between 1963 and 1967. I still cart them around with me to wherever I am living at the time. I also have 33rpm records, including 'South Pacific', which of course I played on the deck of the ship on my portable record player as we sailed through the South Pacific on the way to Tahiti, where the film was made.

Carole Baldwin

Mitcham, Greater London, The Majestic Cinema 1959 M296057x

Saturday Morning Pictures

Saturday morning could not come quick enough for our family. Me and my brother Marty would walk five miles to the morning show with a shilling between us. We looked forward to cartoons with Mickey Mouse, or to on-going serials with the Lone Ranger or Flash Gordon, where the film finished with the hero about to come to a nasty end, so you had to come back next week to see what happened next. The shows usually started with a sing-song generated by a compere, then a different game show like eating a doughnut on a string the fastest or, my favourite, a singing contest. I won my first one by singing 'She Loves You' by the Beatles. I won a big bag of mixed sweets that we shared with all our mates.

Through the tough winter of 1963 we walked up to our knees in snow to get to the cinema, and we were most annoyed to find it could not open. I remember thinking 'Well, I walked five miles, what's the problem!'. That's how much we enjoyed our films.

John O'Connor

Morris Men

The lovely village green and pond at Chalfont St Giles (bottom left) are next to a splendid pub called Merlin's Cave. This is a very popular summer evening venue for morris dancing, and the dancers and musicians can soon draw a crowd of onlookers.

For many summers one of the local morris sides which danced here was Whitethorn Morris – often performing as guests of other dance sides, including Grand Union Morris and Lord Paget's. I played my piano accordion as leader of the Whitethorn Band. On occasion our band had nine or ten musicians, which at times outnumbered the usual team of eight dancers. Our morris band included drums, accordions, melodeons, whistles, and even a musical crowbar. The red, white and blue dresses of the Whitethorn Morris dancers made a colourful and energetic spectacle. The band played toe-tapping dance tunes in jig and polka tempos, and a good time was enjoyed by all.

John Howard Norfolk

Chalfont St Giles, Buckinghamshire c1965 C498043

Whitethorn Morris

For many years, morris sides danced in the road in front of the pub garden of the Red Lion at Coleshill. This was a popular venue to celebrate May Day morning at dawn. Whitethorn Morris and their Whitethorn Band made it a really exciting way to kick off the dancing season in the dark pre-dawn, with a slowly growing crowd of sleepy Coleshill villagers emerging from their cottages to come and watch.

I played my accordion, and sometimes had to shelter under an umbrella to keep my keyboard dry. The jolly landlord came out and passed around a hipflask of strong liquor to encourage both the musicians and the dancers. As dawn broke the music and dancing became more vigorous – no doubt helped by the drink.

Our dancing companions from Grand Union Morris and our Whitethorn Band and Whitethorn Morris Dancers then went into the Red Lion along with scores of villagers for a traditional English cooked breakfast. The landlord and his staff had to make perhaps a hundred huge cooked breakfasts, which were served at the bar and all eaten by 7am. What fun and what memories!

John Howard Norfolk

Coleshill, Buckinghamshire, The Red Lion c1965 C496009

More Morris

To the right is the spot where the dancers and musicians of Dartington Morris and their guests Heather and Gorse Clog Morris performed in August 2008. The view shows some village women sitting on the low terrace where a crowd gathered for the dance performance just recently!

There is now a plaque on the front wall of the inn inviting people to try the village stocks.

I brought my piano accordion along and played in the band for Heather and Gorse, and also enjoyed a pint of lovely Flowers Best Bitter. There were probably a hundred folk gathered around the front of the inn and also standing in the road enjoying the show.

John Howard Norfolk

Stoke Gabriel, Devon, The Church House Inn 1918 68537

Maidenhead, Berkshire, Boulters Lock 1956 M7052

Maidenhead, Berkshire, Boulters Lock 2004 M77701k

Pandemonium on the Water

Summer Sunday afternoons were often spent at Boulters Lock when I was a child. We would have a walk along the river and end up at the lock to sit and watch the boats go in and out.

There would be the people who thought they were the bee's knees in their blazers and straw boaters but who usually managed to make a mess of getting in and out of the lock. And the dogs that would jump off the boats into the lock, causing pandemonium. Fortunately they all seemed to get rescued, either by their owners or by someone from the crowd that was always there sitting on the side of the lock.   *Linda Ellis*

Far from the Madding Crowd

In 1964 I moved to Keswick to work as the assistant manager at the then Royal Oak Hotel, just past the Moot Hall on the far left corner in this photograph. The Royal Oak and the George hotels, across the street from each other, were owned by Sir Percy Hope, a local dignitary. I lived in my own room in the hotel, which was managed by Mr Peverett and his wife. I hardly had any free time and earned just £12 a week.

On my few days off I escaped the even then 'madding crowds' and hiked the fells by myself all day, hardly ever seeing any living thing other than sheep. I vividly recall finding a spot in the tufts of grass out of the wind, taking a bag lunch break above Stickle Tarn and writing poetry, or being caught in a hair-raising lightning storm near Wastwater, or struggling in the high winds on Helvellyn's knife edge, or being clamped down in a pea soup fog above Buttermere.

These experiences were a great antidote to the busloads of elderly American tourists 'doing Britain in three days', obediently shuffling along behind their bus drivers for lunch in our Poet's Dining Room, and the winter-time banquets of evening-dressed local folks attending our many special functions.

There was an ornery old gent called Isaac who would always chase out anyone who dared to take his fireside seat in the tiny Ingle Neuk bar. Before he left, after his customary several half pints of Worthington E (off the wood), he would announce in broad Cumbrian 'Ah's garn yam!' (I'm going home).

Dylan Rivis

Keswick, Market Square and the Moot Hall 1951 K12056

Helvellyn, Cumbria, Striding Edge 1912   64343

Rousdon, Devon, The Landslip and Whitlands Cottages 1900 45263

Our Favourite Outing by the River

My family and I often walked to the River Usk (right), down Pentre Road and across the Brecon Road. We had picnics on the side nearest St Mary's Church in Llanwenarth, and looked in the water for tiny fish and insects. I particularly liked the flowers I found in the meadows nearby, and picked large bunches to take back to my grandparents' house. On the banks grew quantities of a flower called Jumping Jack, Touch-me-not or Policeman's Helmet,

which I called a netflower. At one point there was a chain ferry, with a sort of flat punt-like boat, and it was fun crossing the river in it.

Diana Dioszeghy

Abergavenny, Gwent, The River Usk c1955 A9035

Landslip Cottage

My great-grandmother and great-grandfather lived at Landslip Cottage for many years, providing cream teas to visiting locals and tourists alike. My own mother married a Gapper, who was born at the bungalow higher up the cliff. The visitors' books for the cottage teas read like a script from P G Wodehouse – with very reserved English expletives referring to the wasp population. The cottage was already a ruin and overgrown when I was a boy, although Auntie Lizzie and Auntie Annie, born at the cottage, still lived on the estate.
Gwyn Gapper

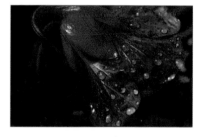

My sister Margaret and I (née Rayner) were evacuated to the home and care of a friend, Olive Tuck, who had a cottage next to a farm just out of Combpyne. Across the fields where we played was the path to Landslip Cottage. When mum and dad came to visit, a special treat was to have afternoon tea at the cottage. I remember a pathway of bright orange nasturtiums, the wooden tables and seats, and the path (forbidden) to the beach, which was festooned with barbed wire. I am sure we had afternoon tea, but think the adventure made the visits more memorable.

We visited the farm to watch the cows being milked. Unfortunately I contracted bovine TB and spent the next year in a convalescent establishment.

I remember going to the station to meet our parents and watching the steam train puffing its way through fields of wheat. Being wartime, the roads were empty of traffic, and we had freedom unheard of in this day and age. On a windy day the wires would sing along the road.
Jean McKern

Up the Hills

When my sister and I visited my grandparents in Cheriton, we would go up the hills straight away. When the wind was blowing, the trick was to see how far you could 'lie' on the wind. There was a place behind the hills where the original channel tunnel was started in the 1940s. My mother was disgusted at the idea of cutting through the hills. When she died, my sister and I spread her ashes on the hills overlooking the new channel tunnel, and whenever I go through it I say a silent prayer: 'It's OK Mum, only me!'

Su Knight

Cheriton, Kent, Caesar's Camp 1908 60391

A Wet Weekend at the Youth Hostel

The Youth Hostel in Cynwyd (below) was a converted watermill. It was very old and very damp, and I stayed there one wet weekend in April 1967 with my girlfriend as we were heading towards Snowdon. I had a top bunk and banged my head on the low roof beams. The following day we moved on from Cynwyd and stayed at Llanberis before our attempt on Snowdon. The weather was so bad that the mountain rescue teams were out forcing everybody back from the mountain, so forty years later I STILL haven't been up Snowdon!

John Howard Norfolk

Cynwyd, Clwyd, The Old Bridge 1936 C372013

Inebriated

The Anchor Inn at Irby (right) was one of my mum and dad's favourite haunts. When my husband and I were courting in 1984, we went in one evening and there was a gentleman (quite inebriated) perched on a stool, cigarette in one hand and a whisky in the other. He fell backwards, stool and all, and landed with cigarette and glass of whisky, still intact, clutched in his hands.

Beverley Sharp

Irby, Merseyside, Thurstaston Road c1955 I42015

Potter Heigham, Norfolk, The Bridge 1934 86381

Potter Heigham, Norfolk, The Bridge c1960 P167059

Too late!

As I read out the memorable words from a guidebook about the low bridge in Potter Heigham, warning boats to be extra careful, I was greeted with the words 'Too late!' as we rammed the bridge. Thirty years after this photo, we were still causing havoc!
Lorna Cowen

6 *Invariably the chain would cover him with more mud, much to the joy of the onlookers on the bridge* 9

Just by the road bridge on the Yarmouth side was a pub with a long grass garden which went down to the river. On the bank was a post with a notice on it which read 'Don't disturb the water otter', and tied to the post was a rusty chain. The road over the bridge was like a grandstand overlooking the garden. People in the garden would encourage a friend to pull the chain, and the people on the bridge, who knew about its secret, would cheer the person on to pull the chain VERY slowly so as not to disturb the water otter. Most people in those days dressed up to go to the pub. Slowly the MUDDY chain was pulled in, spreading mud on the victim. At last a large, muddy, smelly kettle came out of the river, at which point the victim would throw the hotter back into the water – and invariably the chain would cover him with more mud, much to the joy of the onlookers on the bridge.
John Hopthrow

The National Caravan Rally

My parents kept our caravan at Overstone – on the far side near the lake. One year, 1953, I think, the National Caravan Rally came to Overstone, and the field filled up with hundreds of caravans. I think this photo (right) is the milk queue!

David Marklew

Overstone, Northamptonshire, The Solarium Hotel c1955 O104020p

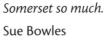
Overstone, Lakeside c1955 O104052

Happy Holidays

My husband and I spent many a happy day fishing in Merry Lane. Well, he fished and I read a book. We stayed in a caravan in the field at the last farm down the end of Merry Lane. One holiday we arrived early, parked our caravan and had a sleep. We awoke to find the caravan wobbling about. Looking outside we saw a herd of cows pushing the caravan. We had parked on the route they went to be milked. They didn't know they could walk round the caravan until the farmer shouted at them. Another time we parked in the apple orchard and through the week we watched cows eating fallen apples.

The panels of the caravan banged with the wind, and we decided not to go back on the motorway until the winds died down. When we first went to Somerset there was no connection to the M5, and we had to go right into Bristol and take the old road to Bridgwater where we were staying on another farm.

We had lovely holidays in the Bridgwater area with my parents and our Alsatian dog.

Years later when I was doing our family tree, I found out that my husband's maternal line started in Somerset, and I have often wondered if that is why he loved Somerset so much.

Sue Bowles

Bason Bridge, Somerset, The River Brue and Merry Lane c1960 B869318

Clifton Hampden, Oxfordshire, The Barley Mow Inn 1890 27010

Grandfather's Favourite Inn

This was my grandfather's favourite inn at the time the photograph was taken. He was coachman at the Manor House at Long Wittenham, a short walk along the 'Maddy', a road from the inn to Long Wittenham following the river and very prone to flooding. It's a family story that he would often spend too long here, and Granny would have to prepare the horse and coach and dress up in his clothes to fetch the master of the house from Didcot station several miles away.

Mr B K Seeney

Kidsgrove, Staffordshire, Mow Cop Castle c1965 K145003

All Uphill

Our dad used to take us for a walk up to Mow Cop Castle on a sunny Sunday. We would set off from Talke with a bottle of pop and a jam butty, walk along the canal for a while, then through the lanes in Scholar Green past the Three Horseshoes, and up the steepest hill to the castle. We would sit inside the round window at the front and try to see our house in Talke on the other side of the valley. We could see so much on a clear day, but never really understood what we were looking at. The Welsh mountains were part of the view, and we were always trying to spot the beach in Rhyl, North Wales. Jodrell Bank (where we thought the spacemen lived) was another part of the view. We would have our jam butty and pop on the grass behind the castle, and then moan all the way home because our legs ached.

If Mum came with us we had to go in the car, a red Austin 7, and take a picnic – more jam butties and pop. Then we would walk part of the way back with Mum and look for nice flowers to pick. Dad always picked us up on the Scholar Green level, and then took us for a 'run out', either to Cheshire to see Jodrell Bank, or to Trentham Gardens for an ice cream.

Tina Stanyer

> ❛ We would have our jam butty ... and then moan all the way home because our legs ached ❜

Wading in the Bristol Channel

It is quite possible that the little boy to the right in this picture (right) is me at age six. My family used to stay at a friend's caravan in the park above the cliffs. From 1954 to 1958 we stayed there most weekends in the summer and even a few in the spring and autumn. St Mary's Well Bay was not a good beach, for there was a lot of rock and bladderwrack seaweed. My brothers and I would play for hours along the seashore between Lavernock proper, about a mile to the east, and Swanbridge and Sully Island to the west. On the cliffs above this picture was the army camp. This was a shore battery with large concrete emplacements (sans guns), officers' quarters, and other buildings deserted since the war. The gun batteries were connected by tunnels, probably to move the ordnance, and we had a lot of fun exploring them.

It was a time of great freedom. My mum would let us go and do whatever we wanted totally unsupervised all day, just coming back for something to eat. Given the enormous tidal range of the Bristol Channel, which would catch and drown a few people each year, the crumbling cliffs, which we climbed with gusto, and the decrepit military camp (now a 'resort'), it is surprising that we did not get into some trouble. I am not sure I would allow my six-year-old such freedom, but it was magical at the time.

Phillip Armour

Lavernock, South Glamorgan, St Mary's Well Bay c1955 L279012

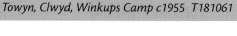
Towyn, Clwyd, Winkups Camp c1955 T181061

A Baby Doesn't Count

When I was 18 in 1955 my mum booked us a chalet at Winkups Camp, Towyn. There was Mum, my stepfather, myself and three sisters aged 5 years, 3 years, and 3 months. Off we went from Huddersfield in Yorkshire in our little Austin 7 – I can remember the excitement now. My mum paid £5 for the week. On arrival we all piled out of the car and Mum went in to register. The lady came and looked at us in dismay and said: 'But you've only booked for four people'. Mum said: 'But there are only four, three adults, two children make another one, and you can't count a baby!'. The last bit was said with almost a note of triumph. No more was said about that, and the lady led us to our 'chalet', which was in fact a hen hut. I'm not saying it had ever been used for hens, but the little gaps that the hens were supposed to use were there, although they had been boarded over, so it obviously was a hen hut, though a very snug hen hut I must say. But despite all that we had a wonderful holiday and sun shone gloriously all week.

Margaret Campbell

Happy Family Days at Jaywick

My family had a holiday in Jaywick every summer, from when I was five up until I was about 15 years old. We stayed in bungalows on stilts. My brothers and I thought this was wonderful, and would run and play underneath. The weather always seemed to be baking hot, and I remember the sand burning my feet.

At night, my family and all the relations who were on holiday with us went to the Morocco Club, and stayed there till closing time.

My mum used to hire a bright orange pushchair for my younger brothers, and we would walk to Clacton Pier, where I went on the Steel Stella roller coaster. I was so scared, as I was only about 7 or 8. The only thing I didn't like about these holidays was the awful smell when the lorries came round to empty the outside toilets.

We went back recently to Jaywick – it looks a bit desolate now, but even so, I had a lump in my throat when I visualised all the happy times we had there.

Jean Soward

Jaywick, Essex, The Sands c1955 J4038

Jaywick, Essex, A 'B' Type Bungalow c1955 J4026

Clacton-on-Sea, Essex, The Pier 1958 C107062

A Frightening Experience!

It was my fourth birthday. We were staying in Caister at the Sycamore Camp in a caravan that my parents had hired for a two-week holiday. The date was 13 June 1958, and we took a trip in Dad's old car up to Lowestoft. After a cup of tea or bottle of Fanta and a ham roll in the Fisherman's Café on Whaplode Road we got on with the business in hand, which was to order some bloaters to be sent home for my grandad.

While we were there we went and sat on the beach close to the old Punch and Judy booth and waited for the show to begin. Suddenly all the kids were totally transfixed by the antics in the brightly coloured booth.

It was at this moment that I had the shock of my short life. Mr Punch announced that a kid from Sheffield called Brian had a birthday that day, and that he was all of four years old. Being a very shy kid I ran the full length of the beach, and when my dad caught up with me I had filled my new pair of khaki shorts.

Since finding this photograph I have been in contact with the Punch and Judy Professor, Bryan Clarke, who has given me the name of the Professor in those days. So the name of Franklin Spence will live with me forever … boy, did he give me the most frightening day of my life!

Brian Green

Lowestoft, Suffolk, Punch and Judy, The Children's Corner 1952 L105079t

Summer Holidays were Invented for Fishing

As a small kid I couldn't wait for the summer holidays to arrive. As the days drew closer I could hardly sleep at night, knowing that any day now we would be packing our suitcases and heading to the caravan site for the whole summer, six weeks without any school.

When the big day arrived we headed to the bus stop to catch the number 14 bus to Pickmere. We were poor and didn't know it, because we were happy. I remember the smell of old leather seats and old ladies' hair spray. All the men wore Old Spice and had their hair slicked back with Brylcreem.

As the bus pulled out of the bus stop, my brother Russell and I had one mission in mind – to look under the benches for money that had fallen out of the pockets of the men's trousers. We were never disappointed. All the money went for one thing, the reason summer holidays were invented: fishing.

When the bus finally turned off Chester Road into Pickmere Lane our summer holidays, filled with endless hours of fishing, were about to get under way. We got off the bus on the corner of Pickmere Lane and walked the final half-mile down Mere Lane to Platts Farm, where we and other family members had caravans.

Within minutes we legged it down to the pond on the caravan site to see what was going on. Very rare was it that some old timer wasn't down there with something to show us in his keep net. 'Hey mister, what you caught?' we would ask in unison. 'Come on, give us a look then', we'd say. And just like any fisherman, he was more than happy to show off his catch. On seeing the man's catch we would tear off to get our fishing tackle out of the shed. We'd dust off the cobwebs and scrounge up some maggots 'til we could ride a bike or walk into Knutsford to the tackle shop to get some of our own.

We didn't have any fancy tackle, but that didn't matter – the fish weren't smart enough to know the difference. Our tackle was mainly old hand-me-down rods and reels, enough 6lb test to tie up a cow, split shot that was made of real lead that we collected off the discarded lines of someone's tangle, a few rusty hooks gathered from the same location, a disgorger for removing hooks, and lots of beautiful floats in many shapes and sizes. My favourites were the long slim ones, black with a couple of contrasting coloured bands near the top, usually yellow and red or white and red; they came from reed beds and tree branches, or were washed up on the shore after other fishermen's lines got snagged or snapped and they were not able to recover their float. Being a young lad, nothing got in my way of retrieving a float that took my fancy.

The fish we were after were tench, carp, or (the prize of this pond) the mirror carp with their fancy scales. We got our education in how to fish, and more importantly how not to fish, from the older men. They were more than happy to show you how to tie the right kind of knot so your hook didn't come off the line when

you had a fish on, how to thread the maggots on the hook so they stayed on longer, and how to liven up the maggots by taking a few and placing them under your tongue for a few minutes to warm them up. 'Maggots that wiggle attract more fish', they would say. I sometimes wonder if that was just a joke to see if we would really do it. I did, and the maggots really did liven up, but I don't ever remember catching more fish because of it.

Darren Crumbleholme

Mackerel Fishing in Newhaven

Many's the time we wandered along the edge of the harbour and up and down the landing stages, studying the leathery-faced fishermen's busy hands as they worked on the nets or repaired lobster pots. We'd peep around huge metal doors and gates clad in rusting wire mesh to get a glimpse of the boat yards beyond, and if we'd enough in our pocket for a cup of tea, we'd stop at the café that looked across the harbour, and out towards the bridge on the left. The owners always had time for

Newhaven, East Sussex, The Harbour c1960   N20054

us, and if they had any stale bread and cake, they'd let us have it to feed the swans that swam among the boats just a few steps from their entrance – though the swans only got what was left after we'd picked out all the edible bits.

It was from Newhaven that I had my first fishing trip. A family friend took us out in his small fishing boat, and the fact that he'd lost a finger made an impression on me. He told us that he'd basically worn it away from many years of guiding the fishing line across the joint. We fished for mackerel with fishing lines with lots of hooks in a row, and feathers attached to them. We caught a good many, and in the evening fried them over an open fire, then enjoyed them with thick slices of wholemeal bread and butter and cups of sweet milky tea.

In the background of the photo (above) you can see the shearlegs, the long poles that form a triangle on the left. They were used to lift masts into place and manoeuvre boat engines before cranes were commonplace.

Things changed a great deal during the years around 1965. Much of the land around the harbour was bought up and fenced off to be 'upgraded' into a marina. Once commercialisation hit the small seaside town, for us it lost its appeal, although that's maybe because we grew up and could no longer see it with the naivety of a child.
Kathy Farmer

Eels in the Dyke

As a child in the early to mid 1960s I had many holidays here in these wonderful bungalows. My elder brother used to catch eels in the dyke that ran alongside this place. I was very squeamish when he returned with them but thankfully they were never served for tea.
Gina Reeves

Trusthorpe, Lincolnshire, Radio Holiday Bungalows c1955   T217045

Sunday Roast – and Jelly

Coming across this picture sparked memories of happy times I had on my summer holidays in a chalet at Seaview. It was not unusual to stay for four or more weeks in one of the chalets and spend practically every waking hour on the beach or walking into Whitstable or Herne Bay. I remember rummaging along the beach finding bits of pottery from the houses that fell into the sea where the cliffs had eroded towards Herne Bay, and the time British Rail sent our luggage to Chesterfield in Derbyshire only for it to be located some fortnight later. Even the mud at low tide had its attraction, and the huge shallow pools left behind were a delight for sailing model boats in.

One day my sister came back to the chalet with a bowl of jelly she had found. It would seem that a lady had made this as a treat for her family, and had placed it under their balcony to cool and set. It was returned by my embarrassed mother, along with sister in tow to apologise. But the highlight was on a Sunday, when we went to Mrs Murray's guest house. We would have a roast lunch there, and it was such a treat.

Roger Steer

Swalecliffe, Kent, Seaview Holiday Camp c1955   S545019

Halcyon Days Out at Southend

I remember travelling to Southend with my family on a steam train from London. My sister and I used to put our heads out of the windows. More often than not when we sat down our faces would be black with soot from the smoke of the train, and our mum would try to wipe us clean with her hanky.

When we arrived at Southend it was off to the beach for a paddle and a play, and then a ride on the boats in the boating lake. At lunchtime we walked up the hill to have our lunch of pie and mash, or fish and chips, then a Rossi ice cream for afters. In the afternoon we would get on a boat to the Isle of Sheppey, and spend the rest of the day in the Kursaal. My fondest memory of the Kursaal was the bowl slide, where you were taken to the top of the slide by an electric chair. Once at the top, you were given a coconut mat to sit on. At the end of the slide there was a big wooden bowl to catch the riders in. It was such a thrill. I remember how lovely and shiny the wood on the slide looked through constant use. At the end of the day we headed to the train station, stopping to buy seafood that was sold in straw bags. As you were walking along, the liquid would seep through the bag. Those were the days. How I long for my grandchildren to be able to ride that beautiful slide, which is now long gone.

Jan Rennie

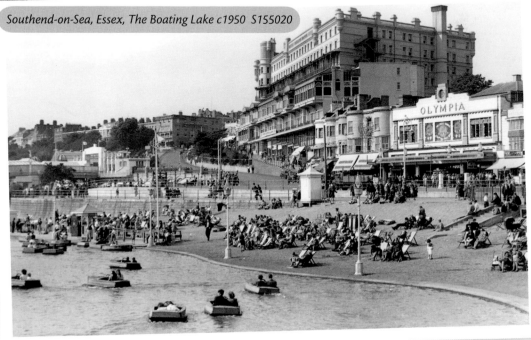

Southend-on-Sea, Essex, The Boating Lake c1950   S155020

One-Armed Bandit

I noticed with some surprise this photo of myself aged about 12 years. I am the girl on the left with the ponytail – the year is about 1960. I don't recall the boy's name. But it looks as if we are standing by the machine that used to print letters of the alphabet. I think it cost one old penny for 20 or 25 letters. There was a metal dial with a brass pointer like the hour hand on a clock, and when it was pointing to the letter you required you pulled down a lever on the side (a bit like a one-armed bandit) and the letters were embossed on a strip of metal.

Chris Rowe

Lyme Regis, Dorset, The Promenade c1960   L121244p

Wild Seas

I stood at the end of the Cobb on the day of the worst storm this winter, and both saw and felt the sea spray as the waves hit the top of the sea wall. It was just as exciting as shown in this view of 1910 (below).

I was visiting for the day with our friends Julian and Janice Dent. Julian took photos of the angry sea – it came almost to the top of the shingle bank where the fishing boats were laid up. We went on to the shingle and threw a few pebbles in the sea, getting our socks and trousers wet in the process, but it was fun, and a lovely memory of a great day out!

John Howard Norfolk

Crabbing

When we were kids, me and my friends spent most of the day in the summer holidays with string and a safety pin. We'd stick some mussel meat on the pin from the mussel bed from the other side of the jetty, and then we'd tie a stone to the string and lower this down the side of the jetty to catch an unsuspecting crab. You had to be very careful pulling it up from the water, as sometimes the crab would fall back in, and then you'd have to start again, but we would have great fun watching the crabs running all over the place, especially when the tourists were waiting for the ferry. They would scream and scurry away from the approaching crab.

Eric Butler

Knott End-on-Sea, Lancashire, The Ferry and the Slipway c1950   K128006p

Lyme Regis, Dorset, The End of the Cobb c1910   L121301

Shoeburyness, Essex, Shoebury Hall Farm Camp c1955   S275026

Basic, but Fun

I was so pleased to see this photo, as the caravan by the brick building was my grandparents'. We had another one right opposite. I was born in 1949 and used to be down there every summer until the site closed in 1972. My grandparents had the caravans well before I was born. I can remember all the men getting their chairs all in a line – this was to watch the people with tents who didn't know the light shone through. We kids used to have water fights, and one of us used to watch for Captain Townsend, the owner, to come along. I can remember one year my friend and I were on the site and I didn't book us in. The Townsends gave me a right telling off.

Mary Wash

The site at Shoebury Hall Farm Camp was pretty basic then, not like today's caravan sites. There was no running water, so one had to go to one of the taps (hot and cold) scattered about the site and bring it back in a metal jug. We used to wash in our shed next to our caravan. The toilets were situated in two blocks, one on the east side of the camp, the other on the west, and it was a fairly large site. From about the age of ten I would often go and get the water. I learnt never to spill it, especially the hot. Cooking and lighting were by calor gas – there was no electricity. We did have a camp shop that sold all you could want – bread, bacon, ham, cheese, milk, sweets, comics and ice cream. In the evening one of the men from the shop would go round the site shouting 'Evening News' and 'Standard'. In the 60s at the start of the Beatles and Stones era they even got a jukebox, much to the annoyance of the shop staff, as we teenagers were forever grouped round it playing the same stuff over and over again.
Alan Perry

Mumbles, West Glamorgan, The Pier 1898 40925

Slot Machines on the Pier

Mumbles Pier was a place of penny-in-the-slot machines, and there were lots of opportunities to spend your pocket money and have fun. On the Laughing Policeman exhibit, a penny in the slot started an unusual and rather scary model

of a policeman, complete with helmet, swaying from side to side and laughing. There was also the Haunted House, where a further penny opened up coffins and cupboards and skeletons, and all sorts of ghosts emerged from the spooky house. There were even the naughty machines where we turned handles to show 'What The Butler Saw' – where a further few old pennies were used up! Innocent pleasures, but a real treat.

A bag of chips, in newspaper of course, the bracing sea air, and the lengthy walk back along the sea wall towards Norton made the day complete.

Gaynor Wingham

The Swan

My dad took me for a walk through Stapehill Gardens when I was five years old. I always remember the large swan with the flowers around it. I often go back and take a photo of it. It's a beautiful scene, and I shall visit again this year.

Joseph Halyckyj

Burton-on-Trent, Staffordshire, Stapehill 1961 B286007

Scarborough, Yorkshire, Children's Corner 1890 23454

Bucket and Spade Holidays

All our family holidays when I was a child were taken at Scarborough, where my parents and I stayed with old family friends in Whin Bank. I first went in the early 1960s, and my last visit was 1973. I loved those holidays, whether taken during the summer, or occasionally at Easter: roaming along the cliff top birdwatching, or with a bucket-and-spade on the beach, enjoying ice creams, seeing 'The King and I' in Peasholm Park (what year was that?) and a young Tom Baker in a Noel Coward at the Theatre in the Round, or journeying inland to the lovely Moors or down to Spurn Point (birding again!). The walk through Raincliffe Woods and by Throxenby Mere was a pleasant ritual. Occasionally we would venture to Bridlington, Filey or Whitby, but we knew that Scarborough was the best!

Jonathan Hutchins

Scarborough, Yorkshire, From the Fish Pier 1890 23466

Scarborough, Yorkshire, The Beach c1955 S71148

Sunday School Outings and Slot Machines

Every year we went on our annual Sunday School outing to Walton on the Naze from Upshire in Essex. In the early days we went by train from Waltham Cross, one train picking children up from stations along the line and taking us all out for the day to Walton, and in later years we travelled by a coach or double-decker bus. The outing was the highlight of the year for many of the children, as it was the only time we ever saw the seaside. We would leave at 8am, and each child would bring their own lunch, which was normally eaten on the train or bus before we got to Walton. We stopped at the 'Half Way' café for toilets and refreshments, and then travelled on to Walton where we met up with hundreds of other children, all out for their Sunday School outings as well. Children and adults herded together to the nearest beach, then deck chairs were purchased and the adults would settle down for the day – dads rolled up their trousers, undid their shirt necks, put on their hats and lay back for a nap, whilst mums got the children changed into swimwear and then relaxed with a good magazine. Us children would be in and out of the sea all day if it was fine, but if it was wet we sat under the pier or by the breakwaters and, using umbrella and plastic sheeting, would make the most of a wet day. Some of the children came with lots of money and (under the eyes of a watchful adult) would spend lots of it on the penny slot machines on the pier, or go onto the fairground.

At 3.30pm we packed up and moved from the beach to the pier, to visit the Pier Restaurant. The restaurant had long trestle tables laid out with paper cloths, plates,

knives and spoons, cups and saucers for adults and plastic beakers for children, and we all sat down to a 'high tea'. We enjoyed white bread sandwiches, then cakes and ice-cream to finish off. Tea and coffee was served from large urns on every table, and squash in jugs was passed along the table for the children. It was really fun having tea here as we could see the sea beneath our table through the cracks in between the wooden floor boards, and listen to it lapping round the supports of the pier. When tea was over there was usually time to enjoy the pier amusements, which included the Hall of Mirrors, Ghost Train, Bumper Cars, Catch a Duck, Throw a Penny, Coconut Shy, The Big Wheel or a trip up the pier on a small steam train.

The coaches left Walton at 5.30pm. To me as a child, looking at the sea as we were going home, the waves seemed gentle and inviting and I always felt that I was leaving the best behind. The coach trip home was normally uneventful as most children would be fast asleep before we reached the Half Way House, and soon we would all tumble out of the coach to the waiting mums and dads.

Christine Brooker

Dunstable, Bedfordshire, The Downs c1960 D69014

Orange Rolling

Orange rolling took place on Good Friday afternoon up the 'orange pit'. There used to be crowds of people all chasing little oranges down the hill.

I was never quite sure what you did if you caught one. I'm sure it wouldn't have been fit to eat! Is this peculiar to Dunstable?

I know of cheese rolling, where they chase a Double Gloucester cheese down a hill in Leckhampton (near Cheltenham), but I haven't come across anything else similar elsewhere.

Merv Thomas

Hunstanton, Norfolk, The Fun Fair c1955 H135117p

Beloved bricks and mortar

MEMORIES OF BUILDINGS

River Clyde, Strathclyde, The Cloch Lighthouse 1897 39823

Biddulph, Staffordshire, The Old Hall 1898 42166

Destroyed by Cannonballs

This was the seat of the Biddulph family: it was built in the early 16th century, probably to replace an earlier Saxon, possibly fortified, house that has been identified on Bailey's Hill, to the south west of the Old Hall. It was partially destroyed in the Civil War by the immense cannon Roaring Meg, some of whose cannonballs have been discovered in the nearby millpond of Biddulph Old Mill (by the Talbot).

My clearest memory of the Old Hall is driving from Biddulph to Congleton when I was about six; it was winter and the view of the hunting tower from the road was excellent. When we came back that way later on in the day, it had been snowing quite heavily, the snow had outlined the tower and the sunshine was glinting off it – it was simply stunning.

Lauren Hughes

Living at the Cloch

I was a lighthouse keeper at the Cloch lighthouse from 1967 until 1972. I lived there with my wife Edna and our two children Andrew and Karen. Karen should have been born there, but she was overdue, and so had to be born at the Rankin Hospital in Greenock. The midwife was very disappointed that she was not going to deliver a baby at the lighthouse, which would have been a first for her.

John McIntyre

Chased by Longleat's Furious Llamas

I have many fond memories of Longleat over the last 46 years, including the freedom we all enjoyed as villagers to roam across the estate – the sixth Marquess was always very generous in this respect. The remains of the American hospital were still much in evidence then; dad would drive the car to one of the old stone ramps so that he could work underneath it! Before the wildlife reserve was built we'd walk across the park from Corsley, and when it was finished and the lions introduced, we all worried that one might escape, but to our knowledge, they never did.

Other memories include the pop concerts mounted on the front steps of the house. I seem to remember the Rolling Stones, but sadly the Beatles never played at Longleat – something we hoped for. Various TV shows were broadcast from Longleat including the children's show 'Tinker and Tucker'. I remember seeing Viscount Weymouth, as the current Marquess was then, driving up to the house in his open-top sports car and looking very cool.

In the Rushpool area of the park where the giraffe house now stands, llamas ran free constrained only by deer fences, cattle grids and gates. I can honestly claim to be one of very few Wiltshire schoolboys

Longleat, Wiltshire, Longleat House c1966 L190077

Longleat, Wiltshire, The Lions c1966 L190302

to be regularly chased on my Molton Mini bicycle by furious llamas. In the 70s, baboons were an early addition to the menagerie. They escaped many times and ran up into the parkland, but to my knowledge never caused any harm or damage. The estate and surrounding farmland was very well maintained, with gamekeepers, carpenters and various trades employed to keep everything in order. As kids we were welcome to wander – with the exception of the pheasant pens there were no boundaries, and we appreciated it.

During the 60s motorcycle scrambles were also held in the parkland, and there were hill climbs up to Heaven's Gate. In the 70s and early 80s the Lombard Rally included Longleat as a stage. From Park Hill a small aeroplane operated, giving people an aerial tour of the estate for £5. I believe Park Hill had been a small airfield used by the USAF during the Second World War for bringing in casualties to the hospital.

Finally, there was Carpet Walk that linked Heaven's Gate with the car park on the Horningsham road. In those days it really was like walking on a carpet of green. Maybe one day the grass will be allowed to recover and it will once more be known as Carpet Walk.

Geoff Pridmore

A Cure for Burns

This cottage was in Bedford Lane. I lived in a house called Connemara, which still stands in Bedford Lane. My father, Samuel Frederick Richardson, and his brother George were bricklayers. They had the job of demolishing this cottage and they were burning the thatch. My brother John was playing dare. He walked through the outer edge of the white ash and dared me to walk through the middle. Unfortunately I did, and was very badly burned. Mother rushed round all the houses, collecting tealeaves to put on my legs. (In those days people didn't empty their pots after every brew – they just topped them up with a little more tea and hot water.) I still do not know where Mother got the idea of the tealeaves. It certainly worked. I was left with just a few little scars, and they are hard to find. After demolishing the cottage, Father and Uncle George built a pair of red brick houses. A Mr Fairminer lived in the first of the pair, and I went to school in Frimley Green with his son.

Mr D F Richardson

The First Home I Ever Knew

The photograph below shows the first home I ever knew. It remains the one I hold as the true definition of 'home'. Waterloo House was where I was brought as a newborn in June 1974, and where I lived so happily until 1980 when we were forced to sell up and leave. I have countless memories, from tobogganing down the fields in the deepest snow ever (which sometimes blocked the doors and entirely covered the downstairs windows – my dad had to climb out of the upstairs to dig us free) to standing in the sunshine waiting for my daddy to return from work over the crest of the hill along the road.

I believe the house to have been haunted quite extensively. Certainly not one of my family can report that nothing unusual happened to them while they lived there. But then that's personal opinion. What do you believe?

Also worthy of note is the view from behind the house, surely one of the most magnificent in England for a child to wake to every day. It has left me with an inability to truly feel free unless I can see across hills into tomorrow. This is my home.

Claire O'Brien

Whitchurch, Oxfordshire, The Mill and the Cottages 1899   43001

Heptonstall, Yorkshire, Waterloo House from Slack Top c1965   H205006

Great-Grandmother's House

The house in the centre of this photo, Mill House, was the childhood home of my great-grandmother, Sarah Jane Bushnell. My mother said that a photo similar to this was displayed on trains to advertise beautiful British places, and my grandmother used to point it out as her mother's home. Some of my forebears worked in the mill, and the millpond sadly took the life of at least one child.

Gaynor Wingham

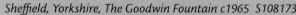

Sheffield, Yorkshire, The Goodwin Fountain c1965   S108173

Magic and Mischief

When the fountain was new, the changing colours of the floodlights that swept round the fountain and tinted the sprays looked so futuristic and bright. You could stare at them waiting for the cycle to run over again. At times the water froze into grotesque lumps, but the most amazing sight was when students put Teepol or other industrial-strength soaps into it and the froth flowed down the street. Equally impressive was the fluorescent dye that gave the water a yellow-green radiance. The fountain was much abused, but ever entertaining. It's a shame it has gone – did it offend Health and Safety regulations?
Mike Toohill

Ottery St Mary, Devon, The Cottage Guesthouse c1960 O28036

Island House

I lived in Riversdale as a child of nine in 1950-51. We rented it from the owner, the delightful Sylvia Townsend Warner, the author, who lived there with her partner, Valentine Ackland. The house stands with one wall literally in the River Frome. Paintings by John Crask which hung about the house must have had a special significance for the couple. You could sit in the library and watch the rabbits on the opposite bank, and herons would sometimes come there too. There was a music room, with a grand piano, overlooking the river. In 1951 the Frome flooded, turning the house effectively into an island.

Richard Leveson

Frome Vauchurch, Dorset, Riversdale 1906 54568

Lordy's Cottage

How funny! We now own and live in the house in the photograph above. It has barely changed since this photograph, although it is no longer a guesthouse and its name is different. We believe the people who ran it as a guesthouse were Mr and Mrs Cecil Haywood. He had been a manager at the factory in Ottery. Mrs Haywood was famous for her cooking. They rented it from Lord Coleridge (known as Lordy). It was called The Cottage because it had been Lady Devon's Cottage, a dower house for the Courtenay family.

It was originally built in the 17th century as a Huguenot weaver's dwelling; there are four other cottages nearby that share the same origin and design. This part of Ottery is known as Dunkirk because of that French connection. The house then consisted of only the left-hand section. The larger central section of this house was added in the 18th century, and the grand drawing room with Gothic windows on the right is Victorian.

A number of people have lived here since, including a well-known High Court judge. For many years it was lived in by a Miss St Quintin,

known as Quinnie, who had a pet monkey which lived on her shoulder. She played croquet on the lawn in the foreground. At some point it must have been bought from the Coleridge Estate, because it is no longer rented. It has also belonged to a sculptress, a dentist, another descendant of the Dukes of Devon, a writer, and a retired navy captain. We believe at least one owner – possibly Cecil Haywood – died in the house.

One of the bedroom windows has an ancient signature etched on the outside, possibly from the ring of a builder or decorator; it reads 'Govier', which is a well-known local name.

Robert Baker

Frome Vauchurch, Dorset, The Village 1906 54575

Little Heathens in Ruffled Collars

My family lived in Waltham Abbey from 1955 to 1961. I attended Waltham Holy Cross County Primary School, and at the ripe old age of 8 auditioned there to become a chorister. The teacher was Mr Goodger who was a kindly old man. I passed the audition and went to the abbey and met Canon A V G Cleall, who taught me to understand Roman numerals, and the choirmaster, who was known by all the boys as Moppie on account of his long(ish) silver hair.

Well, Moppie took me through a whole bunch of scales, which I could sing with ease – this made me later think that choir practice was a waste of time. I had no idea other members wanted and needed the practices. I was by no means a Christian in those days, and church was the ultimate in boredom. My reason for being in the choir was purely mercenary. They paid me. I got five bob a month and sixpence for each service, with threepence deducted for each practice missed. Springtime was great, as we were paid half a crown for weddings. I can remember going to six in one day once. I felt rich.

The most notable memory I have of the choir was at the 9th centenary celebrations in 1960, with everything decked out and spruced up, and the abbey was packed. We processed outside, and I think I was chosen to sing a verse of one of the hymns solo. I remember feeling very proud. After the celebrations all the choir members were presented with silver engraved medallions to mark the occasion.

Our head (boy) chorister was a guy named Peter Lilley, who wasn't averse to keeping all the boys in line – not only with words, but with often painful action. I was terrified and jealous of him. Terrified because when I got out of line (which was quite often) I got thumped, and jealous because he had this large silver chorister's medallion on a purple ribbon which I coveted! It was so much better than everyone else's oval-shaped brass Royal School of Church Music medallions. The colour of the medallion ribbons, incidentally, was a mark of seniority. White, yellow, blue. I only got to blue.

Christmas and Easter were also times of much pomp and ceremony. I loved singing the high note descants to many of the Christmas carols.

Most of us young boys got up to all sorts of mischief almost all of the time. We were anything but the little angels we looked as we processed down the nave in our red cassocks with ruffled, starched, collars, spotless surplices and coloured medal ribbons to the choir stalls at the front of the abbey. One piece of potentially fatal naughtiness occurred in those very stalls. They were installed during my time as a chorister, with overhead book lights. These were strip lights. You could take the insulating end piece out of the tubes – being careful not touch the metal on which our psalters and other books were placed. Looking along the row of boys we would catch an unwary one, singing with concentration, with his hand on the metal. Then three or four of us would touch hands and the guy next to the unwary one would touch him and we'd all get an almighty boot of electricity. This didn't do anything to improve our choral harmony and Moppie got pretty angry.

I have many other memories of the old abbey and believe, despite my somewhat heathen outlook, that my time as a choirboy there was instrumental in my eventual conversion to Christianity. I am one of those people who was so clearly confronted by Christ that it was impossible for Him not to get my attention. What happened next was tears such as I've never cried before or since, followed by the reality of being forgiven and restored.

I live in Australia now, and have been a Christian for longer than not. Now, I wouldn't (and couldn't) have it any other way. My remembrance of the abbey itself, as well as the town, will always be close to me. Some day I hope to visit again. Soon perhaps. God bless you all.

Bill Waring

Waltham Abbey, Essex, The Old Gateway c1955 W14005

Waltham Abbey, Essex, The Abbey Church 1921 70167

Two shillings fourpence farthing an hour

THE WORLD OF WORK

That Sinking Feeling

My grandad worked at South Kirkby pit for many years, so growing up I was forever hearing stories of his days down the mine. He lived on the Northfield estate, which was also known as Little Wigan. I am told this is because of the miners who moved from that area. Being a very inquisitive child I spent hours exploring, even though my grandad told me how dangerous it could be round the colliery.

One day I was staying at my grandad's waiting for my tea. I'd been in all day as it was raining heavily, so when the rain stopped I couldn't wait to get out. My grandad said 'Don't be long', and I was on my way. I walked over towards the pit to amuse myself for an hour before tea. I didn't notice at first, but I walked straight into a slurry pond which is a big area of mud and water that you sink into, a bit like quicksand. By the time I realised what was happening I'd sunk all the way up to my midriff. At this point I was starting to panic, but the more I did the more I seemed to be sinking. As luck would have it there was a log nearby, so I grabbed that and hoped that someone would walk by. Half an hour passed, but still no one did. As time went on I was sinking in more and more so I started shouting for help. Luckily for me, a stranger was walking his dog and heard my cries. He came over and pulled me out. This is just one of many memories that I have of many usually pleasurable hours spent exploring at the pit. This was, however, one I would prefer to forget.

Mark Adams

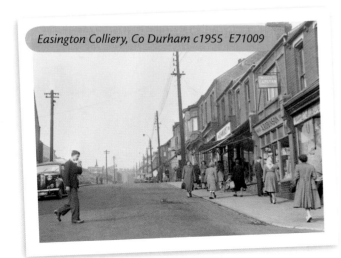
Easington Colliery, Co Durham c1955   E71009

Easington Colliery, Co Durham, Seaside Lane 1961   E71033

Easington Colliery, Co Durham c1960   E71027

The Miners' Strike, 1984-85

We met at the Easington Colliery Club coming up to 26 years ago. Not long into my married life the miners' strike began and that lasted until 1985. Life was very hard. We had to adjust to being married and with not having much money. Soon after the strike started I became pregnant with my first son, Graham. We struggled to buy a pram and cot and other essentials for a baby. But with the help of my dear grandparents we came through this difficult period. Soon after the strike we went into a colliery house, as we lost our first home because we had not been able to pay the mortgage.

I was hairdressing at the time of the strike, and I worked until I was seven months pregnant, whilst Jeff went picketing to get his £2 a day. Jeff made all the meals and did the housework. He made his first spaghetti bolognaise, which was very good, and he has been a keen cook all our married life. One day I came home from work to find Jeff in the yard making coal with coal dust and cement. He had burnt his finger ends badly, and he ended up with finger pokes on each finger.

I suffered badly with morning sickness, and was late for work on many occasions. My head was always down the pot to the point where one morning I missed my bus. I walked down to the next bus stop, which was near the pit. The miners were picketing outside the gates and the police were everywhere. Jeffrey was there to get his £2. He spotted me walking to the bus stop and he came running over, as he thought being near the pit was dangerous for me. I could have been caught up in the angry crowd and hurt.

Coming up to Christmas 1984 was bad for us, as I only had a month to go before giving birth to Graham. I wondered what I was going to do to have a good Christmas. Our parents were in the same boat as us, so they could not help. Everyone you knew was suffering to some degree. People who owned shops tried to help. Mr Snowdon, who owned one of the shops in the village, let people pay on tick for groceries. What a kind man he was.

My grandparents saw we were struggling. One day they came over with a big parcel. It was a food hamper they had

made themselves, and inside was everything from teabags to jars of pickled onions and packets of cake mix. You name it, it was in that box. I was flabbergasted. Along with the box was a carrier bag containing a very large chicken – at first I thought it was a turkey. My grandad's brother had a small farm and he gave the chicken to Grandad, who gave it to me. I sat and cried for ages. I could not stop.

My grandparents did not think that what they did was wonderful at all. Their only thought was that they were helping their granddaughter.

That Christmas made us aware of what Christmas is all about. It is about families being together and helping one another.

After Christmas, on 10 January I gave birth to my first son, Graham. I was in hospital a week at Little Thorpe. I prayed the miners would get back to work soon, as I now had this little bundle to bring up. It was a different ball game when Graham came along. Jeff was able to help with the baby, and we took it in turn to do the night feed. Because Jeff was on strike, we could get milk vouchers – but it was the only real help we got. My family rallied round with items like a cot and blankets.

I was glad when the miners got back to work in March 1985. It took a while to get back on our feet. We moved into a colliery house and tried to make a fresh start. I believe the miners' strike has been a solid foundation to our marriage, as since then we have been able to cope with whatever life throws at us.

Karen Surtees

My Hard-Working Dad

My father worked at the marine colliery for over 20 years. His name was Jack Bedford, from Brynmawr, a hard-working man. In 1964 there was a pit fall where a friend and workmate was killed – my father brought the poor man to the surface. I remember him coming home crying. I had never seen him cry before. Those miners worked with a pick and shovel in awful conditions, up past their knees in water. I'm always going to be proud of my dad and what he did for his kids. He had a beat knee, where his knee just rotted from standing in dirty water for hours – God bless you, my beautiful dad.

Jackie Haynes

Stacksteads, Lancashire, Glen Top c1950 S552007

Cwm, Gwent, The Colliery c1955 C517009

The Old Brewery

I well remember the building in this photograph. I believe it was built as a brewery, and I worked there in 1957. I was a joiner, and was sent to carry out joinery repairs. The firm I worked for was J Greenhalgh of Rawtenstall and the brewery was called Baxters, and was taken over a few years later by Beverly's beers. Shortly after that it was demolished, and now all that can be seen is a large area of grass.

Pete Nicholas

Abercwmboi, Mid Glamorgan, The Phurnacite Plant c1955 A190001

Smoke and Smells

The first time I saw this photo it brought back old memories, because when I got up from bed every morning and opened my curtains the first thing I saw was the smoke from the Phurnacite plant. This was because we lived in Park View Terrace, not more than a few hundred yards from the site. The pond in the picture was where we used to swim in the summer, and also where we did some fishing.

The men that worked at the plant had to put a yellow cream on their faces so that the tar would not burn their skin. Some men who worked on the coke ovens had to wear wooden clogs because the heat from the ovens was so hot that everyday working boots would have burnt up because of the heat.

David Williams

Wigan Clogs

Wigan-made clogs always did have a reputation even way back when. I've even discovered that one of my ancestors made his living as a boot and clog repairer. I never did get to own a pair - but oh! how I envied my school friends who did wear them, and could make sparks as they walked along the pavement.

I did get a few demerit marks for my house at school in Essex because of clogs – thanks to a few extra notes I added to those I wrote up following a geography lesson on the Lancashire cotton industry. Somewhere along the line, when visiting one of the Wigan mills with a teacher from St Michael's (we were buying muslin to make the angels' costumes for a Christmas nativity play), I was told that the reason the mill girls wore clogs was to protect their feet when they were working. This was particularly true in the spinning sections, where to keep the humidity levels high to prevent the thread snapping as it was wound, the floor was kept awash with a couple of inches of water in the old mills. In the modern mills humidity levels could be technically controlled, so swirling water on the floor was no longer a factor, and the wearing of clogs was more of a custom than a necessity. I never did find out why my additional notes were so frowned upon – whether the information was incorrect or not, or if perhaps it was just a case of teaching a pupil, who thought he knew more than the teacher, a lesson in showing the right kind of respect for the teacher's knowledge! Lateral thinking and constructive argument were definitely not encouraged.

It's interesting, though, to know clogs do still have a valid use and are still going strong.

John Morris

Cippenham, Berkshire, Bath Road Trading Estate 1965 C442033

Demolition

There was a man called Twinch, Henry I think, owner of Cippenham Manor, and Twinches Lane was originally his shortcut. The photograph (above) is taken from the footbridge put up for the Girls' High School pupils to cross the road to get their buses. The school was sold in the 60s for housing and a retail park. The bridge was later removed. Twinches Lane is on the left.

The land on the left, originally all farmland, was covered by Nissen huts during the war, with an AA battery protecting the trading estate. After the war people were gradually re-housed and the huts demolished. One of my Uncle Albert's first demolition jobs was to take the bases up. Uncle Albert, my brother Pete and I broke them up with a sledgehammer, levering them up with a length of 2in shaft and then 'popping' the bases with the sledge. We loaded them onto our old ex-Navy Ford V8 lorry.
Dave Hill

Charlestown, an Ancient Port

I briefly attended Charlestown Infants' School in 1942, as it accepted children a year earlier than Mount Charles Infant's School a mile away.

During the war years the quaysides around the inner dock had corrugated iron buildings that were used in the fitting out of inshore minesweeper vessels. These boats were built at nearby Par and had their engines and machinery fitted at Charlestown. The sheds were removed at the end of the war, and once more the harbour looked very much as it had when it was built by Charles Rashleigh in the last decade of the 1700s.

St Austell, Cornwall, The Clay Workings c1955 S6052

In spite of wartime restrictions, locals were permitted access to the beaches, and the one on the eastern side of the harbour entrance was our destination whenever the weather allowed. As we grew older, mother would be waiting for us there with a snack when we raced down the hill after school. The beach was very pebbly, but with the breakwater to dive off and the wonderful rock pools to play in at low water spring tides, we ignored the pain of walking over pebbles as only preoccupied, very happy kids can.

During the late forties and fifties, water polo matches were played in the outer harbour during the summer, evening tides permitting. The Charlestown team played teams from Fowey, Mevagissey, Falmouth and others, both home and away. There was also an annual regatta and swimming gala, and a memorable event was walking the greasy pole erected out over the harbour wall.

The harbour was very busy during those years with the export of china clay from the clay pits around the St Austell area. The dried clay was loaded into small coastal ships (200–300 tons) which transported it to the Continent. It was always exciting to watch a ship that had lain anchored in the bay awaiting high tide come into the harbour under the guidance of the port pilot Tommy Coates. The entrance was very narrow, and entailed a 90-degree turn towards the lock gates that retained the water in the inner harbour. Manually operated capstans, mounted at strategic points along the harbour wall, were used to winch the ships into position,

so that with the engine 'very slow ahead' the ship would creep into the inner basin with only inches to spare on both sides. At that time the two massive wooden gates were also opened and closed manually with capstans, but some years later these were replaced by a hydraulically operated gate that was lowered into a horizontal position to allow ships to pass over.

Peter Marks

Charlestown, Cornwall, The Harbour 1912 64784

Woolpit, Suffolk, The Old Mill c1960   W442030

An Old Mill

My ancestor William Irving lived at Low Mill, Grassington (below) with his family before 1820 until his death in 1843 aged 84. He was a woolcomber. His son James Irving also lived here with his family until his death in 1873 aged 93. He was an overlooker. The mill in the photograph has three sections. It is only the centre section which has been demolished. The other two sections are now used as houses, and the largest building also incorporates a dental surgery. In the 17th century a smelt mill was built to the left of the stream near Low Mill, but that too has been demolished.

Christine Booth

Grassington, Yorkshire, Low Mill 1900   45784

Elmer's Mill

Harry Elmer, my great-grandad's brother, owned and ran this mill into the 1940s. There are some wonderful images of him resplendent in the very gentlemanly working clothes of a miller of his ilk, and still working in his 80s.

Anecdotally Elmers Mill in Woolpit and Drinkstone Mill close by were dead ringers for each other, except that they ran (their sails rotated) in the opposite direction to each other. This has recently been questioned on the Suffolk Mills website, which has some memories posted about the structure of Elmers Woolpit Mill after it was tail-winded in 1963 and collapsed. The site says that Elmers Mill was built of 'inferior materials', and therefore of much more recent (perhaps 19th-century) construction than the recognised ancient (and still-standing) Drinkstone Mill. Its recognisably old design would seem to counter this argument, and it's more likely, I believe, that the 'inferior materials' found after it collapsed may have been due to the need for successive and ongoing repairs, required owing to the hard life a constantly used mill was subject to.   *Harry Elmer*

Grassington, Yorkshire, The Wharf and the Old Mill 1926   79062x

Fylingdales, Yorkshire, The Early Warning System c1960 F91002

Early Warning

In 1962, my family (father, mother, one brother, and I) lived in Whitby and Goathland while my father, a mechanical and electrical engineer, was working on the design and construction of the Ballistic Missile Early Warning Signal System at Fylingdales, a co-operative project of the United States and Great Britain. These 'golf balls', as they were called, loomed over the moors. To find photographs of the installation 45 years later has been wonderful. I understand that it has since been replaced with other structures.

Margot Eddy

Fylingdales, Yorkshire, The Early Warning System c1960 F91004

Working at the Gamecock

I moved into the Gamecock in 1963 with my parents Norman and Jean Bennett and my brother Bryan. I was only two years old. My parents were landlord and landlady.

The Gamecock was well known for appearances by club artists, and every night there was some sort of entertainment going on. The pub was known for a good

night out for miles around. It also had an extremely busy off sales where people could buy beer to take away. There were no shops then open after five, and no supermarkets, so the off-licence was packed at night.

There was a separate lounge and tap room and a concert room which had a stage, and the cellar was the stores. Even as a young girl I was allowed to help by serving and collecting glasses, and sometimes I sat under the serving hatch so I could listen to the bands playing.

Over the years there were lots of changes at the pub. When I was sixteen there was a major refurbishment. The concert room became the tap room, and the front of the pub was knocked into one and became the lounge as we know it today. It was extremely busy up until the mid 1990s, when the pit closed, and the old communities started to dwindle away. My father passed away in 1987, but Mum continued to run the pub until she retired in 1996 – they had been there for 33 years.

I remember beer being sixpence a pint, and the only choice being between bitter and mild – lager came later! Cherry b's and babychams were best sellers with the ladies. I remember decimalisation and Dad giving the barmaids lessons in the new currency. The tills were manual, and everyone added up in their head – there were no calculators.

Harworth, South Yorkshire, The Gamecock, Bawtry Road c1955 H482010

Eleanor Hipwell

My Grandfather, a Tenant Farmer

The gentleman with the scythe over his shoulder (right) was my grandfather. His name was Joseph Jackson, born in 1849 at Bootle in Cumberland. He spent most of his life as a tenant farmer, first at Canleton Farm near Egremont, also in Cumberland. He then moved to Lane Ends Farm at Haverthwaite (then in Lancashire) owing to the subsidence of the land due to iron ore mining from the nearby Florence Mine. He retired from farming in 1919 to Penny Bridge, where he spent the rest of his life.

Mr J Jackson

Greenodd, Cumbria, Main Street 1921 70700

Clowne, Derbyshire, Mill Street c1950 C403009

Woodcutter and Footballer

The gentleman pushing a cart in the foreground of this picture (left) is my grandfather, Ernest Pearce (1895–1970). The cart was used to transport bundles of sticks that he cut for sale as firewood. They were sold for 4d a bundle to supplement his wages as a miner and later, as in the photo, during his retirement.

The history of woodcutting in the family goes back to his father, James Herbert Pearce, who leased a plot of land at Whitwell Woods and cut wood for sale from his horse and cart.

Grandad was a sniper in the First World War. He was very lucky, as he survived being shot in the head. We were allowed to feel the metal plate that had been inserted to treat the injury.

Before the First World War, Grandad played football for Sheffield United, and he often walked or cycled to Sheffield to play. June Harvey

On Duty

The police officer standing on the pavement is my great-grandfather, Thomas Rees, PC No 2, who served from 1903 to 1911 in Carmarthen town. He was one of the twelve 'coppers' of Carmarthen town, also known as the 'Carmarthen Shilling'.

Paul Rees

Carmarthen, Dyfed, The Guildhall 1906 53738p

Busky Tripp

This photo (below) shows a rowing boat which probably belonged to my great-grandfather 'Busky' Tripp, who ferried people across the river at the nearby staithe. He also rowed to Lowestoft fish market and back nearly every day with a load of vegetables from his market garden. He would bring back fish to sell in the village.

Ann Morris

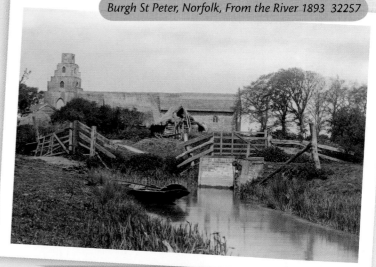

Burgh St Peter, Norfolk, From the River 1893 32257

Grandad's Donkeys

I was most surprised to see this photograph, which shows my late grandfather William Mannall and possibly my Uncle Paul with Grandad's donkeys, which he had for many years on the beach at Hemsby and which Uncle Paul also had later at Newport. I had many gratis rides to encourage others, and I used to help with the tack and grooming.

Don Bullen

Hemsby, Norfolk, The Donkeys c1955 H306068p

Gardener on a Grand Scale

My grandfather, William Simpson Bruchshaw, is the man coming out of the greenhouse with a plant in his hand. He was head gardener to Mr Munro Walker until Mr Walker died. My grandfather's youngest brother, Henry, was farm manager on the estate. While at Pell Wall, my grandfather experimented with growing tomatoes on potatoes – this was in about 1908, I think. We still have the photos in the family. After he left Pell Wall my grandfather lived in Little Drayton. He died aged 91 in 1952.

K D Hill

Pell Wall, Shropshire, The Hall 1899 44440

Pell Wall, Shropshire, The Kitchen Garden 1911 63372

Landlords at the Windmill Inn

My grandfather Edward Chase kept the Windmill Inn on Pitch Hill, and my father, Robert Chase (Ted) worked for him.

My father joined the Surrey Yeomanry during the First World War and served in France with this cavalry regiment. He returned to Ewhurst after the war, not in the best of health having been wounded and gassed. He married my mother, Mona, the daughter of the landlord of the Bull's Head in the village of Ewhurst.

When my grandfather and his wife retired, my father and his new wife took over the licence at the Windmill Inn. They ran it up until the start of the great depression. As well as the usual services of a village inn, they provided hotel accommodation to walking parties down from London. When the walking parties were no longer popular during the depression, father moved away, and the family took an inn at Minster on the Isle of Thanet where I grew up.

Michael Chase

Ewhurst, Surrey, Pitch Hill 1911 63165

Redhill, Surrey, The Hospital 1908 59627

Nursing at Redhill General

This picture (left) is of the old East Surrey Hospital where my mother was an in-patient for many weeks around 1954. As children we were not allowed in the wards, and I can remember waving to my mum through a window.

I did my nurse training at Redhill General, starting as a pre-nursing student in 1965 and qualifying in 1970. We went between two sites – the other one was Smallfield Hospital in Horley, an old wartime hospital. I trained in the days when every hospital had a matron, and there was very strict discipline. We wore starched caps and aprons, and the stiff collars were very uncomfortable.

The wards at Redhill were named after places in Surrey – the medical wards were called Chipstead and Chaldon, and the surgical wards were Bramley and Brockham. The children's ward was in a part of the hospital that had been the old workhouse, known as the Spike. The isolation ward was also very old.

Despite the age of the hospital, some innovative surgery was carried out there in the 1960s. It was here that some of the first hip replacements were done by Mr Peter Ring, who perfected a special technique that was used for several decades.

Each ward had its own designated cleaner who took great pride in the ward – we must have had very low infection rates despite there being only a very small proportion of the antibiotics that are available today.

The hospital was in a beautiful position on Redhill Common. The training I received there is still being put to good use as I continue my long career, now in Australia.

Sally Pashby

Dovedale, Derbyshire, Reynards Cave 1914 67604p

Refreshments and a Rope at the Cave

My great-great-aunt, Annie Bennington, like her mother before her, carried refreshments and postcards to sell from Milldale down to Reynards Cave. She also fixed the rope from the cave, and visitors paid for its use in helping them up and down the steep climb. She is the lady with her back to the camera in this photo. *Stephen Mather*

Cave Guide and Shopkeeper

When he was a boy, my father, Donald William Stevens, used to show visitors through the Pixies' Caves for a ha'penny per person, using the light from a candle for illumination. After the Second World War he followed in his father's footsteps as a Chudleigh shopkeeper, and opened a shoe shop at 7 The Square, or Fore Street, as some preferred to call it. This shop was in business for 39 years, and sold all types of footwear from wellies and plimsolls to brogues, although there was not much call for ballet shoes.

Richard Stevens

Chudleigh, Devon, The Pixies' Cave 1907 58497

Chudleigh, Devon, The Square 1907 58490

A Family Business

I am the lady at the door with my husband Don Weston. The date is about 1959, because that is the year we had electricity in the village and started to sell ice cream. Hence the Walls sign. My parents, Mr and Mrs Caesar Evans, started the tearooms here in 1922, and after my mother died in 1952 my husband and I ran this little business together very happily for 52 years until his sudden death three years ago. But I have managed to keep the business going with the help of many good friends. I am now nearly 85, and affectionately known by many customers as Auntie Vi. We sold Frith postcards for many years.
Mrs Violet Weston

Bosherston, Dyfed, The Tea Gardens c1959   B468060

I, along with very many local girls over the years, helped out at the Tea Gardens at Bosherton (left) during the school holidays. I remember going to the front door a few times to ask if they had a job for me, and being so scared that I came away with an ice cream instead. I need not have worried, as Aunty Vi and Don were so lovely. I enjoyed several happy years with them until I left school and the village to work away. Now it's 40 years later, and I still look forward to seeing Aunty Vi whenever I go 'home'.
Susan James

Singing Cliff Richard songs led to Romance

Minehead, Somerset, Butlin's Holiday Camp c1965   M84253

Penguins

When I was still at school I helped out in the evenings and weekends at the zoo, and one of my jobs was feeding the penguins.

Julie Knighton

I was born in Minehead, and worked in Butlin's Holiday Camp at Minehead from 1962 to 1963.

This was the first full year that the camp was opened. Most of the time I was working the rides in the amusement park. I helped build the Big Dipper, which was 70ft high, but it is now gone.

Some nights I sang on the stage under the name of Elvis the Second, singing mostly his and Cliff Richard's songs. When I was at the camp there were three dance floors, one for rock and roll, another for ballroom dancing, which once hosted the Come Dancing competition for the BBC, and the third for general activities. I danced every night in the ballroom. I was disappointed when I went back to the camp in 2006 and found that there were no ballrooms there now, just the building that housed them. I still go dancing twice a week. In the summer of 1963, I met a girl from Wales who was on holiday there. I moved to Wales, and we were married. We have been married 43 years, and have two children and four grandchildren.
P Aden

Wellingborough, Northamptonshire, The Zoo c1950   W279021

Whelking

This is my grandfather standing beside his whelk house looking at the boats as they unload. He died after a motor car accident on Beach Road in 1934.

P L Matsell

Wells-next-the-Sea, Norfolk, The Quay 1929 81998t

Hop Picking

Paddock Wood and in particular Beltring, the home of the famous Whitbread Oasts, was the centre of the hop gardens of Kent.

The gardens were set out with rows of elevated wire trestles, supported at intervals by poles. In the spring, the shoots from each hop plant (which was cut back to ground level every year) were trained up – this was known as 'twiddling'. A new hop twined up, and was tied from a metal hook in the ground up to the overhead wire. There were usually four shoots per plant. By midsummer's day the shoots would reach the wire and flop over the top.

In early September the hops would be ready for picking. Hop picking in Kent was carried out mainly by London families who came down for a working holiday. Some farms had hop pickers' huts in the hop gardens for their use. Some families even used to bring their own wallpaper to make it seem like their own home. Cooking and heating water was carried out on a wood fire outside. Paddock Wood even had its own 'Hop Pickers' Hospital'.

Where I lived in Southborough near Tunbridge Wells, we went hop picking at a farm called Nightingale Farm, and the farmer's name was Mr Podmore. It was a much smaller enterprise than Paddock Wood, being a mixed farm. Every morning at 7.30am we walked through the fields to Vauxhall Lane, pushing an old pram with the kettle and the day's food. The start of the day's picking was signalled by the farm foreman shouting 'Pull binds'. Hops were picked into bins made of two poles from which a sacking 'cradle' hung. The poles were supported on crossed wooden legs at each end of the bin. Some families had whole bins. Others, less prolific, had half a bin shared with others. The bin was divided down the middle with a sacking partition.

By the time the hops were ready for picking in September, the hop twine was almost rotten, and all that was required was a good tug to release the bine from the top wire. Sometimes you would find a big hairy caterpillar on the bine – we called these 'hop dogs'.

Paddock Wood, Kent, Hop Picking c1950 P220020

Paddock Wood, Kent, Measuring the Hops c1950 P220008p

Every day Mr Podmore the farmer would come round with the farm secretary and the farm foreman to measure your hops. If you had 'dirty' hops – leaves and stalks in with the hops – he would shout out 'Dirty hops' and pass you by. He measured out the hops with a wicker bushel basket, and you were paid at so many pence per bushel. As he measured them out, he would shout 'One-a, two-a, three-a' etc, and the secretary would note your tally for the day. The hops were measured out into big sacks called pokes, which the foreman held whilst Mr Podmore measured out the hops. The pokes were filled until they were almost solid, and then loaded onto a flat horse-drawn cart. They were then taken off to the oast house where they were dried over a charcoal fire.

Lunchtime was signalled by a shout from the foreman – 'Dinnerrrr!'. Our lunch was assorted sandwiches and my mum's meat pie followed by apple pie and a cup of tea. The tea was brewed in a black kettle, which was stood on two bricks with a fire of dry hazel twigs in between the bricks.

The end of the day was signalled by a cry of 'Stop pickingggg!' from the foreman. Home was a trek across the fields with the pram, and then you needed a good wash to try and get the hop smell and stains off your fingers.

I remembered that smell when years later I lived at Goudhurst. I would go into the village shop – Burges Stores – on a Saturday afternoon after the pickers had been in for their shopping, and be overwhelmed.

Michael Willcocks

Belchers

Running parallel to the back of the church (St James's) in the photograph below is the High Street, where I was born, as generations of my family were.

The two pot banks on the right represent just a fraction of the 'belchers' that existed in Longton in the 30s and 40s. They dominated all who lived amongst them with their endless stream of black smoke belching out six days a week and covering all the buildings with soot and dirt. Night-time brought short relief,

until the next firing. Wash days were a nightmare. Clothes went on to the line clean, only to be covered later on with black spots that poured down relentlessly from the heavy smoky skies. White washing was unheard of in the Potteries until the eventual closure of the pot banks.

Perhaps, on reflection, in the late evenings when the kilns stand like silent sentries, silhouette outlines in the night skies, we should remember the generations of potters who worked endlessly in all this grime to give us an industry that was once second to none.

Barbara Johnson

> ❝ *White washing was unheard of in the Potteries until the eventual closure of the pot banks* ❞

Longton, Staffordshire, The Pottery Kilns 1955 L541015x

Woolwich, Greater London, The Market 1963 W460024

Fanny by Gaslight!

Woolwich Market – what a hoot! I can hear the stall keeper at the far left there back in 1959 …

''ere y'are luv … step right up … step right up … see these 'ere brand new silk bloomers … never seen dayloit, never seen moonloit, and never seen Aunt Fanny by gasloit 'aven't these 'ere bloomers … wot'lyer give me then … three pairs a shilling then … come on nah …'

I lived on Mill Lane up by the barracks. Used to love wandering around the market on a Saturday, I did.

Dylan Rivis

The Bank of England

The Bank has occupied this site since the late 17th century. Although you cannot see it from either this view or indeed from the street, there is an exquisite garden and lawn in the centre.

I started my career in banking with the Bank of England in 1963. It was quite awe-inspiring as a teenager to enter the massive front door that was held open by a top-hatted Bank messenger dressed smartly in a pink morning coat. He would gently tip the brim of his top hat and say 'Good morning, Sir!'. He only raised his topper when the Governor entered.

Relics of the very early 1900s still remained in the Bank when I began work. Many of the vaults had telephones installed, and unbelievably these were of the old-fashioned 'candlestick' design. It was difficult to remember to hold the separate parts of the phone to ear and mouth. Weekly deliveries of gold bullion came each Wednesday, on the Union Castle Line, and docked at Southampton. The bullion was transferred to an armoured train and taken to Waterloo and then by security van to the Bank's rear bullion entrance. Security precautions were everywhere. In the 1960s a picket of Army sentries was provided every night, so each time I worked overtime I needed to have a password to reply to the sentries' challenge!
John Howard Norfolk

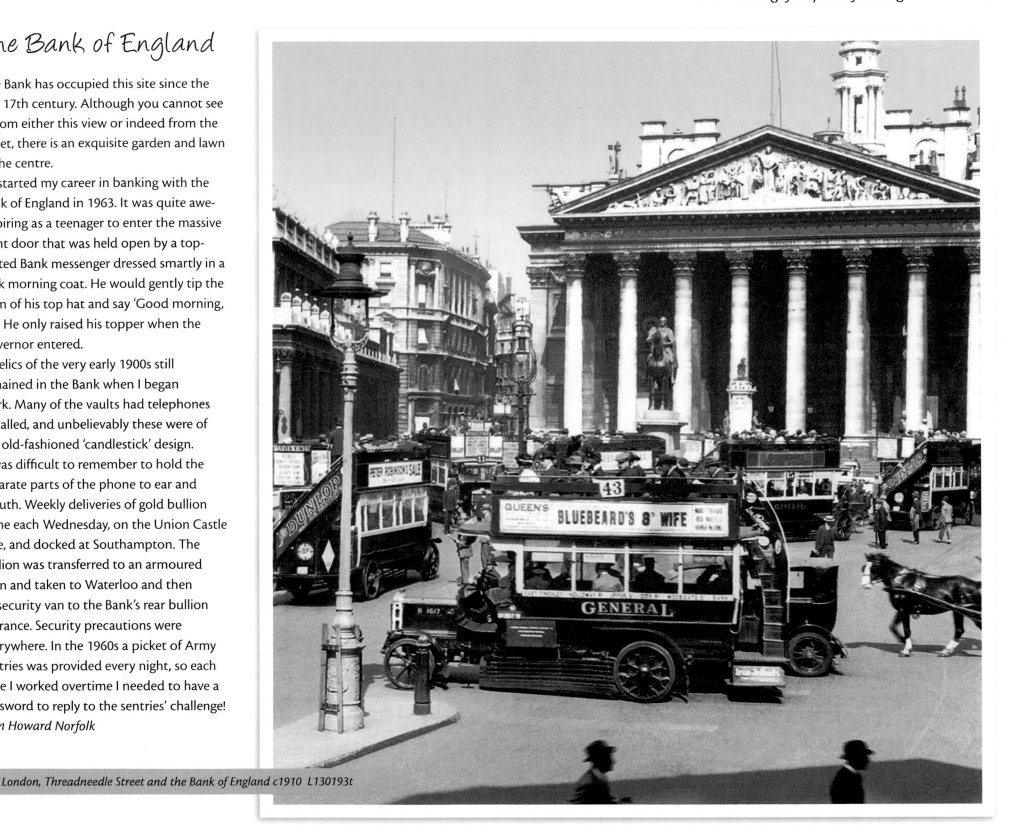

London, Threadneedle Street and the Bank of England c1910 L130193t

Gas Lamps and Coal Carts

I remember the lamplighter lighting the gas lamps along Dicconson Street in Wigan, and insisting that someone hold me up at the window so that I could see him at work. I also remember being taken to see the first Belisha beacon erected at the corner of Mesnes Street, or that's where I think it was.

I also recall the wonderful horses that drew the coal carts to the house and the acrid smell of the delivery men with their blackened faces, how they would throw the coal down a chute to the left of the front door after lifting the heavy metal manhole cover, and the noise as the coal rattled its way down to the lower basement. Only when the delivery was complete was I allowed to go outside and ask if I could look at the horse brasses that the horses wore, a love which has lasted to this day. A memory of these horses is brought to mind every time I look at my collection.

Thelma Hurly

Hatch End, Uxbridge, Middlesex c1965 H404051

Christmas at the Post Office

On the extreme right of the picture (left) is Hatch End Post Office. I worked there as a Christmas Casual in 1965. I had a lovely time on the parcels counter – the permanent staff would weigh parcels and write the postage price and take the money, then throw (yes, throw) the parcels to me at the end of the counter, where I had a huge ledger of stamps. It was my job to stick on stamps to the value pencilled on the wrapping.

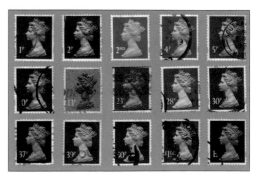

Of course this quickly bored me, so I livened things up by arranging unusual combinations of brightly coloured stamps – at this time there were some particularly lurid green sevenpenny stamps, and I used so many huge blocks of these on the heavier parcels that I single-handedly ran Hatch End Post Office out of 7d's. There must be a lot of very happy stamp collectors around the world with unusual blocks of green stamps in their albums! A fortnight's work was paid at the princely rate of two shillings and fourpence farthing an hour. And I had a deduction for a National Insurance stamp to be stuck on my NI card.

John Howard Norfolk

PC at Piccadilly Circus

I was a young constable in the year 1951 and, fresh from Peel House, Westminster, I was assigned to the Savile Row station known as CD. I lived at the Section House on Broadwick Street, Soho, named after Lord Trenchard. Many times I was assigned to Piccadilly Circus, on the early turn or between 5pm and 1am for a two-week period. There was a police box adjacent to the stairs to the Piccadilly tube station and at the corner of Swan and Edgar's store. When the blue light flashed I would answer the call from the station to go on details in the vicinity.

I was stationed there the day John Christie was arrested for the murders at 10 Rillington Place, and for some time during the Coronation festivities – the line-ups were around the corner from my position and on to Regent Street. After serving in the Met, I emigrated to Canada and served there from 1955 to 1989, but I enjoyed my short time of service in London with a fine bunch of lads.

Nelson Jones

London, Piccadilly Circus c1960 L1305086t

Robin Hood's Bay, Yorkshire, New Road c1955 R41054

The Goodchild Delivery Service

The horse and cart in the picture above belonged to my husband's uncle, Harry Goodchild. He worked with Len Pennock delivering coal and other goods around Robin Hood's Bay and Fylingthorpe. The man at the back of the cart wearing the cap is Len Pennock, and the man in the middle of the picture walking towards the cart is Harry Goodchild.

The delivery business was started in the late 1800s by James Goodchild, the local agent for the British Rail parcel delivery service in the area. Because of the steepness of Bay Bank (it was 1 in 3) a special metal shoe was placed under one of the wheels to prevent the cart running away.

Lynda Eastwood

Robin Hood's Bay, Yorkshire 1901 46794

Love at the Headland

I worked at the Headland Hotel during one summer in the 1960s. It was a wonderful summer working in the garden, and the views along the cliffs and out to sea were magnificent. Pickles was the manager. He was a tyrant, but I seemed to get the better of him. I wrecked the lawnmower by running over a rock while pushing it up and down those front lawns in the picture. He tried to make me pay for it out of my £4 10s a week pay – I refused.

I fell in love with Margaret from Quinton who was working that summer to practise the cooking skills she had learned in Birmingham Catering School. The gardener teased me, saying I was the darkest horse he had ever known and that I had stolen the best looking woman (Margaret) for many a mile from under the noses of all interested parties.

In the early mornings I polished any shoes left out by guests, then had a cup of tea and a cigarette (it was good for you in those days) with the chambermaids, who were also from Birmingham. They had the shortest skirts you could believe! I sometimes worked washing up in the kitchen, removing bottles from the bar, and helping in the still room.

Best of all were the tips I had during the Saturday morning change-over for lugging guests' bags down the stairs for those leaving and back up for those arriving. I sometimes earned half as much again of my wages for heavy work over two or three hours.

The staff quarters were OK except for the TV room, which flooded when it rained. We sat in there surrounded by water two or three inches deep, with our legs up on an old beer-crate.

There used to be a village dance in the corrugated hut overlooking the sea a little away from the harbour. We walked from the hotel down to the hut to dance, or let the locals glare at us. I knew one or two from school, so it was mostly friendly. The walk back along the cliff-path in the moonlight was unforgettable.

During the winter, I was the only live-in at the weekends when there was a function on. I hitch-hiked from the other side of Helston out to the Headland on Friday evenings to work out there. In the unpredictable Cornish weather I walked many miles without getting a lift through some wild nights before arriving soaked to the skin.

I have very fond memories of my sweetheart Margaret. I still have this vivid picture of her in my mind. When she finished work in the kitchen, she would come to see me where I was still working in the high-hedged garden. She was in her whites. She would undo the scrunchie holding her hair up, then, shaking her head, she shook that wonderful hair out, allowing it to cascade over her shoulders. In the sunlight it was amber and gold, and she was the most beautiful thing I had ever seen.

Steve Gilvear

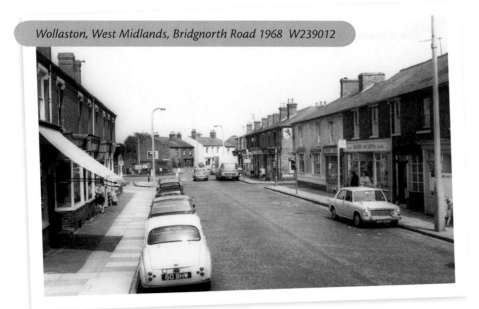

Wollaston, West Midlands, Bridgnorth Road 1968   W239012

One Carrot and One Parsnip? Certainly!

I worked at this fruit and veg shop (owned by Mr and Mrs Evans) from about 1962 on a Saturday when I was at Stourbridge Girls High School, and after I left school I worked full time there. I lived with my parents in Cobden Street, and I remember the race to the top of the road when I was late for work! Very happy memories were made in this shop. In those days there were no calculators and the totals were added as I went along, and we were happy to sell one carrot and one parsnip if that was all that was needed – a far cry from supermarkets now! I worked with Mr Evans at West Bromwich market on his veg stall – I loved to banter with the customers there. I also remember waiting for the Kinver bus at the stop (I now live in Kinver). I also spent time in the general shop by the crossing with a friend of my mum's where food was weighed out and put in small bags.

Carol Wakefield

Skating and Pea-Soupers

My first job after school was directly responsible for my being in Canada now. I worked as a secretary to the Manager of Wembley Stadium, and at lunchtime in the arena caféteria I'd sit and talk to the Canadian hockey players who'd been imported to play for the Wembley Lions. Players like Curly Leachman, Claire Smith and coach Sonny Rost enthralled me with their Canadian accent and stories of their home towns. It was more than this British lass filled with wanderlust could stand, and three weeks after my eighteenth birthday I kissed Mum and Dad goodbye and took to the skies for Montreal and a whole different slice of life.

The fifties was the time to be a teenager. I had graduated from tap-dancing to ice-skating at Wembley arena. I fancied myself as Sonja Henie or at least Yvonne Sugden as I whirled around the ice to the strains of Perez Prado's 'Cherry Pink and Apple Blossom White'. While the girls watched, the boys showed off, and they raced at top speed to Lonnie Donegan's 'Jump down, turn around, pick a bale of cotton', then the girls tried to keep

up the pace to 'Sweet Georgia Brown', the record the arena kept on hand for appearances by the Harlem Globetrotters. Those were the days! Mum used to say if I wore my skating skirt any shorter I'd be wearing it for a collar.

But it wouldn't be right to say I grew up British without mentioning our pea-souper fogs. You didn't worry about walking the streets alone – no-one could find you! From Burnt Oak Station, if the buses had stopped running in the fog, I'd have to count the number of curbs I stepped up and down to keep count of the streets I'd crossed until I got to mine. One time I miscounted, and so similar were the adjacent cul-de-sacs that when I opened the front door (never locked) and yelled 'S'me, Mum', a total stranger yelled back 'Wrong mum, love!'.

Heather Rohrer

Wembley, Middlesex, The Stadium c1960   W314064

Blackjacks, the two-bob gun, and a parrot

SHOPPING MEMORIES

Sweets from the Post Office

I was born in 1955. I was six months old when my parents moved into Magna Close and I have many warm memories of my childhood in Great Abington, some of which relate to the post office. Harry and Hilda Jaggard owned and ran it, with Harry seeing to the post office and Hilda looking after the shop. I still remember the Penny Arrows, the 2d bars of Cadbury's chocolate, the Toffee Cushions, the Winter Mixtures, the Fruit Salads and the Blackjacks, liquorice (comfits, bootlaces, pipes and Catherine wheels), all manner of spellbinding goodies. And Hilda, bless her heart, she had the patience of a saint – we village children would take forever to try and get as many sweets as possible for our 3d or 6d.

Great Abington, Cambridgeshire, The Post Office c1955   G349010

The vegetables were tumbled into the vast brass dish of the weighing scales, and Hilda would pick up the weights and place them on the other end to see if an extra potato was needed to reach the requested weight. If you couldn't find an item that was on your list, Hilda would go down to the cellar to find what was required. Nothing was too much trouble. Harry Jaggard was just as nice. He stood behind his glass window, usually with a cigar for company, attending to the post office needs of the village folk. He had unlimited patience with us children – we would offer him a small hand under the bottom of the glass so that we could get stamped! We'd be thrilled to bits with our very own postmark – until he told us that we were being sent to London!

Harry and Hilda had two daughters, Helen and Jackie, and a huge Airedale dog called Trigger – he was rather frightening. The photo of the post office shows it as I remember it as a child. Many times huge lorries would mount the pavement and knock the corner of the building above the door. In those days the A604 was the main road, and it was incredibly busy. I'm sure there are many former pupils of the school who will remember the Turner's refrigerated lorry that ended up in the front playground. Being children, we thought this was exciting. As a result, crash barriers were placed outside the school.

I have another memory of the post office. There used to be a machine on the outer wall where one could purchase either cigarettes or chocolate outside opening hours. The cigarettes had the correct change inside the outer wrapping. We didn't want the cigarettes, but we would push our small hands up inside the machine and obtain the boxes to get the money. The chocolate was just a bonus.

Chris Cooper

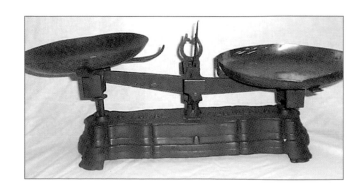

New Haw, Surrey c1960 N183011

Beating the Shopping Bounds

I have lived in New Haw most of my life. My family moved from Kings Road to Farleigh Road in 1949. Pocket money in the 1950s was not very generous – but at the age of five I clutched 2d in my hand and made my way to Hunt's to buy either four Blackjacks and four Fruit Salads (1d for four) or a packet of Polos. Mr Hunt first ran the shop solely as a sweet shop, but he later branched out by selling wallpaper, paint and all things DIY. Today the shop specialises in nail extensions and manicures.

Next to him was the jeweller Mee's (now a hairdresser's) – I used to do a lot of window shopping there. Kendal's used to sell corn, chicken feed and hardware. The shop had a very peculiar smell – grain mixed in with turpentine. The butcher's floor was always sprinkled with sawdust. Mr Cole ran the fish and chip shop – and Mrs Cole always had a cigarette hanging out of her mouth.

Christine Beddows

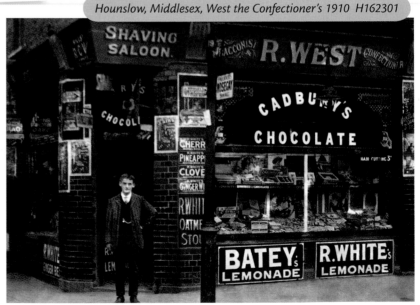

Hounslow, Middlesex, West the Confectioner's 1910 H162301

St Neots, Cambridgeshire, Roper's Shop c1965 S37060

' The shop had a very peculiar smell – grain mixed in with turpentine '

The Two-Bob Gun

At the top of Queens Road in Buckhurst Hill was a small newsagent's shop. It was owned by Mr and Mrs Silk. The shop sold papers, magazines, cigarettes, sweets and a few toys. The little shop did a roaring trade. I attended school at Taunton House about half way down Queens Road and passed Silk's going to and from school. My mother always let me stop for a minute to look in the shop window.

One day I saw a toy revolver like the ones the cowboys used in the Wild West. It was a cap gun, and with the holster cost two shillings. I asked my parents so many times if I could have that gun. Each time I was told no, as it was too expensive. After several months of hoping and asking I still received the same answer. One day I looked in the window and it was gone! I was heartbroken. Someone else must have bought it, and now I'd never see it again.

When Saturday came, my dad handed me a package. Inside was the 'Two-Bob Gun' complete with several rounds of caps. Dad said I could only fire it outside, as the noise upset my mother. I must have spent the rest of the day playing Cowboys and Indians with that gun. I cherished it till I had grown up, and then I gave it to a much younger boy to play with.

Denman Lalonde

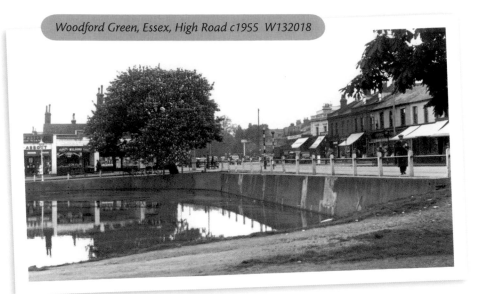

Woodford Green, Essex, High Road c1955 W132018

A Very Special Toy Shop

Oh, yes, I remember this area during the war. Shops were open at their regular hours. The locals bought their necessities, and everyone came and went as usual. The general feeling was 'To hell with Hitler, we'll carry on regardless'.

This also meant that birthdays for children went on as usual. My aunt from Manchester, Auntie Burley, came to visit us at Buckhurst Hill. She helped to celebrate my birthday on 21 June. One year she said: 'We are going shopping, just you and I. I would like you to have something of your own choice as a special treat'.

It didn't take me long to decide what I wanted. We boarded the 10A bus at the top of Hills Road and headed to Woodford Green. Right across from the pond near the corner was a big toyshop. They had a large selection of Dinky toys. The one I wanted was the barrage balloon lorry. It was a very long lorry with a silver barrage balloon on the top. I knew it cost quite a lot of money, and silently thought that perhaps it was too much. But without hesitation, Auntie asked me if that was really what I wanted, so I smiled and said 'Yes please'.

Soon we were back on the bus heading for home. I made sure I held my lovely gift carefully as we rode the short distance back to the top pond on the High Road. Auntie said I grinned all the time we walked down Hills Road to Epping New Road, where we crossed to our cottage at number 58. Mum and Dad said the present was rather extravagant, but my aunt insisted, saying she was happy to be able to spoil me now and then.

Denman Lalonde

Nuts and Bolts – and Fork Handles

The photo (right) brings back lots of memories for me as it shows High Road, Woodford Bridge (later it was renamed Chigwell Road) where the old-fashioned ironmonger's that my family owned was situated. There had been an ironmonger's on the site since the beginning of the 20th century, but we owned it from 1973 until my father retired in 1987. I particularly remember 1974, when the River Roding, which ran along behind the shop, burst its banks and flooded the yard. It was under about seven feet of water and the cellar was full up. My sister and I sat with the trap door open grabbing things as they floated by.

In later years I worked behind the counter on a Saturday and during school holidays, and so did my two sisters. I used to go down there every morning with my father and help out for fifteen or twenty minutes, before school.

We were well known as a specialist ironmonger's for builders and engineers, although we also had a lot of non-trade customers. The job I hated most was when a delivery of nuts and bolts had come in. I always seemed to get this job on a Saturday morning. They were all oily and greasy, and were always packed with the nut already on the bolt. Unfortunately we sold the nuts and bolts on their own, so the job of taking the nuts off the bolts always seemed to come to me. I hated it. The only way to get your hands clean after that job was copious amounts of Swarfega.

The Two Ronnies' sketch about fork handles could have been filmed here. The shop was the same, right down to the zinc-covered counter and the old-fashioned wooden boxes, even the brown overalls! So many people made comments following that programme that my mother even went as far as buying the staff new overalls in a rather fetching shade of blue.

Jane Manley

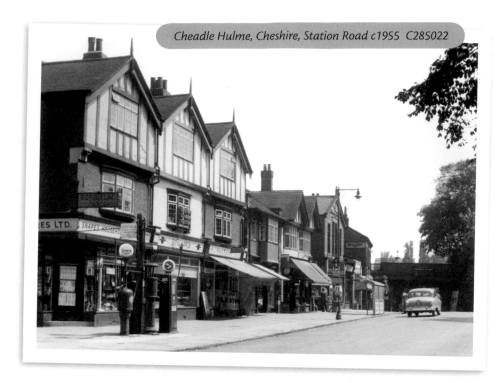

Cheadle Hulme, Cheshire, Station Road c1955   C285022

The Shops on Station Road

This is a picture of Station Road, with Snapes's hardware shop on the corner. The petrol pump was no longer in use by then, but the paraffin one was. Opposite Snapes's is Oak Meadow, where we used to play on our bikes and climb trees.

Also in Station Road was the Elysian cinema, a lovely little picture house. I saw 'Where Eagles Dare', 'Carry on Camping', 'The Jungle Book', as well as 'Kes' (to my mum's horror).

Further on, just before the railway bridge, was Pimlott's the butcher's with an abattoir at the back which was still in use then. Just past the railway bridge on the right was Williams & Deacons Bank on the corner of Mellor Road. Further up Mellor Road was Church's the grocer's. Mum worked there for Mr Church. Just past Church's was a sweet shop. The chap who ran it was a foreign gentleman, possibly Polish. I would choose each sweet from the counter, and he would repeat my 'One of those' with 'Vonne of sose'. I once put my old penny in the chewing gum machine outside his shop and it didn't work, so I thumped it – and down dropped a pocketful of pennies. I promptly went into the shop and announced my little windfall and bought some sweets. The poor old chap never said a word, and let me make my purchases with my ill-gotten gains. What a gent.

Bryan Baskerville

Great-Grandmother's Shop

The shop in the middle of the picture (right) with the two awnings used to belong to my great-grandmother Eva Cadel. It was a wool and toy shop. My grandmother and great-aunt ran it until 1971. My grandmother Joan ran the toy side, and my great-aunt Mary ran the wool. Many people still tell me that their first pram or doll or train set came from the Cadel shop.

Nicola Best

Witney, Oxfordshire, The Market Square c1955   W256017

The Moat Tea Room

My parents Angela and Leslie Jecks-Wright bought the house on the right and ran the Moat Tea Room from there. Our house was at 64 Fore Street. We used to get coaches visiting the castle, and we were kept very busy by the crowds. We used to let the college boys use the upstairs room as a sort of clubhouse and many American GIs used to visit and eat there.

I currently live in California. While waiting in line in the bank one day we all started talking. On hearing my accent one man told me he remembered the tea room and my mother's wonderful cakes. He said to me: 'If you can cook like your mother, will you marry me?' What a compliment from a stranger so many miles from Fram!

Dad had a small vegetable patch in the back garden. Each year he would dig up something of historical interest. Once it was an arrow barb and point, and another time a stone cannonball. The fireplace in the main area was originally made of stones from the castle.

Miss Rivers, a wonderful lady in her 90s, lived in the house at the very end of our building. She was blind, but kept her house spotless. She used a board to wash her floor – the old fashioned way, on her knees – she would wash up to the board, then move the board and do the same.

One day while visiting Miss Rivers, Mother heard a racket going on upstairs in the tearoom. She thought Dad was moving furniture up there. When she went back, Dad was surprised to see her. He thought *she* was upstairs moving the furniture! But when they both inspected the students' clubhouse, nothing was moved or out of place.

My motorcycle (650cc BSA and sidecar) caught fire up against the wall of the pond across the street. A fireman in the Castle pub saw it, and got on his bicycle. Peddling frantically past me, he yelled 'Do you want the fire engine?'. I yelled back 'Yes!!'. He went up and sounded the alarm. The fire engine was a very welcome sight!

The building is all now a private home, but it is still full of memories for me.

Virginia Jecks-Wright

Framlingham, Suffolk, Castle Street c1955 F45017

Framlingham, Suffolk, The Castle 1929 82078

High Wycombe, Buckinghamshire, Frogmore Square 1921 70607t

A Crafty Sip

I had a Saturday job in Woolworth's in High Wycombe, and at the end of the day one of my jobs was to oil the old and dingy wooden floor. I have two golden memories. One was being asked to turn the boxes of loose biscuits around and date-stamp them again a year hence. They had reached their 'best before' date already. The second is working in the 'cage' where the soft drinks were kept. Being very thirsty on a hot day, I would carefully remove the foil-covered tops from Lucozade bottles, drink the top inch and then carefully replace the tops.

Donald Macdonald

The Old Junk Shop

The Old Curiosity Shop in Northwich (right) had solid soil floors. It was full of old junk which might now be classed as antiques. Joe Allman, the owner, was made to leave, as the council ruled that the building was unfit for human occupation.

The shop was situated at the bottom of Winnington Hill, next door to the barrel-roofed house (again destroyed). This was reputed to have been built by navvies, who brought their canal tunnel building skills to use in its construction.

Paul Dean

Northwich, Cheshire, The Old Curiosity Shop c1950 N43002

Plucking Chickens

I was born in Patricroft in 1941 and lived in Mellor Street. After school I used to go to Tommy Cocker's shop to do odd jobs for spending money. One of my jobs was to pluck chickens. He kept them live in his cellar. He would take me down there where the chickens were running around, and he would then screw their necks and give them to me to pluck still warm. Apart from the little cash I received, I also ended up covered in fowl lice! Some job.

Barry Wilson

Patricroft, Greater Manchester, Liverpool Road c1955 P158003

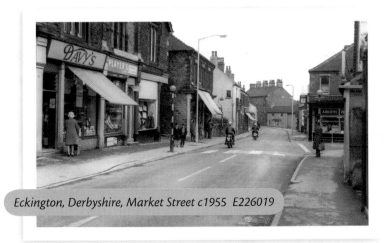

Eckington, Derbyshire, Market Street c1955 E226019

Pea Shooters

As young lads we used to climb up on to the roof of the old betting office over the road from Davy's (left of above photograph), look over the top, and shoot at everyone who came out of Davy's with our pea shooters, using dried peas. We always got a good laugh, but not from our targets.

Roger Bell

Warrington, Cheshire, Church Street 1894 33805p

My grandfather, Isaac Smith, had a hardware and bicycle shop in the building opposite, known universally as the Tudor Cottages, from some time towards the close of the First World War to the late 1930s.

The premises were owned by Rylands Bros, the nearby wire works, where Ike worked at one time, and where his eldest son Arthur later worked until 1955. He set up his business with the compensation he received from being temporarily blinded while working on top secret poison gas research while a foreman at Warrington Gas Works, in around 1916. The whole family, including the children, were apparently required to sign the Official Secrets Act.

In the later 1930s, Rylands Bros persuaded my grandad to move out of the shop while they redecorated it. Isaac was not in fact allowed to return, and the place was converted into a managers' canteen, which it remained until the time Rylands became part of British Steel in the 1960s.

My mother and father did their courting in the shop's loft-like upstairs rooms. As a young boy helping his dad, my father knocked a nail in the plaster wall and exposed what turned out to be stucco work from the Stuart period.

I think the undertaker Henry Hough had one of the remaining three premises – my grandad had the two main rooms on the left as you faced them. A family story tells that at the time of the Spanish flu epidemic in 1918, my grandad remarked to his neighbour that business had been slow that week. To this Henry replied that he 'hadn't buried a living soul all week'.

A plaque on an outside wall says that Oliver Cromwell lodged on or near the spot during his Lancashire campaign against the Royalist forces on 20 August 1648. Given the civic vandalism that demolished all but the facade of the 1870s Parochial School, also on Church Street, as recently as 2002, and even more recently (2005) the listed 1863 building of the Boteler Grammar School on School Brow nearby, one worries that this fine old site, dating to the 1630s at least, may go the same way as many other monuments of Warrington's past, despite its listed status.

Stan Smith

Black Pudding at the Best Market in Lancashire

Bury, Greater Manchester, The Market 1902 48562t

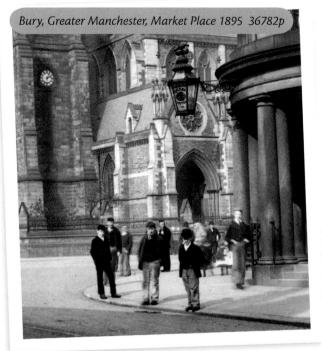

Bury, Greater Manchester, Market Place 1895 36782p

Bury market was famous. We used to go to the market and buy one of Thompson's black puddings, piping hot in greaseproof paper. The man would split it and put on plenty of mustard. There were also the roast potato man, vegetable stalls, fish stalls and the famous cheapjack. He used to gather crowds round his stall with his patter, and sell household goods at knockdown prices. He must have done well – he retired to St Annes on Sea, a sure mark of success. In the late 60s a fire destroyed the old market hall, and the market was relocated. Everyone agreed that the atmosphere was never the same, but the new market today still brings people in from miles around.

Janet Robinson

Droxford, Hampshire, The Village c1960 D198007

The Wonderful Smell of Sawdust

My father was Arthur Harriott, who owned Harriott Brothers butchers' shop in Droxford (which can be seen at the bottom left-hand corner of the picture on the left) together with his brother, Edward. We lived in Old Sarum, which is the white house adjoining, with my mother, Molly, and my Aunt Olive and Uncle Edward. One of my first memories dates from the late 40s when my dad would wrap up parcels of meat and put them in a wicker basket in the iron frame fitted to a bicycle. The meat would be delivered to the householders of Droxford by 'the boy'.

I don't think I ever remember seeing my father without a Craven A cigarette tucked into a corner of his lips – a sublime disregard for Health and Safety, but I don't recall a single case of anyone becoming ill as a result.

The shop floor was covered with a dusting of sawdust, which was always getting trodden into the house and drove my mother wild, but the smell of wood was wonderful.

Pamela Beeching

The Cash Railway at Topliss the Draper's

I wonder if anyone remembers Topliss at 16 Mercer Row in Louth? It was there until 1975, when it was taken over by Boyes. It was probably the last shop in Britain to have a 'cash railway' for taking customers' payments to the cashier and returning the change. The money travelled in a hollow wooden ball, like a croquet ball cut in half. There is a photo on The Cash Railway Website. Cash ball systems were generally superseded by overhead wire or pneumatic tube systems.

Andrew Buxton

Louth, Lincolnshire, Mercer Row c1950 L305009

Louth, Lincolnshire, Mercer Row c1955 L305035

The Tiny Post Office

Mr and Mrs Raines ran a postal service from this tiny shed at the bottom of their garden in 1908. The village was much smaller then: there were only four large families, and no more than a dozen cottages. In the late 1940s the post office moved to a building in the main street. Later, the shed was used to house chickens before it finally rotted away.

The Frith Memory Archivist

North Wootton, Norfolk, The Post Office 1908 60035p

A Noted Umbrella Maker

This photo shows my great-grandfather's shop, nearly opposite the one owned by Jesse Boot. The name S Page (Samuel Page) can be seen on the left-hand side of the street just above the wooden statue of Jonas Hanway holding an umbrella, and the name of the shop was Hanway House. Samuel Page styled himself as 'an Umbrella Manufacturer and Dealer in Ladies' and Gentlemen's Waterproofs and all kinds of Travelling Requisites'.

Jonas Hanway brought the umbrella to this country from China and Japan. At first he was laughed at for carrying such an item, as it was considered effeminate. Samuel Page was a noted umbrella maker because of the excellent quality of the silk that he used in their manufacture. He registered the name Jonas Hanway, and the name 'Hanway' was engraved in gold letters inside each umbrella he made.

J Hammond

Nottingham, Nottinghamshire, Pelham Street 1890 22823

Bletchingley, Surrey, The Village Butcher's Shop c1935 B122005

A Village Butcher

I was sent to Selmes the butcher's to buy my mother, Mrs Dora Maynard, cuts of meat. The floor was covered in sawdust, and there was a little cashier's office at the end of the counter. It always had a very friendly atmosphere, although I used to cry when I saw the animals being unloaded from the lorries into the slaughteryard. Once or twice I saw them escape.

Helen Swabey

The Tribulations of a Butcher's Boy

On the left of photo A158030 (right) is a shop blind that used to protect the meat in the window display from sunshine. That blind was the bane of my life from 1952 to 1954 when I was a butcher's boy. It never ran correctly on its tracks, and I caused many a car to swerve while I manipulated my long pole putting the blind up and down.

The bicycle outside (it's possibly me in the picture) was used for deliveries. When the carrier was full of orders for Maulden and the surrounding area it was a steering hazard, particularly in the snow. One Saturday morning I came to grief down Maulden hill, and spent an hour scraping dirt and stones from the meat with my pen knife. The complaints arrived back at Ampthill well before yours truly. Oh, the humiliation, and all for 2s 6d a week. The humiliation was for being caught out, not for the stony meat. On the positive side, the grumpy woman who lived down Duck Lane never ordered meat again.

Paul Guyton

Ampthill, Bedfordshire, Market Place c1955 A158030

Ingleton, County Durham, The Village 1890 26330

Ingleton, County Durham, The Village c1960 I11063

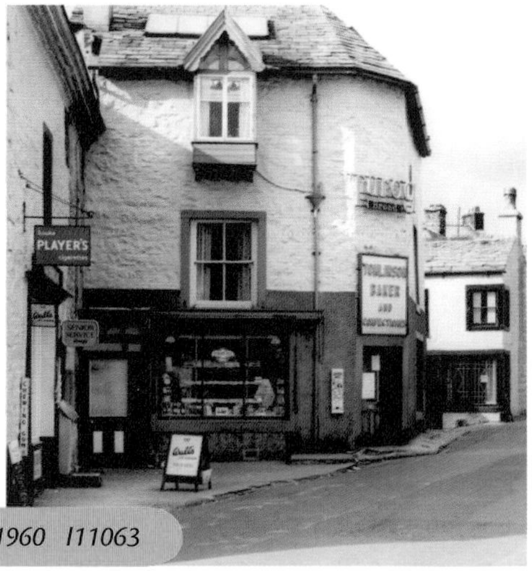

From Printing Works to a Baker's

The 'Printing Office' is where I grew up and lived until my student days. My parents operated a baker's and confectionery business from the premises.

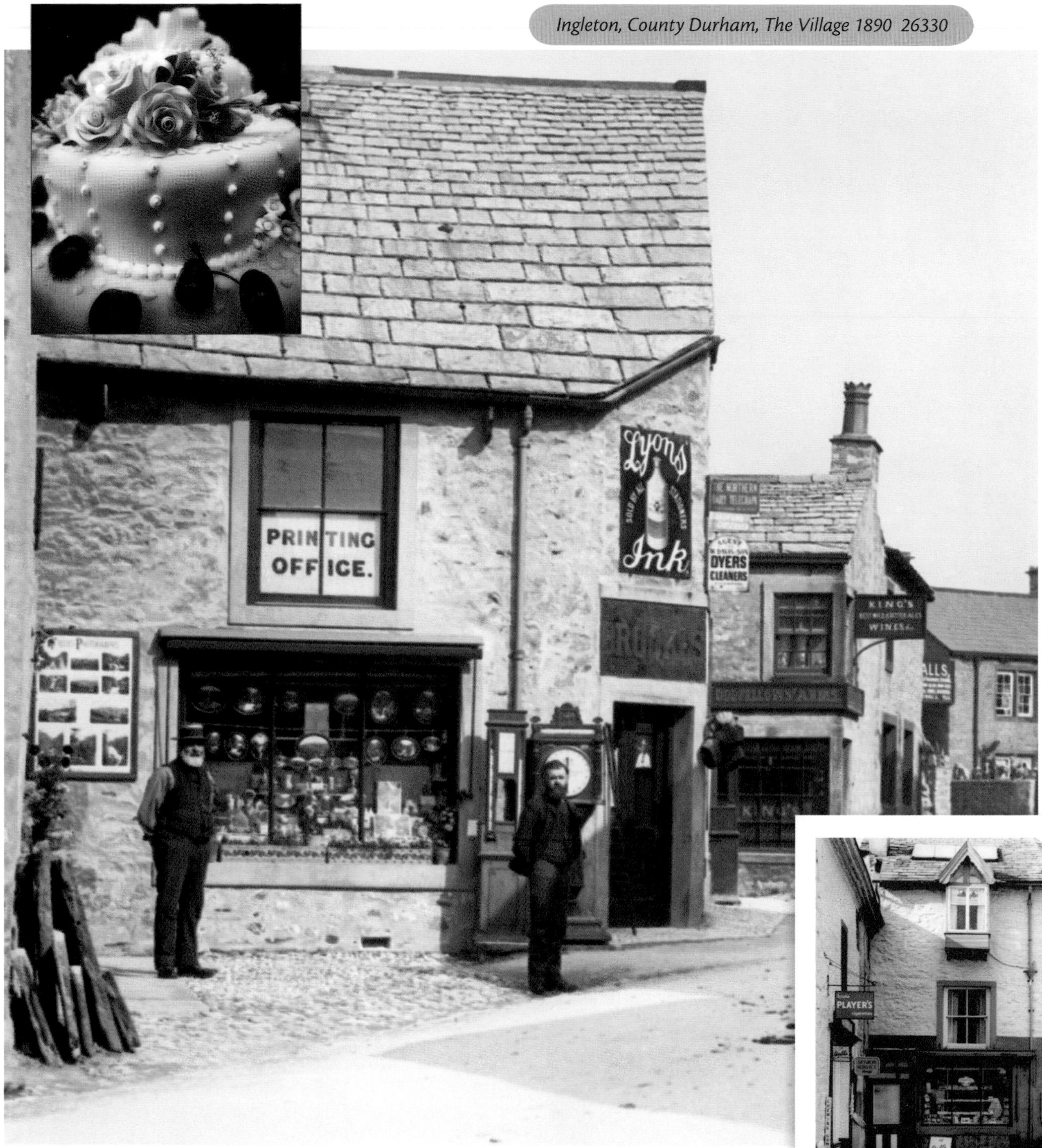

In 1890, when it was a printing works, it was owned by the Brookes family. Their ownership continued until about 1918, when two sisters opened a café (Fells Café) and bakery business. Sarah Fell had lost her husband to the 1918 influenza pandemic, and the sisters moved to Ingleton from Ambleside.

By 1918 the premises had acquired another storey – the roof had been raised to a higher level than this picture shows, and another window had been fitted above the one marked 'Printing Office' (see the photo below). The new top floor was converted to be a bakehouse – with a coke-fired oven on the attic level. My father got a job there and learned the baking trade, becoming celebrated for his elaborately decorated wedding cakes. He eventually took over the wedding business and transferred the baking activity to other premises across the street, while still using the shop and café. The bakery operated under several owners until 1999.

The Printing Office has been variously a confectioner's and café (c1918 to c1945), a baker's and confectioner's, and a clothes shop and bookshop. The Brookes family emigrated to Canada, though the Greta Printing Works continued to exist in other premises in the village until the early 1960s.

Behind the printing works is the Oddfellows Arms, which closed many years ago and is now a shop. The building in the background was originally the farmhouse of Seed Hill Farm.

Dr D R Tomlinson

Hard Labour at Sea View Stores

I lived at Reighton Gap from early 1948 to 1951. The picture of the shop brings back many memories, as I worked there aged 11 during the summer school holidays.

My jobs were the dirty and hard ones. I had to handle the potatoes and the paraffin, and fetch the soft drinks from the back of the store. It was very busy in summer, so I also had to wash up and dry the dishes. My reward was two meals a day and 7s 6d per week pay – I worked 7 days a week from 6am to 9pm. The 7s 6d helped my mother pay half the weekly rent to live in a bus called Linga Longa. We had no water, no fire, just a bus shell – it was a hard life. The two meals a day were a blessing, as we often had no food. The store was only open from 11am to 1pm in winter during the week. Groceries had to be brought from Filey by walking along the sands in both directions.

The owners of the store in those days were Arthur and Joan Russell, who were about 25 years old. Arthur was a professional boxer and had won cups from it. He was either bantam or feather weight. Joan's parents were Mr and Mrs Jack Chambers. He worked at the quarry driving a dumpster owned by Steven Toulson & Son of West Ayton. The foreman of the quarry was Mr Clubley. Frank Black drove the old excavator, and so did Bill Scouson, both from Hunmanby. Stan Bell was another driver. The farm was owned by the Bayes family.

Reighton Gap was a wild, cold place in winter, and the long walk to Speeton school was no fun either. I visited the place in 2006, and although I can still locate the three places I lived in, now demolished, Reighton Gap is just not what it was. It never was much, but for a child like myself it was a wonderful free playground.

Frank Archer

Reighton, North Yorkshire, Sea View Stores c1965   R239068

Post Office Parrot

The post office door at Thelwall had a real brass bell fitted to it. When you entered, if the post master was in the back, the bell would alert the parrot, and it used to scream 'Wipe your feet', followed by 'No stamps today'.

Richard Oxley

Thelwall, Cheshire, The Post Office c1955   T328004

Minster Memories

I used to work in the shop on the corner, where a man is standing outside the door. It was called Langer & Son and was a saddlers, sports and shoe shop. I met my husband there in 1963. We celebrate our 40th wedding anniversary this year, so the picture brings back many memories.

Mrs C Holloway

The lady standing on the bridge is my great-grandmother Hannah Elton, née Churchill, and the small boy she is holding is her grandson, Cecil Henry Stickland, my uncle. He became the verger at Christchurch Priory. Hannah lived with her husband Henry, a carpenter, in a cottage to the left of the photograph (just out of shot). She was the local midwife. At the time this photograph was taken, her daughter Louisa Eliza had returned to her parents' home for the birth of my mother, Ivy Emma Stickland.

Judith Day

Wimborne Minster, Dorset, East Brook 1908   60622

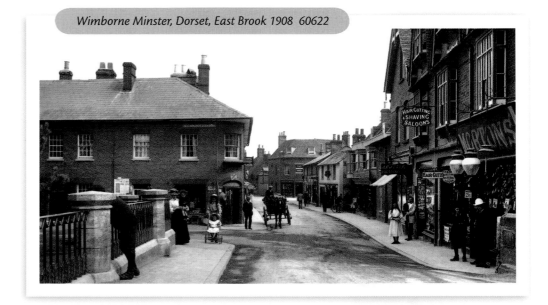

Six Foot's Tiny Shop

To the right of the picture behind the women with prams is Brighty's Electrical, and beyond it the weatherboarded Post Office, the butcher's shop and a big chestnut tree. This tree was one of several trees in the grounds of Dr Ellis's house, which was built in the Georgian era, but was later demolished to make way for a cul-de-sac. The old van parked in the Market Place possibly belonged to Trixxie, who raised poultry up at Lambourne. He was brother to Six Foot, a very small man who lived halfway up Hoe Lane. Six Foot kept a very narrow shop (located behind the van) where large quantities of fresh eggs were sold, hen and duck, and fresh tea was served from an urn. There was just about enough room for the counter on the left, a small alleyway for the customers, and on the right a stool or two and a ledge on which to put a plate and cup. I think you could also buy a sandwich or a biscuit. Next to Six Foot's tiny shop was Bertie Brighty's shop which also had a café at the back. You went down steps to get into these old buildings. You can also see the greengrocer's shop at the end with the Hovis sign on the wall. Fresh bread would be delivered there daily from the bakery at Theydon Bois.

I think I know the two ladies in the foreground with the prams. The lady on the left may be Mrs Peagram, with her son Colin in the pram. The couple with the child in the pushchair outside the butcher's could actually be my parents and me. They might have just stepped off the Number 10 bus – you can see its back parked by the Blue Boar Pub on the left. At the time this photo was taken we weren't yet living in the village, but my parents formed the Leyton Self-Build Group. It started with 100 members, but was left with six committed members who built houses in the semi-detached style opposite Raven's Garage in London Road. My father at this time would have been spending all his spare time in the village building the houses, along with the five other men and also my grandfather, who was a bricklayer by trade. They also had help from Frank Reeves, who was a local drainage expert.

Sue Terry

Abridge, Essex, The Village c1960 A106012

Shillingstone, Dorset, The Post Office and Central Stores c1955 S443004

In Search of an Ice Lolly

My parents ran the Central Stores from 1951 to 1955. Their names were Tony and Eunice Jeanes. The date of c1955 for this picture is about right, as this was the year that my father and mother sold the business to Mr Dean, whose sign appears in the photograph. Central Stores was a veritable Aladdin's Cave to a young boy, full of delights – sweets, colouring books, comics, fizzy lemonade and, joy of joys, ice cream in a huge chest freezer. I well remember being rescued from the cavernous interior by my father after falling in while attempting to reach my choice of ice lolly.

Timothy Jeanes

Cove, Hampshire, The Village c1955 C172008

The Joys of a Jamboree Bag

I lived in Old Coulsdon as a small child and remember walking up to The Parade to visit the sweet shop. We lived down the hill at the bottom of The Glade, and it always seemed a long hard climb up to The Parade. We would cut across through the churchyard. If I was very lucky I was allowed to buy a Jamboree bag in the sweet shop. A Jamboree bag was a mix of different sweets like Penny Chews and Liquorice Sticks, and also a small toy. Other times I would buy a Sherbet Dab or 2oz of boiled sweets such as Rhubarb and Custard, Pear Drops and best of all, Fruit Pips, which were very small fruit-flavoured boiled sweets, so you got lots for your money.

Linda Ellis

Old Coulsdon, Surrey, The Parade c1955 O106007

The Sweet Shop

Going 'down the village' pretty much referred to the stretch of Cove Road between Hazel Avenue and Marrowbrooke Lane where most of the shops were. Once upon a time Cove must have been the typical English village: two houses, three pubs and a church.

Charlie Christopher and his mother owned a sweet shop, opposite what was left of Cove Pond at the side of Cove Green. I helped out in the store around the time that the new counters were installed, in about 1949. They were covered in plastic laminate with sloping glass fronts, very modern. Part of the store was given over to haberdashery where Mrs Christopher sold a few reels of cotton and so on. When the store started opening on Sundays, they had to cover all the counters on the north side and only sell sweets and ice cream. Rationing lasted until well after the war, and sweets were in short supply. Christopher's used to sell liquorice root, a sort of woody substance with a strong flavour that kids would suck on and which wasn't rationed.

Alan Hickman

Lichfield, Staffordshire, Market Place c1955 L45033

A Floral Tradition

My parents had a florist's shop in Market Square in Lichfield from 1932 to1962. I can see our Morris van parked on the square, with the Interflora logo and our name clearly shown. I was in Egypt doing my National Service when this photo was taken, but the cars and fashions pictured here take me back to that era in sleepy Lichfield. The statue of Dr Johnson is still in the square, but all the shops have changed and the square has been resurfaced. I now have a florist's shop in Bird Street, Lichfield.

John Ivison

Aunt Tilly's Tea Room

This photograph shows my great-aunt's tea room and restaurant. She was Mrs Matilda Howells, known in the family as Aunt Tilly. I can clearly remember visiting the tea room on many occasions as a 9 or 10 year old child with my mother Adelaide, who was Aunt Tilly's sister. Her husband (Uncle Jack) did all his own baking in a huge wood-fired oven at the rear of the premises and meals for the tea room were cooked in an equally large wood-fired range in the adjoining kitchen.

Leslie Hobbs

Lyndhurst, Hampshire, High Street 1908   60104

Nylons like Gold Dust

This is Gloucester's oldest department store, Bon Marché, photographed from outside the post office. During the war, part of the store was taken over by the American forces. Many courting couples arranged to meet for a date under the clock on the far corner. I remember queueing outside the store on most Saturdays to buy currant bread for a treat for Sunday tea, and also to buy nylons, which were like gold dust. On the opposite side of the road was the up market store Dentons.

June Jackson

Gloucester, Gloucestershire, The Oxbode 1949 G20017

Gloucester, Gloucestershire, Southgate Street 2004 G20726k

Got any gum, chum?

MEMORIES OF WARTIME AND MILITARY SERVICE

Gasmask, Rifle – and Diphtheria

We had to carry our gasmasks at all times in the square cardboard boxes they were issued in. I remember playing with my dad's rifle when he was in the Home Guard – luckily the ammunition and the bayonet weren't kept at home. People shooting other people was unheard of in those days – except for the war. I can't repeat what my grandma said she would do to Hitler if she got her hands on him.

We saw very little of the war, just an odd gung-ho Spitfire pilot flying low over the housetops. One plane that caught my imagination was the '7 miles a minute' Mosquito announced on the radio, but I never actually saw one. Then there were the strange messages that came on the radio after the news – they were for our agents in occupied countries.

Fortunately all my uncles came back from the war unharmed, though at home lots of people died from TB. A young lad next door aged six or seven died from diphtheria. He was the first person I have been close to who was there one day and dead the next. It was quite a shock.

Peter Butterwort

> ❝ I couldn't repeat what my grandma said she would do to Hitler if she got her hands on him ❞

Father was a Stranger

As a child I lived in Earl Street, Hanky Park, Salford, and then moved to Cottrill Street off Ellor Street. I attended John Street school in the Ellor Street area. I never really knew my dad when I was young. He went in the army when I was four in 1939 and returned in 1946 when I was nine.

During the 1940 blitz of Manchester and Salford in 1940, we all had to go to the Unwin Street shelters for the night when the sirens sounded. But I and my brother Jack, who was five years older, used to watch the German bombers coming over and dropping their bombs over Trafford Park, Salford Docks and Manchester. It was a sight not to be forgotten.

When the war ended we had street parties to celebrate VE day (Victory in Europe). I was playing in the street when a soldier with three stripes (a sergeant) wearing an Australian bush hat and carrying a kit bag came to the door at 28 Cottrill Street. My mother came to the door and said, 'Albert, this is your Dad'.

When he returned from Burma he had malaria and he also had flashbacks at times. He would be fighting Japanese soldiers on the living room floor. It lasted for about a year, but he came out of it. He must have gone through a very rough time. His malaria lasted longer. My dad made up for lost time, but the one thing he would not do was go on holidays, as he'd been away too long with the war. At least he came home.

Albert Morris

American Ships

My friend and I would await the arrival of American ships on their way to Manchester. We would shout 'Got any gum, chum?' to the crews. We would occasionally be rewarded by a packet of sweets being thrown from the ship, it was far tastier than the English equivalent!

Harry Roscoe

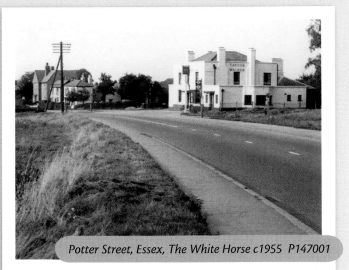
Ellesmere Port, Cheshire, The Manchester Ship Canal 1947 M340501

Warrington, Cheshire, The Manchester Ship Canal c1960 W29088

Potter Street, Essex, The White Horse c1955 P147001

Unexploded Bombs

I was born in the White Horse at Potter Street on 7 October 1937. We used to walk to school across the fields from Hare Street. During the Second World War, Germany dropped incendiary and high explosive bombs, and some of the kids used to try to pull the unexploded bombs out of the holes in the ground where the tail fins of these small bombs stuck out. I remember some bold children throwing the bombs into the brook where a bridge crossed the stream.

George Nicholson

Ice Cream and American Chiclets

Glanamman, Dyfed, View from Penybont 1956   G249012

Glanamman, Dyfed, Main Street 1956   G249016

The shop on the left of the above photograph – with the awning down – was known as Capanini's. They sold the most wonderful ice creams, sodas and coffees. The daughter's name was Bella, and she was a fiery one, older than me, and typically 'Italian'. Further up, was the Billiards and Snooker Hall. In my day the local barber was in there as well, so you could play a game while waiting to have a haircut or shave.

There were lots of worries in those days about polio, and it was suggested that ice cream was a carrier – which caused a big slump in sales. But I always had several when I was there on my holidays.

The Square (Y Sgwar), was a place for the women to gossip, as there wasn't much traffic in those days. We walked everywhere, to Garnant for the Picture House, or down the hill to 'Show Sam,' where I used to watch Cowboys and Indians films, as well as those Pathé newsreels about the war. Walking up to Y Sgwar afterwards wasn't much fun – it was steep. Sixpence! – that bought you the world in those days.

It was also on Y Sgwar that I met my first two American Army soldiers. They were returning to barracks after their weekend leave, as the train at the bottom of the hill would take you anywhere in Wales or England. Whenever you saw American soldiers you ran up to them, and said 'Got any gum, chum?', holding your hand out. A much-prized stream of chewing gum would pour into your hands – many years later I found out that they were called Chiclets.

I remember how they laughed when confronted – two smashing, young black soldiers, who spoke to me in a funny way, but were so nice and friendly – I never forgot them. They were typical Americans, friendly and generous, and they took time to talk to me, a scruffy urchin type of boy who spoke what seemed like a fractured form of English to them – I think that made them laugh even more! I wish I knew where they are today – if they are still alive. They gave me my opinion of Americans, which to this day has never changed.

David Jones

A Chef with Light Fingers

My first posting as an LAC (Leading Aircraftman) chef in the RAF was to 22 Group HQ at Buntingsdale Hall in May 1953. I was 18, and was to become chef to Air Vice Marshal Merton in his residence, Farcroft, in Market Drayton.

I reported to the guardroom and was whisked up to meet the AVM by his PA, Flight Lieutenant Jan Badini, who, I was told, was a Polish count. I think he must have been, as he later told us about hunting wolves on his estate in Poland before the war. I was later to live in Farcroft, cooking for the AVM, his wife (known as 'Aggie' behind her back), Corporal Davis, Pete Redcar, and another batman called O'Gorman. It was a quiet life for about a year before I was moved on to RAF Bridgnorth.

The main thing I remember was Princess Alice, Duchess of Gloucester, coming to dinner and staying the night. I had an audience the following morning with the Duchess, who was still in bed, nightcap and all, while she congratulated me on the dinner and told me that I had 'light fingers'. She was referring to my pastry making, but we laughed at her wording afterwards.

I went back to Market Drayton during 2005 on a 'down memory lane' visit. The old hall was still there with the mist still rising off its still waters, but Farcroft had been pulled down and replaced by a housing estate.

Jamie Smith

Market Drayton, Shropshire, Buntingsdale Hall 1899 44449

> ❝ I was given an audience the following morning with the Duchess, who was still in bed, nightcap and all ❞

The Build-Up to D-Day

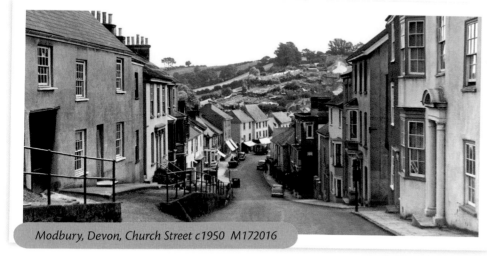

Modbury, Devon, Church Street c1950 M172016

Born in 1938 in Modbury, I remember the latter years of the Second World War. I remember vividly the nights during the months of the heavy blitz on Plymouth, with the beams from searchlights criss-crossing the sky as German bomber formations droned overhead.

The American forces had an army camp in a field across from Modbury School. I would wander through the camp, and the GIs would give us sweets or chewing gum. The roads were lined with trucks and tanks preparing for the build-up to the Normandy invasion, and the villagers volunteered for rehearsals by lying in the streets posing as casualties to be carried off to first aid stations.

In the evenings, some of the GIs sneaked into town and came to our home. My sister Peggy sometimes played the piano for them, and they brought canvas bags of goodies for us. At Christmas time the children in the village were scooped into US army trucks and taken off to a camp for a Christmas party.

My mother occasionally took me to Bigbury-on-Sea. One day we saw lines of American GIs wading out to landing craft with their rifles held above their heads as they practised embarkation. I remember the soldiers marching out of Modbury in single file on each side of the road towards the coast, and the tanks traversing the sharp bend into New Road. One of the tanks hit and damaged the wall of the Red Devon Inn.

I saw open army trucks carrying prisoners of war with a jeep escort front and back covering the prisoners, who were blindfolded and had their hands tied behind their backs. Towards the end of the war some prisoners walked into the town to sell toys they had made.

Once a week we had a cinema show in the upstairs function room of the Red Devon Inn. We sat on wooden benches and waited expectantly as the reels were changed for the next part of the film. On VE Day there was a big bonfire on the Green opposite the school with people singing and dancing in front of it.

Roger Stevens

Sheltering under the Kitchen Table

For two-and-a-half dreadful years, from July 1942 to October 1944, my parents and I survived in three rooms at the top of number 40, Victoria Road, rented from a Mrs Pither. Only the front two rooms, overlooking the street, were habitable, and the back room my father used as a sort of workshop. Water was from a tap a few inches off the floor beside the loo, in a small closet at the top of the stairs. Hot water was boiled in a teakettle on an old gas stove in the 'kitchen'. Washing was done in an enamel basin, and the dirty water was carried out and flushed down the toilet. One of my earliest memories is of going to get water and getting confused with the tap. I couldn't make the water turn off and the pot overflowed, and by the time my mother came to the rescue, the floor was flooded and water was dripping through the ceiling at the bottom of the stairs. Mrs Pither was not amused!

Aldershot, Hampshire, Victoria Road c1955　A31015

The top three windows to the right of the lamp pole in the picture are about in the right place to belong to number 40. The window closest to the pole lit the small room with the gas stove and the kitchen table. The other two were in a bedroom just big enough for my parents' double bed with my bed at right angles to it. The only heat was a two-bar electric fire.

In September 1942 I was enrolled as a pupil at Stanley House School on St Michael's Road. I was only four-and-a-half years old, but going to school got me out of my mother's way. Miss L D Elliff was the school principal. The first term cost £3 6s, which was quite a chunk of money considering that my father made only thirty bob a week working at the Royal Aircraft Establishment.

The school's air-raid shelter was two large steel boxes stacked on their sides, one on top of the other, in the garage. All the pupils were crammed in, and a wire mesh was put up to stop them falling back out. I remember a doodle-bug going over and the teachers standing watching in the open garage doorway. The bomb missed us but sadly it landed on another school not far away.

My mother arrived shortly after in a dreadful state, for she had heard that a school had been hit.

If the school's air raid arrangements seem a little primitive, they were perhaps better than at home. When the warning siren started wailing, my mother and I would sit under the kitchen table. Being under a table in front of a window on the top floor of an old Victorian building at least ensured a quick exit.

Amidst all this I developed swollen adenoids. So I spent a few days in the children's ward of Aldershot Cottage Hospital. My parents visited daily, and once brought their ration of eggs. They seemed quite annoyed that I didn't want to eat them. I didn't care about not eating, but do I remember complaining about some kid who kept crying all night and kept me awake.

For me, all this, the strange way of life with rationing, the blackout and the Home Guard rifle to play with, was perfectly normal, but those years must have been very unpleasant for my parents.

Alan Hickman

Life in a Mining Village

My mother was born in Wakes Yard in a mining village called Wrekenton, County Durham. She lived at Eighton Terrace, a cobbled street with two rows of sandstone houses, darkly stained from pollution from coal-fired chimneys over the years. She was an orphan with her two sisters, and they were brought up by their grandmother, Hannah Watson.

In the war years, there were many shortages. People had to make do with what they had. If you broke a cup, you had to drink from a jam jar if there wasn't a replacement. Often tea was mixed with dried bramble leaves to stretch it out a bit. There were many tea substitutes.

Ginger beer was a popular drink with mining families, and they often made their own. There were many houses in the northeast that had a 'ginger beer plant' fermenting on the windowsill.

The northeast had its fair share of night time raids by German bombers. The sound of the sirens warned you that the bombers were on the way, and you felt frantic as you tried to gather your family together to find a safe place to shelter. The drone of the bombers, the whistle and explosions of the bombs, and the fear of your house taking a direct hit must have been terrifying. If it wasn't a bomb that hit your house, a small incendiary bomb could burn the house down.

One night, German bombers flew over Wrekenton and Springwell. One bomb hit the field where the Springwell Colliery pit ponies grazed, and the bomb killed them all. When morning came, people came to see the damage and saw the dead pit ponies. The ponies didn't go to waste. Soon the field was busy with people who cut up the ponies with their knives so that there was fresh meat for the table.

Meat was a luxury. If you were lucky enough to get your hands on some butcher's bones, then it all went into the pot with vegetables to make a big tasty stew for the family. Mining families were poor, but very tough and adaptable. There was no hot running water. If you wanted hot water for a bath, out came the kettle and pots and pans to boil the water to fill a tin bath in front of the stove or the cast iron range, and we all took it in turns sharing the same water before it got cold.

If you had a hole in the sole of your shoe and there was no money for new shoes, you had to make do with a bit of kitchen lino if you were lucky, or cardboard if you were not so lucky. You cut the lino or cardboard and made it into a sole and slipped it inside your shoe so that you didn't wear a hole in your sock. If you had holes in your socks, they were never thrown away, but were darned instead.

We didn't have an inside toilet, just an outside one. They were cold and damp. Squares of newspaper cut up and hanging from some string from a nail in the wall was used if there was no toilet roll. There was usually just a little paraffin lamp or a candle, as well as a mouse trap in the corner, just in case a little visitor crept in. We did have mice in the house. One day when I was about 6 years old I got the fright of my life when I realised there was a rat in the cupboard. It leaped across a pile of shoes in front of me. Another item I always remember being kept on the top shelf of the cupboard was a jar of goose grease. This was commonly used to rub on your chest and back if you had a cough or cold, and it used to stink!

The winters in the northeast were freezing. There was a lot of snow in those days. One cold winter killed our family cat. I found it curled up frozen stiff on top of the snow-capped wall dividing our house from next door. I remember snowdrifts three feet high against the outside doors. Gloves were a luxury and if we had to go outside we had to make do with socks over our little hands. If a pullover was worn out, then the wool would be unpicked and another one knitted. Not a lot went to waste in our family – they were good recyclers, they had to be.

Ron Summerson

The Cambridge Ghost

The Cambridge Military Hospital was founded as part of the initiative begun by Florence Nightingale (below) after the Crimean War to improve medical facilities for the Army. It was built on a grand scale, and had very long corridors, which seemed to be about a quarter of a mile long.

In February 1969 as a cadet at nearby Sandhurst I had an accident on the assault course. The injury was quite severe and I had to have an operation and physiotherapy, so I spent several months in Ward 7. At this time, the hospital was not full of military patients. It took in overflows from NHS hospitals and there were a number of wards of civilians, including a ward for terminally ill patients and another for children. A young QARANC (Queen Alexandra's Royal Army Nursing Corps) sister, Lt Collinson, came to Ward 7, and she and I as a long-term but 'walking wounded' patient became friendly and had a chat from time to time. On one occasion, having just finished a stint as the hospital duty night sister, she told me the following story.

The ward for seriously and terminally ill patients was on the ground floor, and the children's ward was on the second. Sister Collinson was visiting the children's ward in the early hours of the morning when there was a sudden and dramatic drop in temperature. It was a passing phenomenon, and might perhaps have been passed off as a cold March draught in an old hospital. Later, she toured the terminally ill ward and came to the bed of an elderly woman, who was still awake. Beside her bed stood an empty glass that seemed to have contained milk. Sister Collinson, knowing that milk wasn't available, asked the woman where it had come

Aldershot, Hampshire, The Cambridge Military Hospital 1891 28672

from. The woman told her that she'd woken, feeling thirsty, and had been approached by 'another sister' wearing the usual QA sister's uniform of grey/blue dress and bright red cape, who'd given her the milk. The sister hadn't spoken, and had quickly gone, but the woman remembered that the sister's dress had been strangely long, almost down to her ankles. Sister Collinson thought that as the woman was so ill she had perhaps been a bit delirious but, on checking with the nurses, found that there had been no other sister around and that no-one had given the patient a drink. The woman died a few hours later.

Intrigued, Sister Collinson asked around and was told about the hospital ghost. A young QA sister had worked there during the First World War when the hospital was full of wounded soldiers evacuated from France. Following an offensive, the hospital had filled with wounded soldiers, and the staff were tired, stressed and overworked. One day, a new intake arrived, one of whom was a young officer, the seriously wounded fiancé of the sister. She, coincidentally, was assigned to deal with him. On seeing him, she panicked and accidentally gave him an overdose of an anaesthetic or drug from which he died shortly afterwards. Full of remorse and depressed, the sister committed suicide. From that time on, she was occasionally encountered in the long corridors, mostly around that part of the hospital where her fiancé had been admitted and had himself died.

Thinking back, Sister Collinson realised that the time the milk had been given to the dying woman was just the moment when she was in the children's ward, which was almost immediately above the terminally ill ward. It is said that intense cold often accompanies spiritual visitations, but perhaps it had just been an unusual draught and a delirious old lady. But – perhaps it hadn't.

James Ritchie

Concrete Air Raid Shelters

My father Leon Lalonde was the mechanical engineer for W&C French from 1928 to 1947. He was responsible for the repair and maintenance of all mechanical equipment and heavy machinery. The large yard was located between Fairlands Close and the Reindeer Pub on Epping New Road, Buckhurst Hill. It housed every different kind of machine and piece of equipment a construction company might need, as well as a major repair workshop, a paintshop, a welding shop, and a wood working shop.

During the war Mr Charles French was concerned about the safety and welfare of his staff and employees and their families. He ordered a series of air raid shelters to be built into the side of a hill within the yard. There were to be four side-by-side concrete shelters, reinforced with tramlines from Walthamstow. They would have a roof several feet thick, and walls of equal strength. One was designated as a women's and children's shelter, and the second for men.

Each section had its own set of private chemical toilets. The third section was a storage shelter, which contained cases of tinned and dried foods, bottled juices, rice and other basic foods. It also held three large tanks full of drinking water. The fourth shelter was used by air raid wardens, fire watchers and rescue crews as a command post. The complex was equipped with its own diesel/electric generator, should emergency power be required.

It was said that more than 100 people could survive in these shelters for several weeks. Heavy mobile drag-lines and other earth moving equipment were stored on the roof of this refuge, which gave added protection against bombing.

My parents and I spent many nights in this protective sanctuary along with other families. We'd pass the time playing cards, the men playing darts. Children like me (I was 8 years old) played with our toys or cars or tried to get some sleep in the army cots arranged along the walls. People brought in beer and spirits from the off licence, and sang songs and danced to the gramophone playing records of Victor Sylvester and his Ballroom Orchestra.

Denman Lalonde

> ❝ People would bring in beer and spirits from the off licence, and sing songs and dance to the gramophone playing records of Victor Sylvester ❞

A Kid's Heaven and Hell

A St Marychurch boy, I lived at Hampton Farm Cottage, St Marychurch. I can still smell the tar and the salt from old fisher and other boats pulled up on Oddicombe beach … and I can still feel the beautiful shining pebbles.

Together with my friends Brian and Roy – just two of many wonderful pals – we would spend school holidays at the back of Hampton Farm, scrumping apples, making camp among the trees, eating wild strawberries and loganberries … and at various times of the year picking bluebells and mushrooms and trying to catch a rabbit (we got money for the skin) and collecting waste paper (for pocket money, again). Oddicombe beach was my favourite. I could swim in rough water at the age of four.

And then there were the days of hell. I can still see us running like mad up Hampton Lane and throwing ourselves to the ground to avoid machine gun bullets from enemy planes that were whizzing everywhere. And my dear brother,

home on leave from the RAF … I can still see him – and all the other loving people – digging in the rubble of the church (St Marychurch) looking for survivors after that dreadful Bank Holiday air raid.

And I vividly remember cadging chewing gum and K rations from the Yanks just before D Day … and then all of a sudden they were gone, and St Marychurch and the Babbacombe Downs seemed empty. The pebbles on Oddicombe remind me of all the people I have come into contact with all of my life … some small, some large, some rough, some smooth.

Frederick Watson

Oddicombe, Devon, The Beach c1881 14429

St Marychurch, Devon 1925 78533

Babbacombe, Devon, The Cliff Railway 1925 78528

Anstey's Cove, Devon, near Oddicombe 1896 38609t

Wartime in a Welsh Village

I was born and grew up in the little village of Llanfairpwll. Everyone knew everyone in the village, which over 60 years ago was predominantly Welsh. We were taught in Welsh at the Infants School. Then one sunny afternoon, the excited English voices of evacuees from the English cities of the North were heard. Each home in the village was allotted their share of these children. The war had come to Llanfairpwll. Very soon afterwards, all the trees in the Column Woods were cut down and hauled away, to be used in the war effort.

The grand old house, Plas Llanfair, was commandeered for barracks for Army personnel. First came a Welsh regiment. These were followed by a Scottish regiment, the Lovat Scouts. Their pipe band marching through the village streets was a sight to behold, and it was the very first time I heard bagpipes.

When the Scots departed, the Yanks moved in. I had never before seen African Americans, or Jeeps, or had doughnuts and chewing gum. But we soon got accustomed to seeing the Americans going about their daily business. The great 'Brown Bomber', Joe Louis, visited the troops at Plas Llanfair to give an exhibition. I think that the Yanks must have taken their leave just before D-Day.

My memories of the war were not that bad. We had rationing and gas masks, but the war was never a reality for

Llanfairpwllgwyngyll, Gwynedd, The Village c1950 L311033

me. That is, until one night when a German bomber discarded its unused cargo of bombs over the village. The only real casualty was No 8 Maen Afon, which was totally demolished. The other houses were intact, and even a canary in its cage survived. The other bombs fell into fields surrounding the village. One fell behind the railway station.

The railway station, famous for the long name set up along the platform, played a big part in my growing up. As a young boy, it was from here that we used to catch the Sunday School Trip train to one of the nearby seaside towns, such as Rhyl or Colwyn Bay.

I was later to work on the station as a junior booking clerk, a very happy time in my life. I was surrounded by older workmates who taught me and teased me endlessly. They were all characters, and I remember them fondly. Names that come to mind are William (Information) Williams, a porter, who knew a little about everything. There was Will Goods, and Will Davies who ran the goods yard from what is now the café and souvenir shop. The station house was occupied by the station master and his family. This gentleman was always immaculately dressed and appeared to me like a miniature Welsh Guardsman.

All this changed for me early one morning in April 1953. Case in hand, I was on my way to the station to catch a train to Wrexham. It was the end of childhood, a happy one for me. I had been conscripted into the Royal Air Force to do my National Service. I left Llanfairpwll with a mixed feeling of sadness and anticipation. In the years to follow, I was to further enlist in the Royal Navy, get married and have a family. I was never to settle back in Wales and my village home.

I have lived in Australia for over three decades. It has never felt like home. Home will always be

Llanfairpwllgwyngyll, Gwynedd, The Railway Station c1940 L311031

that little Welsh village. It is where my best and sweetest memories stem from. It is where my parents were born, and where they lived out their lives. Home is the little slate roofed house into which my parents moved on their wedding night, and from which my mother moved to another kind of home in the village. She had lived in her little house for over 70 years and had brought her five sons into the world there. She died very recently at 99 years of age. What a host of memories she would have had.

During my short and rare visits to Llanfairpwll, I am struck by the many changes that have taken place over the years. It has grown, and many of the quaint little cottages have been extended and covered in pebbledash. They in turn have been surrounded by larger and more modern houses. The little green fields, where I romped as a boy, have been taken over by fancy-named housing estates. Welsh is still largely spoken, but English can be also heard in the streets and shops. I know very few people that I meet. For an ageing man, an exile, with only precious childhood memories of the place, the changes I see have not improved my village home, which was always perfect. But I consider myself extremely fortunate. I can go away and retain the memories of Llanfairpwll that I had as a boy, where I lived among caring, kind people.

Glynne Parry

Evacuees

I first arrived in Llanegryn at the latter end of 1939 along with my younger sister and a lot of other kids from my school (St John's) in Birkenhead. I was eight years old and my sister Linda was six. We were all taken to the village hall where people of the neighbourhood came and took us to different addresses. A lady from the next street to me in my home town was with us, as she had two girls of about five and six and a little boy under two years old. They were chosen along with my sister by Mrs Evans of Gessail Farm, but I wasn't included. My father told me before I left home: 'Don't let them split you up from your sister'. I stood in the centre of the hall and wouldn't allow my sister to go without me. Mrs Evans said 'OK, you can come too', and away we went to the farm by Bird Rock.

I had a wonderful time there. It was the first time that I had tasted butter and home-made bread – and fresh milk too. There were two ladies there called Mrs Evans, John and Evan Evans, and a young man called Egrin. It was marvellous collecting the eggs of a morning

and watching the cows being milked – sometimes we were squirted by whoever was doing the milking. At the bottom of the orchard there was a toilet built over a stream with three holes in line – running water, no less. One day a lot of children from my school came around with the teachers and were astonished to find us there. They thought we had gone back home, as we hadn't attended school. We were at the farm for about five weeks, but we had to leave and go into Llanegryn so that we could attend school.

We were placed with Mrs Davies who ran the post office down by the bridge. After that my sister often sat on the wall of the bridge crying because she was so homesick. We went to the school up the lane. We had a field to play in for a playground and a spinney where we used to set snares to catch rabbits (we never caught any). Our teacher, Mrs Garner from St John's School, used to take me out of the class into the cloakroom to comb my head into the sink with a fine-tooth nitcomb – I was absolutely crawling. My sister went through the same routine.

I can't remember if I ever had a bath. My mother came out to visit us, and when she saw the state we were both in, she bundled us up and took us back home and was very angry at what had happened to us. Overall we were evacuated for about ten weeks, and we were back home before Christmas 1939. Mum wouldn't let us go again.

Llanegryn, Gwynedd, The Village c1960 L409195

Llanegryn, Gwynedd, The Village c1940 L409001

' 'Don't let them split you up from your sister' '

We went back to Llanegryn about ten years ago, and we found it a very moving experience. We picked up some slate from out of the river to take back home and a piece of flint each from the gate posts of Gessail Farm. I have them in my garden now. We also met a lady who remembered the 'vaccies'.

Bob Boyd

Bomb Damage

I remember the 118 bus went from Clapham Common to Mitcham Cricket Green. I also remember well those wonderful Leo's ice lollies. After the awful Walls's slabs of lard between two wafers that went soggy, they were magic.

My family moved from Northborough Road to Rosemead Avenue in March 1940, as all the London County Council schools were closed. My sister and I went to Pollards Hill School. Both my brothers went there or to Alfred Mizen some ten years later. I went on to Rutlish in 1946 on the 152 bus from Fair Green up Western Road past the school and the gas works,

where we all held our noses. The first love of my life went to Western Road School, her name was Lileen Townsend and her father was a coal merchant. She gave me my first kiss!

In 1940 we were deeply involved with the blitz and the Battle of Britain. We stood at the corner of Rowan Road, Northborough Road, Wide Way and Manor Road, hiding behind the letterbox and telephone box. The letterbox had funny paint on top to detect gas.

Our house was first damaged by a land mine in the back garden of 30 Rosemead Avenue, and then by a flying bomb that actually lodged in the branches of an enormous oak tree at the corner of Manor Way and Rowan Road. My father claimed that the tree saved our lives. The house was again badly damaged when a

Mitcham, Greater London c1960 M296095

V1 or V2 demolished houses in Rowan Road opposite Sunnymead Avenue.

I remember round-roofed pre-fabs. I am sure they were built by Italian prisoners of war, who used to talk to us through the wire fence. We did see German prisoners too, but I don't know where they went.

Paul Croxson

Porthpean, Cornwall, The Beach c1955 P87005xt

Invasion Scare

During the invasion scare of the Second World War, Porthpean beach was protected from seaborne landings by the Germans with anti-landing craft defences built along the length of the beach – I believe they were built at the low tide mark. An A-frame structure was constructed from scaffold piping. Possibly this had mines attached, but I have found no confirmation of this. On the slope leading up from the beach there were pyramid-shaped concrete pillars about four or five feet high that would prevent vehicles getting any further.
Peter Marks

I spent many happy hours on Porthpean beach, with my family and my friends during the summer holidays. I remember the anti-invasion devices well, as we used them as monkey bars. After the war they became very rusty with many sharp rusty edges to get snagged on. During the war years there were some bombing targets a few miles off the beach, and we used to watch bomber pilots practising their skills from time to time.

Gerry Mewton

The Sergeant's Teeth

My father was a drummer boy at Edinburgh Castle when he was 14 in 1915. He threw the sergeant's false teeth out of the window by mistake – he thought it was just a cup of water. But next day, when the sergeant picked up the cup and said 'Where's my ------- teeth', he realised what he had done. He never owned up. It was a mystery that was never solved!

Eddie Tait

Edinburgh, Lothian, The Castle from Johnston Terrace 1897 39121t

Deal, Kent, Beach Street 1924 76068

A Spitfire in Trouble

In about 1943 a disabled Spitfire landed 30 yards from the beach opposite the Golden Hind café and just beyond the hotel on the right of the photograph on the left. Three or four chaps stripped off, swam out and pulled the pilot from the aircraft. I hope the pilot survived, but I don't know if he did.

Jim Bell

Lamberhurst, Kent, Hastings Road c1955 L323010

Littlebourne, Kent, Oast Houses c1965 L56022

Life in the Land Army

The white weatherboarded house in the photo on the far left was the farmhouse of the farm where my mother, Joyce Clark, worked with three other girls when she was in the Land Army during the Second World War. It was called Cogger's Farm. She was there while the Battle of Britain was fought overhead.

The farm grew hops, wheat, barley, oats and enough vegetables to supply the local school. The oast houses behind the house belonged to the farm. The hops were picked each year by families from the east end of London who came down and made a holiday of it. They slept in stone outhouses in the farmyard on straw pallets. My mother was billeted with Miss Parrot and another Land Girl called Lot in a house just off the photo, in the first road to the left. Every Sunday, Lot and my mother had to sing hymns around the piano, and if they went to a Saturday night dance they had to be in by 10pm.

Anne Allan

Firefighters and the Home Guard

I remember the Town Hall at Cowbridge. The interest for a schoolboy was the Merryweather fire engine that was kept in a garage at the side of the Town Hall. It was great fun to see it being driven out, bell clanging and the firemen in their shiny helmets hanging on.

One local resident and fireman was a Mr Bond, who fought the fires in the air raid on Cardiff in the Second World War. He won a medal for his work that night. The caretaker lived on the premises and when the LDV, later the Home Guard, used it as their HQ, he was the Sergeant Major. The firemen slept there at night, and their duties involved manning a road block at the top of East Street. The officer in charge of the company was Mr R H Williams, Captain Williams, who was the local chemist. The other Sergeant Major was Mr Bishop who was a porter at the railway station.

The pub called 'Jimmy Blair's' situated almost opposite the Town Hall is now gone. Thankfully the Town Hall still stands, for it is an old part of this ancient town. When the town was bypassed, there were fears that its commerce would die. But in fact the opposite happened. It is now a flourishing town, and a popular place to live.

Roy Newton

Cowbridge, South Glamorgan, The Town Hall c1955 C313050

Tramstops, trains and a Triumph Spitfire

TRANSPORT MEMORIES

The Hovercraft – and Knowle's Boat

I remember the excitement of seeing the hovercraft as a child. We spent many days on the beach at Penarth, usually at the pier end, but when the hovercraft visited we congregated at what we called the landing stage end near the yacht club.

The boat in the background was used for a service to Flat Holme run by a Mr Knowle. We called it 'Knowle's boat'. For many years I craved a journey to Flat Holme on Knowle's boat, but never made it. I eventually got there a few years ago, so it only took me 40 years!

Michael Evans

Penarth, South Glamorgan, The Hovercraft 1963 P24184

Woolwich, Greater London, The Ferry 1964 W460028

Over the Smelly Thames

In the 1950s and 1960s it seemed like the Woolwich Ferry was the only way that we could go 'over the water' from South to North London. I remember trips with my Nannie as a child, catching a bus from Eltham to Woolwich and then going on the ferry when she went to visit a Methodist church on the other side of the Thames. The Thames at that time was so smelly that she gave me a hankie with lavender water to hold to my nose! I loved going on the ferry, and I can remember the noise and smell of the engine room and the excitement of landing on the other side. To me it was a journey to another land.

Gaynor Wingham

That Big Archway in the Sky

I was sitting in my classroom at the parish school in Church Street, and I had just put away my plastic counters after a hard maths lesson – I was only five, and 1+1 was very hard. My teacher's name was Mrs Oats, and she was lovely. As I sat gazing out of the window I noticed this huge construction being built in the distance.

When I got home that evening I asked my dad what it was. As we travelled on the transporter bridge every Saturday to visit my grandparents in Simms Cross, Widnes, this was of great concern to me. My dad explained as best he could to a 5-year-old what it was, and that we would have to walk over it instead of using the transporter.

The next day in school I noticed the big arch hovering in the sky, and I cried my eyes out. The teacher called for my parents to take me home as I was inconsolable. When I finally calmed down I said that I wouldn't be able to see my nan and grandad any more because there was no way I was walking over that big archway in the sky as I was too frightened I would fall off. But my parents told me that a road was going to be underneath the arch, and when they had drawn me a picture of it, I calmed down. But I had several nightmares, until I saw it for real when the bridge was finished.

I went with my school to the grand opening and we all stood along the spur road. If you were posh and had money you bought a flag from the school for sixpence, but if like us you weren't and didn't, you bought a hankie for threepence.

Carol Cooke

Runcorn, Cheshire, The Bridges c1961 R67043

Widnes, Cheshire, The Bridges c1961 W97017

Fleetwood, Lancashire, The Ferry 1901 47069

The Family Shipping Line

My great-grandfather, Thomas Newton Croft, was a member of the family that founded the Fleetwood to Knott End ferry. He managed it for the local council from 1896 until his death in 1915. I am told that my grandmother, Alice, used to do cartwheels to entertain the passengers waiting for the boat to come in. The service was re-privatised a few years ago. Being involved in the marine business myself I like to refer to it as 'the family shipping line'!

John Dearing

Rats, Rats and more Rats

This photograph was taken when the road bridge was nearing completion in 1961. My husband grew up nearby, and tells gruesome stories about the plague of rats they experienced when the undergrowth was cleared in the early days of construction. The family cat brought home several rats each day, and local gardens were over-run with them. Worse still, they got into outhouses and sheds, under floorboards, and even into houses.

Alyson Herbert

Saltash, Cornwall, The Tamar Bridge c1961 S50057

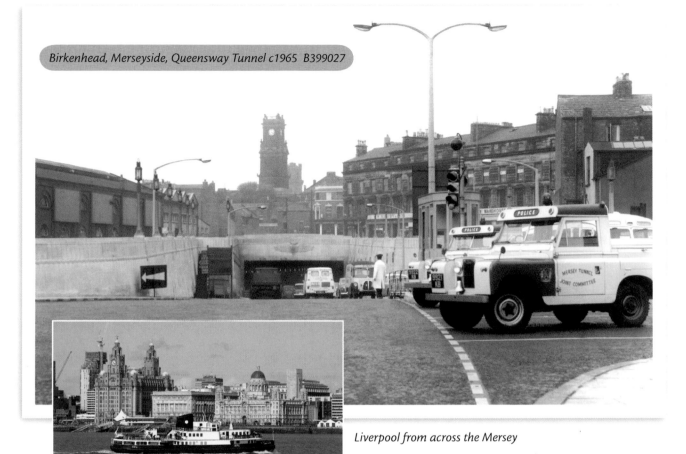

Birkenhead, Merseyside, Queensway Tunnel c1965 B399027

Liverpool from across the Mersey

Tunnel under the Mersey

I clearly remember these Land Rover 'Tunnel Patrol' vehicles, although I was only seven in 1965. I thought that they were real police vehicles and I was puzzled by the cream colour, as ordinary police vehicles were either all white or sky-blue with white doors.

My family used to visit my grandmother who lived in Tranmere virtually every week, and my dad used to play a game on the way home with me and my mother when it was dark. It was called 'How Many Cars in the Tunnel Without Lights?' Each of us had to guess how many cars were in the tunnel without any lights on, and the closest to the actual total won. You were supposed to leave your sidelights on but many

people turned their lights off as the interior of the tunnel was quite brightly lit. In those days the branch tunnels were open more often than not.

I had three older cousins who lived in Croydon. They collected the Mersey Tunnel tickets, which were about 4cm wide and 10cm long. Quite why they collected them, I never knew. They were in various colours. I remember there being a kind of pink, a blue and a light green and they had a broad central stripe with a different coloured edge. They also had a corrugated effect on the edges where the ticket came out of the machine.

Brian Jones

By Train, Boat, and Horse and Wagon

My father was born in Talwrn near Llangefni. Each year we went back there. We went by train to Liverpool and then to the pier head to board the 'St Tudno' which sailed at 10:30am. It dropped people off at about 12am in Llandudno, and went on to the Menai Bridge, where we arrived around 2pm. We always looked to see who could see the Menai Bridge first. Passing Bangor Pier we always knew that my grandparents would be waiting for us with the horse and wagon. The first stop was to my Aunt Mary and Uncle Tom in Llanfair PG, who had a big spread waiting for us. Across the road from my aunt's was a big rock which we climbed up with our cousins while the relatives enjoyed the reunion.

Afterwards we got back onto the wagon and Polly the horse trotted off to Talwrn. It was a long day, and we were all tired. The next morning after breakfast we ran down the lane to see Uncle Will and Aunty Maggie and our cousins and played around a stream that ran through their farm.

Trevor Williams

Menai Bridge, Gwynedd, The Suspension Bridge 1890 23187t

Bangor, Gwynedd, The Pier 1897 40045

Llandudno, Gwynedd, On the Beach 1890 23242t

The Ferry to Hayling Island

In 1955 I would have been taking this very ferry from the Southsea side after taking the trolley bus and regular bus from North End in Portsmouth to make the trip to Hayling. Some of our group drove with Aunty Linda in her old Austin by road, carrying all the sandwiches, blankets and other beach paraphernalia.

I always opted for the ferry as I loved stepping off the dock down into the ferry, which had bench seats alongside the gunwales. Sometimes I stood with my legs apart, riding the swell as we swung out into the heavy running tide. I was in my element with the wind streaming through my hair and the smell of the marshes in my nostrils.

On reaching the other shore we had a pretty long walk. We settled down into the dunes next to the old golf club building.

Hayling was where I managed to get away from my over-controlling and mean step-parents for a while. They settled down amongst the gorse bushes and enjoyed the sun. I took off immediately for the beach, where I spent hours searching for crabs and shells in the tidal pools and running on the sands.

There were some pretty heavy seas coming into Hayling at high tide, but we had a lot of fun diving through the pounding 6- or 8-foot waves as they came onshore, under the watchful eye of my step-grandfather, Pop, or my Aunty Linda. Pop would cruise along on his back like a heavily laden trawler, huffing and puffing, his hands barely cutting the surface of the water as he propelled himself along.

Once Linda saved me from drowning at Southsea when I put my foot down to touch bottom, but submerged as I discovered I was in deeper water than I thought. Her teacher's 'eagle eye' fortunately spotted me going under, and almost instantaneously her hand went under my bum and pushed me back up!

Dylan Rivis

Hayling Island, Hampshire, The Ferry c1955 H400021

> ' I was in my element with the wind streaming through my hair and the smell of the marshes '

Polish Navy MTB to Houseboat

Bursledon, Hampshire, The Bridge c1955 B304008

There are several houseboats moored up to the bank on the left-hand side of the photograph. I lived on the large white motor torpedo boat (MTB) originally called 'Hippocampus', when she was moved from the River Hamble to the River Itchen in 1974. I renamed her 'Whimsical Macgoffley'.

She was built in Cowes at the J Samuel White Shipyard and launched in 1944, one of six MTBs used by the Polish Navy. (Her number was S-8 during the Second World War, and she was eventually returned to the Royal Navy as HMTB 427 at the end of the war.) She was sold by the Admiralty in 1950, and as far as I know was moved to the berth near Bursledon Bridge at that time, until 1974, when she was moored on the River Itchen. She was moored next to the railway bridge in Priory Road, St Denys until 1990, when she was scrapped. I have discovered most of her wartime history, but would like to know more about her from the time when she was moored on the River Hamble.

One of the other six Polish boats, S-10, was, for a time (1954-55) moored downstream and named 'MY Taifun'. She had been used in the film 'The Ship that Died of Shame', starring George Baker, Richard Attenborough, Bill Owen and Virginia McKenna, and was up for sale. She eventually ended up in the Mediterranean where she was used for smuggling – the skipper was Hugh Edwards, the brother of the comedian Jimmy Edwards. She foundered off the North African coast and was lost during a smuggling trip in 1958.

Tim Deacon

Leighton Buzzard, Bedfordshire, The Grand Union Canal c1955 L211049p

Aylesbury, Buckinghamshire, The Grand Union Canal 1921 70564

Australians on the Cut

We left Australia on an open-ended working holiday to England in January, 1974. Who'd have thought that within six weeks of arriving in London we'd be living on a leaky old narrow boat in Braunston near Rugby, and that six months later – still on the boat – we'd be calling Leighton Buzzard home for nearly two years.

The boat was called 'Sadlers Wells', and she looked more like a railway carriage than a traditional narrow boat. She became ours for £200 after we answered an ad in *Exchange and Mart*. Work opportunities in Braunston were slim, so we decided to move within easy commuting distance of

London for more work options. The major problem was that our home did not have a motor. It had never had one – this was a converted butty, the boat that's towed by the motor.

So by pulling, poling and the occasional tie to a motor through locks (not to mention a hair-raising rudderless tow through the tunnels between Braunston and Stoke Bruerne) we tied up at Leighton Buzzard, where we set up home. We were advised that taking the boat further south would incur more interest from the British Waterways Board, and that our semi-legal, semi-residential status would be under threat.

Our mailing address was care of Faulkners Store, and we worked at a local nursing home, the Firestone warehouse and eventually the Post Office. We became part of the canal community based at Leighton-Linslade.

Thirty years later, long back in Australia, with the advantage of the internet I often scan images of the British Waterways and recall our times on the canal at Leighton Buzzard … and wonder whether the boat people we got to know so well are still around. The Faulkner family who ran the store at the canal bridge … Tim and Andy Collier who were still carrying coal in winter, and doing camping canal holidays in summer … Andy and Richard, the boys from

Luton who had a narrow boat called 'York' … Laurie, the London businessman who lived alone on his small boat … the Griffin family who ran the Wyvern Shipping Company and so many others we had got to know during our time there.

We came very close to staying in Leighton, nearly buying a house in Bideford Green, but at the last moment decided that we didn't want to make such a permanent commitment to remaining in England. We sold the boat to an enthusiastic young couple from London who worked for *Time Out* for £100! Unfortunately, in their enthusiasm to undertake much needed repairs to the hull, they opened up old leaks, and the boat sank a couple of weeks after they bought it. We had moved to Luton by then.

Six months later, we boarded the SS 'Australis' at Southampton, bound for Sydney. Our last encounter with a canal was the trip through the Suez Canal on the ship. I often wonder how long the half-submerged 'Sadlers Wells' remained where it sank, just down from the Linslade bridge. We revisited the sad sight just once after moving to Luton. We never saw the new owners again.

Ross Barnard

Market Drayton, Shropshire, Tyrley Locks 1911   63346

Canal Families

My great-grandfather worked as a lock keeper at Tyrley at the time of my grandmother's birth in 1883. He was called William Nixon and married an Elizabeth Timmis, whose father and brothers also worked as lock keepers at Tyrley and lived there. My grandmother Eva Nixon married Henry Thacker, who also lived near Tyrley and worked as a lengthsman on the canal.

Mrs C A Hayes

Bedford, The Embankment 1921 70437

Driver of the 'Silver Stream'

I was the main weekday driver of the launch in this photograph (right) during the student holiday periods between 1955 and 1958. When I drove it, it was called 'Silver Stream', the largest of a set of three electric launches which carried paying passengers for trips from the steps on the downstream, north side of the bridge. Typically this launch would carry about 40 passengers. 'Silver Stream' was magnificent to drive, silent with almost no water disturbance up to the 6 knots maximum for the river. She had a tubular rudder form which surrounded the propeller. This allowed a very tight turning – most of us could turn her round in places where the river was only one and a half times the launch's length.

The two sister launches were smaller. 'Silver Spray' was a shorter, less sleek version of 'Silver Stream', and she had a single section canopy (she is possibly the boat in the background of this photo coming

downstream), and seated around 30 people. 'Silver Foam' was a conventionally shaped craft with square bow and stern and room for 15 to 18 passengers.

During the 50s these launches were owned and operated by a Mr Smith from his home on the riverside near Cardington. The premises, now somewhat extended, are known as the Barns Hotel. The barn was the winter quarters of this fleet for servicing. I was told that 'Silver Stream' and I think 'Silver Spray' started in the pleasure market in late Edwardian times. 'Silver Foam', having a less elegant profile, was probably added later.

Mr P C Hedgecock

Bedford, The River and the Bridge 1921 70435

Watching the Barges

I lived at the house just at the top of the photograph below. The outbuildings can clearly be seen in the field that adjoins our family home. I spent all my childhood playing with my brother and friends here. That was at the time when the barges were horse-drawn. I loved watching the working barges going through the locks. My grandfather was publican at the Three Locks (known then as the New Inn) for 16 years.

Stephanie McPherson

Wheaton Aston, Staffordshire, The Canal 1952 W286008

Stoke Hammond, Buckinghamshire, The Three Locks c1965 S566012b

Chocolate Charlie

During the school holidays the canal and its towpath became a playground for the village children. Several of us caught the fishing bug and used the canal throughout the holiday. We always looked out for a barge called the 'Mendip'. The bargee was a gentleman called Charlie Atkins. His route was from the Cadbury factory at Knighton to Bournville in Birmingham. This was the origin of his nickname, Chocolate Charlie. We always asked him for a bit of chocolate, but his cargo was the raw chocolate crumb before it had been milled, and it was all but uneatable. If he was in a good mood we were allowed a ride up the canal for about two bridges. Then it was 'Get off home to your mother'. Can you see that happening today?

Roy Downton

Thames Barges 1896 38336

Thames Barges and Navy Launches

After the war in 1946 my father, a sergeant in the Military Prison Staff Corps, was transferred to Darland camp in Gillingham, but as there were no married quarters available the family was billeted in the coastguards' quarters on the Isle of Grain. These were a row of houses with a bedroom in the attic from which we could see across the Medway to the Isle of Sheppey.

I went to the village school for a year, and was also in the church choir, but the best fun we had as children was playing in the deserted fort and wading out to the tower when the tide was out. Our parents would have died if they knew what we got up to.

A great pleasure for me was watching the Thames barges sailing up the Medway – those barges have held a fascination for me ever since. Another memory of Grain was crossing over to Sheerness by Navy launch from Port Victoria, then a small oil refinery.

John Gregory

Isle of Grain, Kent, The Beach c1960 I52007

Rowing with 'Borrowed' Money

I vividly remember the day when as an eight-year-old, me and my mate, Billy Sturmey, 'borrowed' 2 shillings from my mother's purse and hired a rowboat from the Portslade foreshore. We rowed around among the cargo vessels tied up on the seaward side of the 'canal', as we called the harbour. We spent the whole morning enjoying what we thought was an amazing experience. The only downside was that crossing the main road and rowing on the canal were prohibited by my parents, so the consequences of doing both and with 'borrowed' money were not pleasant. But the memories of that exciting day are not soured by the discipline I received, even though sitting was not easy for a day or two.

Brian Langworthy

Portslade-by-Sea, Sussex, The Power Station c1955 P728002

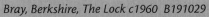
Bray, Berkshire, The Lock c1960 B191029

Ice Creams by the Lock

My friend Jean and I lived at Dorney Reach, and we used to go for walks by the River Thames with my dog. On Sunday afternoons we crossed over the walkway on top of the lock gates to buy ice-creams from the lock-keeper's shop. You could hear the roar from the weir. The children from Dorney Reach loved to help open and shut the lock gates, which were operated manually.

Monica Peck

Bray, Berkshire, The Landing Place 1890 23621p

' The children loved to help open and shut the lock gates '

Sailing across the Atlantic to Canada

Liverpool, Merseyside, The 'Empress of England' leaving Liverpool c1958 L60034

We sailed across the Atlantic on the 'Empress of England' from Liverpool to Montreal, arriving in Quebec City on 30 October, 1958. I wonder if this photo is of that same voyage!

My favourite memory is of the playroom, where they had a rocking horse. I was five years old, the horse seemed huge. I was scared to get on it at first, but soon I screamed if I had to get off it to give another kid a turn. The horse was made of wood and was white and black.

I remember going up to the stern. The captain was there, dressed in white. We saw two whales in the water up ahead. Through the round window, they appeared so bold and beautiful – even at the age of five, I appreciated their strength and beauty.

Our cabin had two sets of bunk beds. The room was quite small. My father slept on the top left as you came into the room. The hallway was very narrow, and as we edged along, we had to hang on to the rails as the ship rocked from side to side. Up on deck it was cold, and there were white wooden deck chairs.

I have read the history of this great ship, and I am proud to have sailed on one of her journeys.

Martine Symington

Brundall, Norfolk, The River Yare c1955 B497016

Launching the Sailing Boat at Brooms

Imagine my surprise while sitting here in the USA looking at pictures of Brundall, the village where I was born. The picture on the left shows my dad, Sidney A Brigham, launching a sailing boat at Brooms Boat Yard in about 1955. He had worked at Brooms since he was around 15 and worked there until he was 65. As a family, we spent many happy holidays on the river.

Peggy Miller

Brundall, Norfolk, The River Yare c1965 B497013

The Great Days of Steam

I have always been interested in trains, and Shillingstone Station gave me some great memories.

I did not enjoy the best of health when I was young, and spent a lot of my childhood down at the station, even on days when my asthma was bad. In the summer months when the line was busy I would take an old camp bed down and sleep in the signal box. When the last down train to Bournemouth had gone at 9.30pm, the signalmen had a drink. Then it was heads down until 3.00am when bells started to ring for the first excursion from the north of England on its way to Bournemouth. I would stay there until the last train up at 11.05pm on Saturday evening.

They were great, those days of steam. The signalmen who gave me the privilege of sleeping in their box were Mr Harry Scammel and George Ainsworth. My father, Jack Newman, was a lengthsman at Shillingstone, and I went fogging with him in wintertime. The porters at the station in those days were Bert Sherlock, Reg Eaton, and Wilf Savoury.

Brian Newman

Shillingstone, Dorset, The Cross and Main Road c1955 S443004

Hell's Angels

I'm not sure if the signal box (right) was still in use in 1965. I remember it better about five years later, when the Hells Angels used it as a kind of den. With a few mates, I used to walk the railway line from the pithead to Broad Lane playing fields. I must have been about 10. We always had a nosey into the box, as it was pretty derelict by then. I look at it now, and can't believe how well the owners have restored it and converted it into a lovely home. I think only goods used the line, which has long been removed along with the pit it served.

David Hector

Daring? Or Idiotic?

When I was 16, I wanted to impress a girl called Kerry from Connah's Quay. I climbed up onto the railway bridge and jumped down onto the roof of a train as it went under, just as it was pulling in to Little Sutton station in Merseyside. As it neared the station I jumped up and grabbed the trellis of the footbridge and hauled myself up onto the walkway. I sometimes lie in bed at night and break into a cold sweat thinking of what might have happened. I don't think Kerry could have been that impressed.

Stephen Owen

Essington, Staffordshire, The Signal Box c1965 E191015

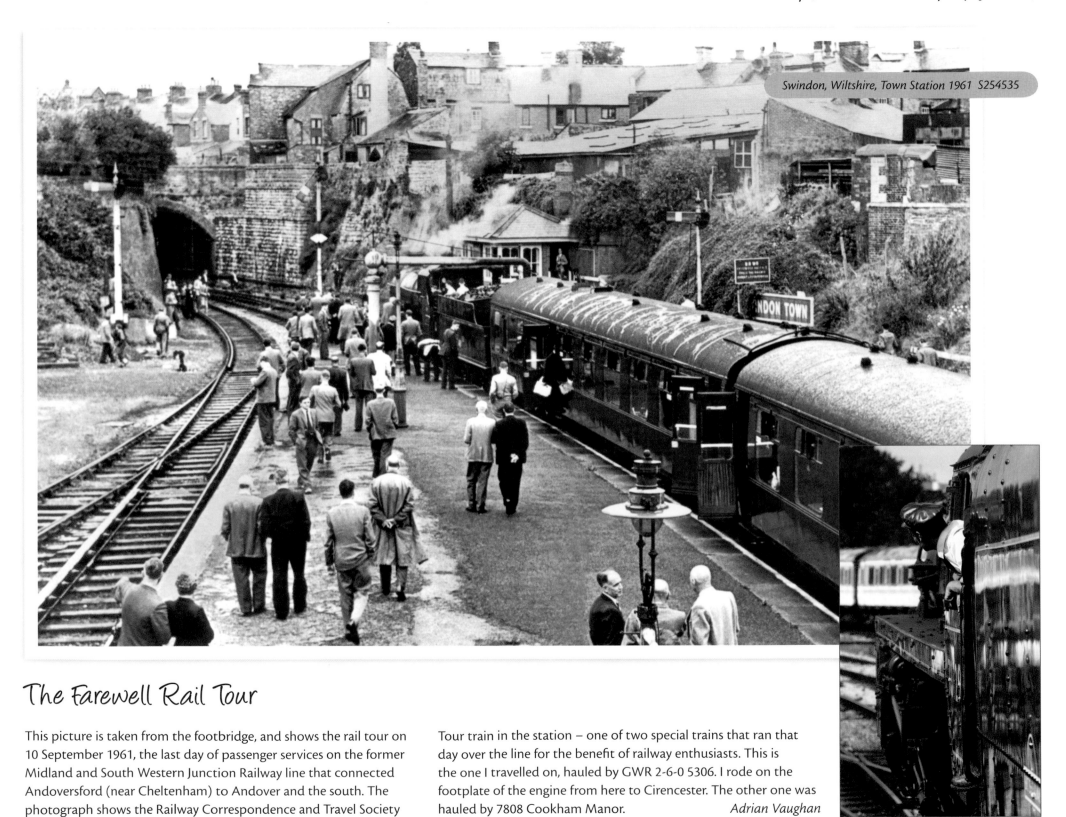

The Farewell Rail Tour

This picture is taken from the footbridge, and shows the rail tour on 10 September 1961, the last day of passenger services on the former Midland and South Western Junction Railway line that connected Andoversford (near Cheltenham) to Andover and the south. The photograph shows the Railway Correspondence and Travel Society Tour train in the station – one of two special trains that ran that day over the line for the benefit of railway enthusiasts. This is the one I travelled on, hauled by GWR 2-6-0 5306. I rode on the footplate of the engine from here to Cirencester. The other one was hauled by 7808 Cookham Manor.

Adrian Vaughan

His Pride and Joy

The man standing on the bottom left-hand side with the white T-shirt and quiff is my grandad! He is now 70. The car next to him was his first car and his pride and joy!

M Paull

Burry Port, Dyfed, Station Road c1965   B472059p

Duston, Northamptonshire, The Squirrels Inn c1955   D202012

A Unique Morris

The Morris car in the photograph above was overhauled and bodied by my father, Arthur Parker, in 1951–52. He had removed the body from a 1937 Morris 8 van, overhauled the mechanics and the chassis, and built from scratch a new shooting brake-style body. As a 7-year-old I was thrilled to be able to help with the work and immensely proud of the result. Unfortunately, when father came to register the car the authorities decided to demand the full purchase tax, which hadn't been levied on the original pre-war commercial vehicle. This sum, in the hard times of the early 1950s, was hard to find, and the Morris sadly had to be sold to cover it.   *Mr C Parker*

Trolley Racing

At the age of 11 nothing was more valuable than a set of old pram wheels. We used a 4-foot plank for the base. To sit on, we fastened a short piece to the back with an axle and two wheels, and then another two wheels at the front but fastened with a bolt so you could steer it. Fix a seat, and you were away. Pull it to the top of the hill and race down. There were only about three or four cars in Dinnington in the 1940s, so it was quite safe. Safe, that is, until Wigmores bus came, and then it was both feet on the ground to stop as best we could. That's what we called burning rubber!
Ramon Fletcher

Dinnington, South Yorkshire, Lordens Hill c1965   D101008

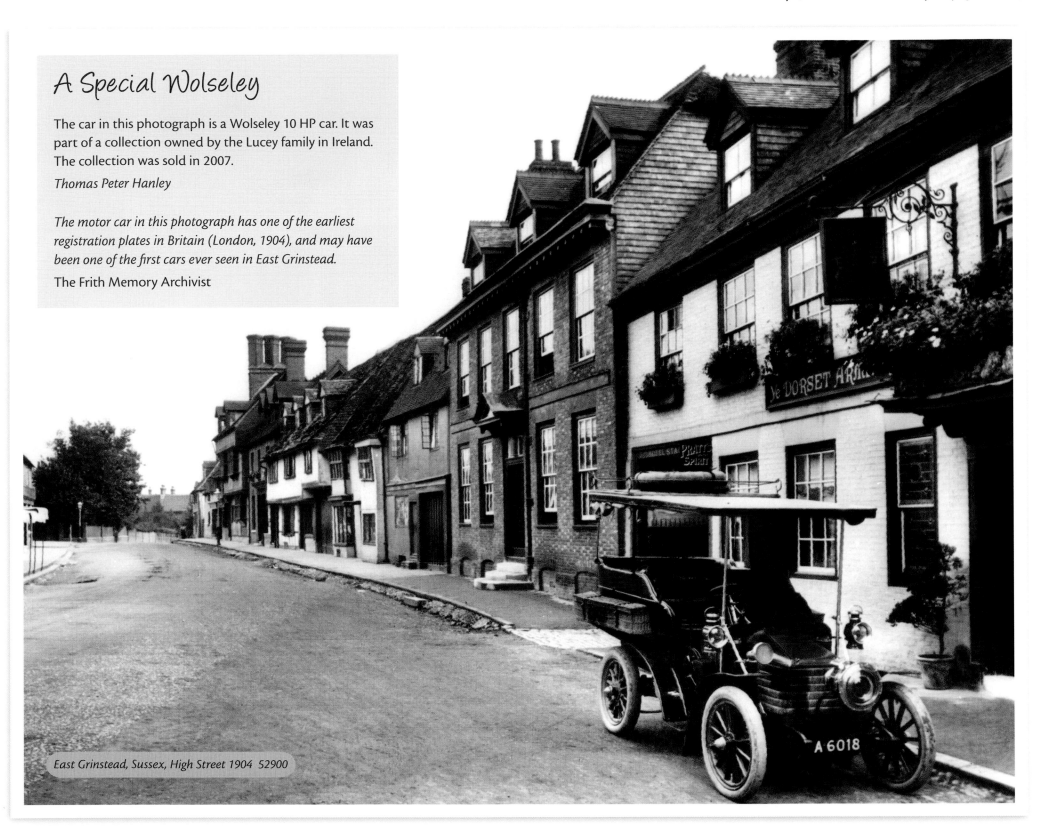

A Special Wolseley

The car in this photograph is a Wolseley 10 HP car. It was part of a collection owned by the Lucey family in Ireland. The collection was sold in 2007.

Thomas Peter Hanley

The motor car in this photograph has one of the earliest registration plates in Britain (London, 1904), and may have been one of the first cars ever seen in East Grinstead.

The Frith Memory Archivist

East Grinstead, Sussex, High Street 1904 52900

My Favourite Car: a Triumph Spitfire from the Cornwall Garage

I bought my favourite car in Hatch End from the Cornwall Garage in April 1970. It is on the right of this view (bottom) beyond the row of shops and the crossroads of Uxbridge Road and Cornwall Road. The car was a 1966 Triumph Spitfire, pale blue with two black racing stripes up the long bonnet over the hard top and down the boot. It cost me £465. I drove it for four years until I sold it to a local fireman in Sevenoaks. He thought he might have the necessary mechanical and welding skills to strengthen the rusty body.

Although these cars did not have large engines, they were blessed with excellent acceleration thanks to a low body weight. Sadly the cornering was not great, and it was possible to hang out the tail in spectacular skids.

The Cornwall Garage looked after me and my car most reliably. As a result I went back there in later years and bought two new cars when they became a Fiat franchise in the 1980s.

There were other garages in Hatch End. In Cornwall Road itself there was a small workshop which specialised in servicing three-wheelers. On the main road was Spurlings, a Vauxhall dealer. I recall my father buying a Vauxhall Viva in a shade of vomit yellow from them in 1969.

On the left of the picture near the junction with Grimsdyke Road was a truly old-fashioned petrol station. Remarkably it was in the midst of a row of shops close to MacPhails the greengrocer's. They turned a handle to pump the petrol through a rubber hose attached to a very long gantry that swung out over the wide pavement. Health and Safety considerations weren't as strict in those days!

John Howard Norfolk

Langwith, Derbyshire c1950 L295015D

Hatch End, Middlesex, Broadway 1964 H404068

Petrol and Dinky Toys

I was born and lived for some time in Boundary Walk in Langwith. When my family moved to Peterborough, I visited my grandparents regularly. They lived in Boundary Walk until the early 1960s.

The garage (above) was always a magnet for a small boy, because as well as selling petrol

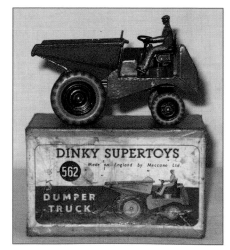

and repairing cars it also sold Meccano and Dinky toys.

I remember my grandmother buying me the Sunny Stories magazine from the newsagent's to the right of the picture.

Alan Fuller

Una Road Cars

I was brought up in Una Road in the 1960s and 70s. My mother still lives in the same house more than 50 years later. One thing that always strikes me now when I visit is the number of cars. I can still name the people in Una Road who owned a car, and the type of car it was, when I was a child. Probably only seven cars maximum.

There were two Morris Minors, an Austin A35 van, a Wolseley 1500, a Reliant Regal van (a 3-wheeler), a Ford Anglia, yellow and white, with an American-style spare wheel holder on the back, and a Heinkel bubble car. We did not own a car, which grieved me terribly, as I have always loved cars.

Richard Webb

Manchester, Greater Manchester, Market Street and Piccadilly Junction c1965 M21046

Parkeston, Essex, AA Port Office c1960 P144002

Trolley Bus Conductor

In 1966 I was hired by Manchester Corporation Buses as a trolley conductor. I was 18 years old, and I worked the last six months of the trolley buses' life on Ashton New Road, working out of Stephenson Square. They were the best years of my working life, and I worked with a smashing bunch of men from all over the UK. Piccadilly was where many of the bus routes terminated. Our canteen was upstairs, and a grand breakfast with a steaming mug of tea could be had for a few bob.

Chris Walker

> ❝ I can still name the people in Una Road who owned a car, and the type of car it was, when I was a child ❞

Llandudno, Gwynedd, The Great Orme Railway c1960   L71693p

The Great Orme Tramway

The Great Orme Tramway is split into an upper and lower section at Halfway station. This photograph was taken on the lower section at the middle passing place, situated on Ty Gwyn Road just above Black Gate. At this point, car 4 takes the outer rails to pass car 5, which passes on the hillward side. The roadway here is 'pinched' (in other words, it suddenly narrows) and has on occasion been the scene of minor crashes with motor cars heading downhill whose drivers have not taken into account the outward swing of the front of the tram.

I was conducting number 4 one day when a brand new motor car heading downhill ventured into the danger zone, despite safety road markings and the tram driver sounding his warning horn. The result was that the motor car had its front and nearside panels brutally filleted by the front left step of the tramcar. The car driver waved his hands as if to indicate to the tram driver (who rejoiced in the nickname of Bob Dog) to steer away – as if he could!

The car was very severely damaged, but the tram sustained only a minor scratch to its paintwork on the step. Our passengers were unharmed, and seemed to think that the 'Brummie' car driver's antics and (understandable) hysteria were very entertaining. When the police attended, they even suggested that his bad driving was entirely to blame – cue for more hysteria and unsympathetic laughter from the passengers! After 20 minutes delay we were off again towards Halfway station, up past Ty Gwyn curve and on to Killens Hill, the steepest part of the lower section.

The steepest gradient is approximately 1 in 39; this is where the yearly safety tests are carried out before the season begins. The tram is overloaded with sandbags, the speed governor is bypassed to allow for a speed in slight excess of 5mph, and when the brake is applied the tramcar stops in approximately 10 feet – fantastic to observe.

The trams in the photo are in the dark blue livery which was changed to a brighter shade in the 1980s. The original livery was Deep Ochre, but this was replaced within a few years of the line opening by a very dark blue which with the application of several coats of varnish appeared almost black.

Today, the Great Orme Tramway is equipped with effective and modern safety and operating equipment. Recent track relaying, and the creation of a modern Halfway depot which incorporates modern engineering, operating and passenger facilities, make a ride a great experience. One of only a few surviving street cable tramways (there are others at San Francisco and Lisbon), its survival is an amazing example of Victorian engineering and a credit to its owners and the men who keep it going.

John Owen

A Four-Legged Passenger

Llandudno, Gwynedd, The Upper Tramway c1905 2197A

This photograph shows two tramcars, Numbers 6 and 7, at the passing loop above the Great Orme Mines. They are painted in the Deep Ochre livery which was only used for a few years after the upper line's opening in 1903. The haulage cables are clearly visible. They are seven-eighths of an inch in diameter, and they roll above ground on 12-inch sheaves, guided by 'top hat' profiled pulleys. Every pulley requires greased lubrication on a daily basis. This is a back-breakingly unpleasant job, but without this, the cables would wear out quickly and would literally scream in protest! One can also see the two trolley poles mounted on each roof, which were used singly for signalling purposes.

It was at this spot that a 'washout' of the track ballast took place in the late 1990s. This caused the upper section to be temporarily closed for reballasting and the installation of new pointwork equipment. A safety camera was found to be necessary, for there had been several attempts to tamper with safety equipment here.

About 100 feet from this spot the tramway passes through a low cutting in the hillside. It was here that one of the drivers – we'll call him Bill – was driving No 7 through morning mist in 1993 when a mountain goat jumped from the embankment onto the front platform of his tram! Bill was butted almost off the platform, and only just kept his grip on the handrail. The goat wasn't very happy with his perch, and jumped off. Now, all of this tripped the safety switch. This caused the two trams on the upper section to stop suddenly, throwing Bill off the platform altogether. When he radioed to the winding house what had happened, the response was peals of unsympathetic laughter, and for several years after, his colleagues warned new acquaintances of Bill's fatal attraction to the hillside goats!

John Owen

Old Colwyn, Clwyd 1921 70827x

Trams at Colwyn Bay

The grey-painted tram in the photo is heading for the Queen's Hotel terminus, just over half a mile away. It took just over five minutes and three tram stops to reach the terminus, where the brakes would be wound on full to counteract the falling gradient. The conductor held on to the trolley pole rope, pulled it down and tied it down to the front bumper. He would then untie the other trolley pole rope at the Penmaenhead end and carefully allow the trolley head to rise upward into contact with the overhead wire.

He would then have to check for any lost property left in the car from the last journey before entering on his waybill the numbers of tickets that he'd sold since the start of his journey. Maybe he had time for a quick, illicit cigarette with the driver. No chance if they thought an Inspector was around!

Photos of the trams that ran in Old Colwyn are very rare. This one dates from the last three years of their running beyond Colwyn Bay. They were succeeded by the buses of North Wales Silver Motors, New Blue, Royal Blue and for a very short time indeed, White Rose Motors.

John Owen

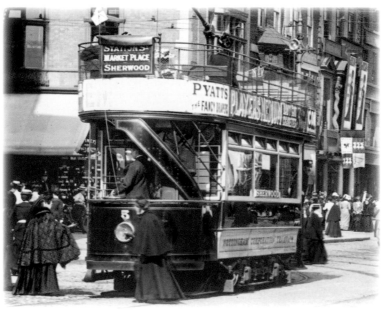

Denham, Buckinghamshire, The Airfield c1965 D183015

Looping the Loop

My father, Edward Wyatt, spent every spare moment flying his glider at Denham airfield. We lived in Higher Denham, and were taken to the airfield on many a Sunday. I was six in 1953. My brother, sister, and I were strapped into the back seat of the glider and off we would go. My father often insisted that we take the controls. I remember the winch letting go, and then we soared up to what seemed like the heavens. My dad also had a small plane, and would take us flying to high altitudes to help alleviate whooping cough (I think). We looped the loop, and felt sure we would fall out of the open cockpit.

We moved to Canada in 1955, but when my dad passed away in 1983 he requested that he be buried in Denham churchyard. This was where his heart was always, particularly on the airfield.

Jennifer Schinkel (née Wyatt)

Living with Planes – and Other Things

In about 1961 my father became the manager of Blackbushe Airport, near Camberley in Surrey. As a result my mother, brother (16) and I (9) moved from our comfortable house in Cheltenham to a large mobile home attached to what was then the middle of the long terminal building. We weathered high winds, blizzards, beating heat, pounding demolition, aircraft running to within inches of the front window, and eccentrics using our roof as an escape route, and we enjoyed crowds of drag racing fans, air shows, and trials for land yachts, fibreglass sports cars and mono-planes.

We watched the making of TV adverts, serials and a film with Robert Mitchum, met with various film crews and celebrities including Dick Emery, and experienced wonderful wildlife, horses, dogs, cats and goodness knows what else.

For my father it was an opportunity to develop an airfield from a derelict site to a successful business. For my mother it was a bit of a nightmare, with little control over her life, less privacy than she would have liked, and a job bringing up two children in very difficult circumstances. But for my brother and I it was a five-year adventure that has left me with a profound respect for those who fly and a deep love for very open spaces!

Nikki McAllister-Freeman

An Aeroplane Crash

I was only a toddler when a light plane landed in the cricket field beyond the allotments at the bottom of Regent Street, Church Gresley, in Derbyshire. Everybody around dashed down to see the spectacle. Few had seen an aeroplane actually on the ground, and it was common to run outside to see one actually in the air. (This was before the Second World War, when it was possible to count dozens or estimate up to a hundred or more.)

The pilot was a woman, and she had apparently lost her bearings. Eventually she decided to carry on her journey, but to take off in such a short space would have been a challenge to the best of pilots. She became airborne, but didn't get beyond the local treetops. I was told that someone was hanging on the tail-plane for a ride as the aircraft was taxiing for take-off.

Brian Venning

I am still Nat Lofthouse

SPORTING MEMORIES

Wembley, Middlesex, Olympic Way, Cup Final Day c1960 W314029

The Leeds and Sunderland FA Cup Final

I watched so many Cup Finals on television when I was a boy, never dreaming that I might actually be there. But it happened in 1973. My neighbour was a long retired football referee and received two tickets for every Cup Final. He hadn't refereed since the 1940s, and yet he continued to get his tickets.

Anyway, he made my dream come true, and sold me his tickets for a face value price of just four pounds each, so my wife Elizabeth and I could see the Cup Final. The touts in Olympic Way were offering big money to buy tickets, and Elizabeth thought it would be a good opportunity to finance a shopping expedition in the West End. But I told her that the Cup Final was a magic occasion, part of her education, and an event to remember for the rest of her life. And so it was in 1973 – a first division team beaten by the underdogs from Sunderland. Oh, how I enjoyed that day, thanks to my lovely neighbour. By the way, he didn't want to go as he was blind.

John Howard Norfolk

Watford FC in the 1950s

I first saw Watford play – in their old blue and white colours – at the end of the 1955-56 season. The only cover was the Main Stand. On the opposite touchline was the Shrodells Stand named after the nearby Shrodells Hospital (now Watford General Hospital). I stood behind the goal on the left, as the terrace was steep with plenty of barriers to lean on and high enough to give a view of the whole pitch. Halfway through the second half, newspaper sellers walked around the terraces selling the *Evening News* or the *Evening Standard* with the half time scores from other grounds, and sometimes even

a short match report for the first few minutes of other games. The Watford ground staff hung numbers on hooks at the edge of the greyhound track with half time scores too. The code letters for the other games were printed in the programme. I went to most home games, and sometimes even reserve games, as I was so keen. It wasn't a particularly strong team in these mid 1950s years, which is probably the reason why I can remember the defenders rather than the forwards. I wonder where Bell, Shipwright, Catleugh, McNeice and Chung are now.

John Howard Norfolk

The Virtual FA Cup Finals

On the field above, the FA Cup Finals were played – but only in the imagination of young boys, of course. It also served as a picnic venue, and for blackberrying with Mum and my sisters.

Today it is a playing field with a small park for the youngsters. Sunday League football is played here now, but never with Tom Finney, the Stanleys Matthews and Mortenson, or Bert Trautmann (the German goalie). And even at 60 years old, whenever I pass the field I AM STILL NAT LOFTHOUSE!

Mum's gone, my sisters have moved. But I still see it every day.

Mick Potter

Football in the River

Every year in Bourton-on-the-Water there would be a game played in the river using the bridges as goal posts (left). As far as I am aware, it is still played today. Around 1955 my father, Frederick Tarte, was a referee at local football matches. He refereed over a number of years at the games in the river, as he was stationed at RAF Rissington. One year Fred arrived in a bowler hat and holding a briefcase. Upon his arrival he opened the briefcase and pulled out his referee's whistle, rolled up his trousers, and entered the water ready for the match. In subsequent years the referees also arrived in fancy dress. This summed up my dad – who was certainly a joker at times. I am proud to be one of his children.

George Tarte

East Ham, London, The View from Town Hall Tower c1965 E100030

Up the Hammers!

My grandfather, John Williams, lived in a Victorian terraced house in Seymour Road in East Ham with his parents and four brothers. The house was knocked down and replaced with the large block of flats you can see in the distance to the centre of the photograph. It stands right next to West Ham United's stadium, the Boleyn ground, which has been there for over a hundred years. My grandfather and his brothers were regular visitors to the ground, being avid fans, a tradition which he passed down to myself and more recently my son. As a boy one evening John and his brothers decided to honour the club by redecorating the football ground with slogans such as 'Up the Hammers'. They were caught by the local bobby from Bow Street, who gave them a clip round the ear and made them repaint the ground as a punishment.

Julian Hight

Cricket on the Green

I always remember the cricket green at Mitcham as the lazy hazy days of summer. My father played cricket here. I don't remember the name of his team, but we had to sit and watch him. I liked it when the crocuses poked their heads out of the ground at the beginning of the season. They appeared in glorious colour in all the corners of the green, with the cricket pitch in the middle. We were never allowed to play on the green. If we wanted to run around or fly our kites on a bit of grass we went to Commonside East or Commonside West, just up the road, where there was plenty of room and no one to tell us off. The cricket green was reputed to have been played on since the 17th century, but the first recorded match was in 1711.

The photograph (right) of Lower Green shows the cricket green bus stop and the Cricketers Arms, where a lot of male spectators went during breaks in the cricket matches. Carole Baldwin

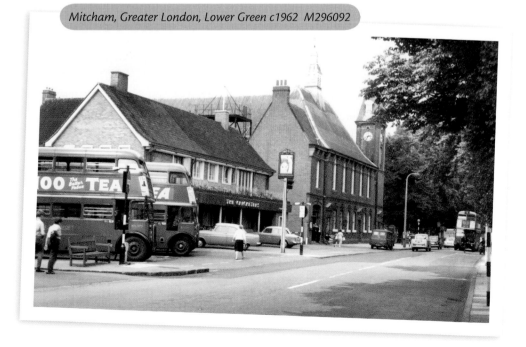
Mitcham, Greater London, Lower Green c1962 M296092

Wembley, Middlesex, Empire Pool c1960 W314052

The 1948 Olympic Games

My father Thomas Patrick Holt represented Great Britain in the 1948 Olympic Games. He and his brother John and two sisters were on the swimming team. Unfortunately, Thomas came fourth in his event, as he was struck down with a tummy bug prior to his swim. He had over-indulged in the lavish food supplied for the competitors. As it was just after the Second World War, dear old Dad could not resist the temptation of food he had not tasted for the duration of the war.

He trained without the assistance of a coach, a dietician or any financial backing and inspired me and all of my siblings to swim, and to try our best at everything we attempt.   *Maurice Saunders*

During the Second World War I went to the Empire to watch ice hockey. The teams playing were mainly teams of Canadian servicemen from various UK stations. The one I remember best was from Down Ampney, an airfield a few miles north of Cricklade. It is the unusual name that has stuck in my mind all these years.

Later, in 1948, the Olympic Games were held in the UK. I managed to get tickets for two events, one of which was swimming in the Empire Pool.
Daphne Poynter

Cinder Track Racing

High Beech, Essex 1911 63887

My home was in Buckhurst Hill, but on Saturdays in the summertime my dad would sometimes take my mum and I to the cinder racing track at High Beech. My memories of those Saturday afternoons come back as clear as a photograph, each one enhanced by the smell of Castrol Oil, the lubricant of choice for the motorcycle daredevils.

The grandstands would be full, and the men selling choc-ices would wander the stands trying to earn a few shillings while getting to watch various racing heats. The 'gate' would fly upward, and as many as ten young men (and sometimes a young woman) on brakeless motorcycles would dive for the first turn. In unison they would make their bikes lie down, almost touching the ground. The riders' left knee had a steel plate strapped on it, and their left shoe had a steel toe protector. Races of five, ten or more laps would determine who would be in the final. The din from these finely tuned machines was as deafening as the race was thrilling.

Names like Vic and his brother Ray Duggan were top riders of the day. Their brightly coloured leather suits and helmets were all the fans could see amid the blue smoke which made that unique smell and the clouds of flying cinders. Many bikes were powered by the small but powerful JAP engines.

This very noisy and smelly Saturday activity amid the quiet green countryside of High Beech was a great contrast to the way we usually appreciated the countryside. It drew supporters from London and many of the suburbs. Dirt track cinder racing all but disappeared when war was declared and I don't remember if it ever came back to High Beech after the war, but I seem to recall the race track stadium being torn down in the years after the Second World War.

Denman Lalonde

> **As many as ten young men ... on brakeless motorcycles would dive for the first turn**

Camberwell, London, The Bowling Green, Ruskin Park c1955 C516027

Old Blokes in White Coats

Sometimes on the way to the Green at Camberwell we would watch the men walking up and down the bowling green. They really took things seriously. The green was mown with precision, and I'm sure the bloke that cut it measured the length of the grass with a ruler. When the player was preparing to bowl, my brother and I would shriek to put him off his run. Since we did this most weekends, I bet they really hated us. We thought it was great fun.

Denise Masters

Prehistoric Cricket

I lived in Plymouth around 1951 to 1953, and our family spent two or three holidays in the village of Darite. My father organised cricket games in the field where the Trethevy Quoit stands. We played three or four times a week, and a lot of the local lads would join in. My mother sat beneath on the base stones and did her knitting.

John Stanyon

Darite, Cornwall, Trethevy Quoit 1890 24475

The Chalk Pit and the Hunt

The chalk pit at Odiham looks much the same today as it did over 100 years ago, but most of the buildings are no longer there. A story I heard in the Bell pub mentioned the local hunt gathering in Bury Square on Boxing Day some years ago. They left in the direction of the chalk pit on a foggy morning, only to lose half of the poor hunting dogs over the sheer face of the cliff. It seems the wily old fox had the better of them on this occasion.

Julian Hight

Julian's hunt story is almost right. I was living at the chalk pit at the time, and still do. It was a Saturday lunchtime about 1981, when the hunt came over the top, but it wasn't on Boxing Day. The hounds were chasing hares. The leader of the hunt knew there was a main road, so he directed the hunt across the field. The hare was chased through a hole in the hedge at the top of the pit, and the dogs followed through. From about 34 dogs they lost 18. Mr Cleverley, the local vet, had the sad task of ministering to the injured dogs. To my amazement the kennel maid knew every dog by name, and sat in our barn with the survivors. I've not seen a dog hunting near the pit since, though we have had dogs fall over the top. And on one sad day a local man fell to his death.
Sally Tunstell

Odiham, Hampshire, The Chalk Pit 1903 49208

❝ To my amazement the kennel maid knew every dog by name, and sat in our barn with the survivors ❞

I lived to tell the tale

MEMORIES OF UNFORGETTABLE OCCASIONS

Our Honeymoon – A West Country Idyll

We spent a week of our honeymoon in the 16th-century mill at Lydia Bridge. Across the lawn was a view of the brook and the early spring flowers. We stepped outside to the sound of the waterfall across the narrow, winding road. From the bridge, the view of the waterfall was spectacular. A path along the brook led to the ancient church where we wandered around the cemetery and the historic interior. Then we explored the village of South Brent, little changed since these pictures were taken. We ate at the tea room, feasted in the pub, and cooked local produce in our quaint, antique studded cottage.

Up the hill from our cottage, the lane twisted and turned, sheltered on both sides by tall hedgerows.

The lane was only wide enough for one car. Half way up the hill we stopped to take photos of a sudden pastoral vista of cloud-speckled sky over hills and fields and lovely homes. Later we pulled through a gate for a walk on the moor dotted with sheep. On still another day we drove to a village on the moor and stopped to watch wild moor ponies.

We hope to return next year or for our 10th anniversary.

Elizabeth Goehringer

South Brent, Devon, Lydia Bridge c1890 S360503

South Brent, Devon, The View from Lydia Bridge c1960 S360006

Dartmoor, Devon, Ponies c1965 D6135

Liverpool, Merseyside, St George's Plateau c1881 14071t

Liverpool, Merseyside, Lime Street and St George's Hall 1890 26661

A Romantic Interlude

Yardley, West Midlands, Bakeman House c1965 Y18011

My wife and I lived here for a month in December 2006. It was a romantic experience, and I will always be grateful for it ... The excellent view towards the Coventry road, the unusual sunlight during the late afternoon and the buses and vehicles making their way through the Coventry road gave us a great feeling. The lovely chill and the cold we could sense through the window created an amazing atmosphere. The street lights and the car headlights made us feel alone as the nights stole up on us. So many unforgettable moments we shared at lovely and lively No 4 Bakeman House.

Ananthakrishnan Ramasubramanian

Receiving my Certificate

As a youngster I attended a presentation at St George's Hall in Liverpool, where I received a beautiful certificate in recognition of an essay I had written. I can't remember what I wrote about, but since the RSPCA awarded the certificate, then I assume it must have been about animals.

As a very shy, not-at-all-confident child, I remember nervously waiting and waiting for that moment to come.

> ❝ I immediately tripped and went sprawling at the feet of the adults seated there ❞

At last, I climbed the few stairs alongside the stage – and as I stepped forward onto the old wooden stage, I tripped and went sprawling at the feet of the adults seated there. I lived to tell the tale, but didn't think I ever would!

Lynne McCarrick

Royalty at Milford

In 1962 I was in Cledwyn Evans's class at the primary school in Milford. In the summer terms Queen Elizabeth the Queen Mother used to visit King Edward's School in Witley, and Mr Evans led his class to the roundabout to see her go by. He was ragged about it by the other teachers. We all stood just by the walnut tree on the left of the picture. We waited, but not for long. The Rolls Royce came whispering up to the roundabout and sailed past us. Then I saw the Queen Mum lean forward to tell her driver to pull up, and he reversed the car back to us. Mr Evans gulped, she waved and smiled at us through the window, then suddenly they were off towards Witley. Mr Evans was very red-faced.

Mike Taylor

‘ *We had something called 'vol au vents' for lunch. These were considered by us to be a complete denial of a child's right to a square meal!* ’

Milford, Surrey, The By-Pass 1935   86776A

I can add to Mr Mike Taylor's story about being taken to see HM Queen Elizabeth the Queen Mother in 1962. I was a pupil at King Edward's School in Witley at the time of one of her earlier visits, which I believe was in 1956. Mr Gordon Humphries MA was Headmaster at the time, and it was the only occasion upon we had seen him at all flustered.

HM had lunch with us in the dining hall, and the two things that stick in my mind about the day were meeting this tiny, smiling lady, and that we had something called 'vol au vents' for lunch. These were considered by us to be a complete denial of a child's right to a square meal! To this day I find it difficult to picture royalty eating without envisioning their plates being full of little crusty puddles of French goo.

Mycroft Holmes

The Queen's Visit

On the left-hand side of the road (below) you can see what was at one time the post office – it later became a carpet shop. On the right-hand side of the road was Harold Jones's coal merchant's yard, and next door to it was the greengrocer's shop which was run by his wife. Everyone was very excited because they were going to see the Queen.

Ledsham Road and Chester Road were lined with people penned back behind metal barriers with policemen trying to keep the heaving throngs back. The rain poured down, and no one could see for umbrellas. Everyone was soaking wet. The Queen came speeding around the corner in her black, shiny car and everyone cheered and waved their flags even though no-one could see her properly. Luckily I was sitting on top of Harold Jones's wall with my sister Margaret and Doreen, Harold Jones's daughter, and for our trouble we got a fleeting glimpse of a tiny figure huddled up in the back seat.

Kathleen Green

Little Sutton, Merseyside, Ledsham Road c1965 LS58050

Leeds, Yorkshire, Briggate 1951 L28012

Scaling the Heights for the Festival of Britain

This photograph (above) shows a Wednesday afternoon, early closing day, which explains the low volume of traffic and few shoppers. The year is definitely 1951. On the left are myself and my apprentice electrician – we are manhandling the long ladder outside William Timpson's shoe shop. I worked for a company that for many years maintained the electrical installations at the two Leeds branches of William Timpson. On this occasion, to celebrate the Festival of Britain, shops in the city centre were invited by the various trade organisations to enter a competition to find the shop with the best display.

We were illuminating the upper part of the building, which involved fixing a light fitting at the apex of each of the two dormer windows shining downwards, and two lights fixed to the shop fascia facing upwards. The ladder only reached the lower part of the roof, so I had to scramble up the roof and then crawl on my stomach along the ridge of the dormers and then try to fix the light fittings. The shop came third in the competition, and the lights became a permanent feature of the building until it was demolished in about 1958. After almost 60 years in the electrical business, this task was my most terrifying experience.

Ken Greaves

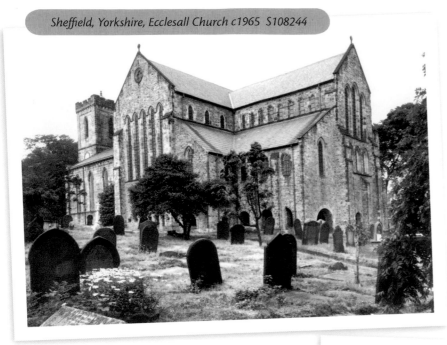

Songs of Praise

This was the church I went to as a child – mostly I had to go as a condition of attending Brownies, but it was always both imposing and comforting. The most outstanding memory I have is from the early 60s, when the BBC visited to broadcast a live service. Normally the church was about two-thirds full, but that day, there were far more people than spaces on pews, and the BBC chaps on the door were 'vetting' people as they tried to enter. Luckily Mum was dressed in a new outfit which was the height of fashion. I don't remember her smart skirt suit, but I do remember her dark maroon hat with a rakish feather. The BBC man sent her straight down to the front pew as a suitable candidate to appear on live TV. They didn't reckon on me and my younger brother, however.

Neither of us could take our eyes off the cameras – we spent the whole service staring at them, and several times someone came over to Mum and asked her to stop us staring at the cameras.

Jean Smith

A Ghostly Experience

The date was somewhere between 1972 and 1974. I had a horse called Shamrock that I kept in Sandon, and I used to ride him through Danbury and Little Baddow all the time. I went down Grace's Walk one day, from the Little Baddow end. When we were about level with the house, my horse suddenly froze and snorted. He was normally very calm, so I was surprised, and I looked down the bridle path in the direction of his gaze. Down by the stream and the bridge I saw a figure of a woman dressed in black, standing very still looking straight up the track towards us. She wore a long gown which was certainly not modern dress, so I knew that this was a strange happening. I stared too for a minute or so, and then she vanished. It was almost as though she was still there but we just lost the ability to perceive her.

Heather Chaplin

Halloween Haunting

On Halloween night 2007 some friends and I wanted to do something different for our Halloween night. Where better to do it than at the old Bodmin prison?

Off we set at 9 o'clock. We spent some hours in the darkest depths of the prison, and we are convinced we saw a ghost of a man in the Naval Wing. We did some filming and we took some pictures of what looked like 'orbs'.

It is not the place to visit if you are easily shocked, as the prison has an odd smell to it

and you hear a lot of strange noises and see a number of shadows that are not there when you turn around.

Trisha May

Bodmin, Cornwall, The Prison c1955 B129042

Revolver

Southsea, Hampshire, The Beach 1890 22762

On this beach I once dug up a fully loaded revolver. When I showed it to my step-grandfather, he grabbed it out of my hand and tossed it angrily out to sea for some other kid to find, and shoot himself with no doubt! Who knows … it might have been a murder weapon? More likely it was left over from the Second World War.

Dylan Rivis

A Tragedy

Around 1957 I was walking down Hereford High Street (below), on my route home to Bradbury Lines, when I saw the wife of an officer from the Army camp in great distress with some policemen outside the grocery shop.

She had left her small baby in the pram outside the shop while she went inside to shop – not unusual in those days. Something about the scene told me that something had happened to her baby, and I went home and told my step-parents about it. Since they considered me a ne'er-do-well, they scoffed at me as if I was an idiot.

It didn't take long for what I had seen in High Town to spread out to Bradbury Lines, where the woman and her officer husband were billeted. My step-father came back from the Officer's Mess with the terrible news (that I had accurately perceived) that a woman who had escaped from the mental home had snatched the baby, taken it to the old Roman bridge and tossed it into the river, where the child perished. They found the body the next day floating among the tall underwater weeds near the river bank.

Dylan Rivis

Hereford, Hereford & Worcester, High Town 1949 H74043

Margaret and Wallflowers

The year was 1950. I was 13 and walking along this beach with Margaret, her brother John and my eight-year-old brother, Peter. When we arrived at the spot where the man is sitting in the photograph, I looked up and saw wallflowers growing on the cliff face. I decided to climb up and pick some for Margaret. When I was level with the flowers, I held on with my left hand and picked a few with my right. The rock here is very loose and crumbly, and the piece I was holding came away in my hand. I remember looking at it and beginning the slow-motion fall. I landed on my back with a large boulder under my lower back. I was unable to move. The rock and the wallflowers were still in my hands.

My brother was frightened for me and ran all the way home to tell our parents. He got no reply so he ran all the way back to the scene.

I was in some pain, but enjoying Margaret's caring ministrations. A little panic was creeping in when a young couple strolled towards us. He was a big chap who tested me for damage, picked me up, and carried me home, followed by his girlfriend and my companions.

Dr Pardoe was called and diagnosed a severely bruised pelvis and ordered me to 'Stay in bed and rest for three days'.

Word travelled fast in Portishead in 1950, and a school friend, Dennis, heard that Anthony Warren had fallen down a cliff. He told the school, and they assumed that I was dead. At assembly that morning they all prayed for 'the repose of the soul of Anthony Warren, who tragically died on Sunday'. Fortunately, every part of me was 'reposing'. I went back to school on the

Portishead, Avon, The Beach 1887 20188

Thursday, and was very surprised at the reception I received. 'You're supposed to be dead!' they said and I did feel a bit of a fraud, being responsible for a wasted prayer from 600 or so people.

Tony Warren

Brighton, Sussex, Eastern Terrace c1955 B208069

A Tragic Suicide

The building set at right angles in the distance was a hotel. My mother, Florence Starkey, was studying in the Teacher Training College on the top floor when she looked out of the window across the angle into an open hotel window to see a woman hovering strangely at the back of the room. Their eyes met. My mother looked away, and as she did so the woman threw herself from the window and was impaled on the area railings below, directly next to the entrance to the college. All the students were confined to the college for hours whilst she was prised off the railings – just one small, anonymous tragedy.

Wolstan Dixie

The 'Annie'

The boat M26 in the middle of this picture (below) was the 'Annie', owned by my grandfather George Rowe. The 'Annie' was wrecked near Goscar Rock in a severe storm. My grandfather was found half drowned by my grandmother on the beach. From accounts given by my father it seems that the rudder broke in the storm, and so there was no way to control the ship. It ran aground on the only rock on the north beach between Goscar and the harbour.

My grandfather was also a member of the lifeboat crew. On one occasion it was swept down to Swansea and the crew returned three days later – but not before the families had assumed they had been lost. They had gone to help the Hardwick lightship.

Pat Devlin

Tenby, Dyfed, St Catherine's Rock 1890 28064t

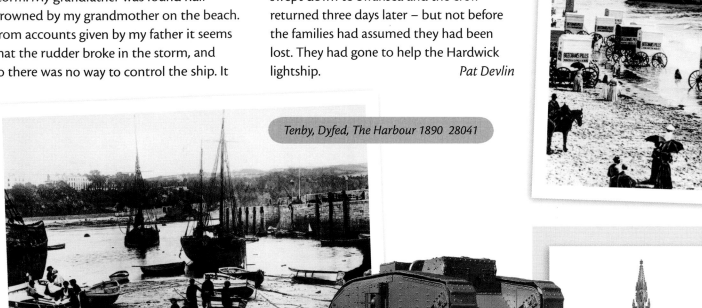

Tenby, Dyfed, The Harbour 1890 28041

A Fatal Explosion

The First World War tank behind the water fountain in the photograph (left) was removed because little boys used to go inside it and use it as a toilet. It exploded when the welder went to work on it, not because it was still loaded with ammunition, but because there was still petrol in the fuel tank. The welder flew across Kingsbury and landed, dead, in front of Ivatt's shoe shop .

Doug Caton

Aylesbury, Buckinghamshire, Kingsbury 1921 70556

No Head for Heights

We spent a day in Edinburgh on our way back from holiday. We also went up to the top of the Scott Memorial. I was keen to do this as Sir Walter is reputedly one of my ancestors.

All went well on the way up the monument and we spent quite some time examining the memorabilia in the top chamber. The return down the narrow winding staircase became a nightmare when one of our party announced that she was scared of heights, and after informing us that she couldn't go down those stairs again, proceeded to pass out on us. Have you ever tried lugging a semi-conscious near-hysterical person down a narrow spiral staircase that isn't wide enough for two people to pass one another with ease?!

Thelma Hurly

Edinburgh, Lothian, The Scott Memorial 1897 39111x

Watford, Hertfordshire, High Street c1955 W40019

> 6 All of a sudden there was a herd of cattle coming very fast down the High Street and stampeding 9

Stampede!

In around 1954 my mother took me to Watford for shopping and the market. We lived in South Oxhey, and caught the train from Carpenders Park Station and got off at Watford High Street station, in the lower part of the High Street. This particular day I was walking up the High Street holding my mother's hand, when we saw a lot of people running and panicking. My mum held me tight and rushed me into a shop front. All of a sudden a herd of black cattle came very fast down the High Street and stampeded

past us. I was petrified, and so was my mum. Someone said that they had escaped from the slaughterhouse and broken free.
Babs Earley

The Silver Jubilee Parade 1935

On the occasion of the 1935 Silver Jubilee of George V there was a parade through Lulworth. My mother and several other mothers dressed six of us young boys as toy soldiers, and we had to march in the parade. The best thing in the parade was a model of the 'Queen Mary'. It was loaded over a car. You could not see the car, only the majestic liner floating through the village. It was a wonderful occasion, and we had a party that evening in the Parish Hall when everyone

was presented with a mug to commemorate the occasion.

My family lived at 19 West Lulworth, just opposite the war memorial. We were Church of England, but my mother insisted on sending us to the Roman Catholic School in East Lulworth. She had heard that Miss Yarnitsky was the best teacher in Dorset, and that was enough for her. On days that my sister and I missed the bus we had to walk to school.

My mother died in 1943 and together with my father is buried in the churchyard overlooking the village. I think there are still some relatives of mine living in the village. I hope that they enjoy their life there as much my family did.

Albert Spavins

West Lulworth, Dorset, The Village 1904 52709

Floods

In 1947 my parents, my sister and I moved to Datchet. The shops in this photo, taken 2 years before, are so familiar, even now. Not long after we moved, snow, which had lain thickly on the ground for many weeks, began to thaw. The Thames eventually broke its banks and the whole of the village green was under water. Our house was not flooded, but I remember my parents taking up carpets and moving furniture upstairs, just in case. I also remember coming down to the water's edge by the International Stores and waiting for the punts bringing food and other supplies across the water, and the people trading from their boats. As no buses could get through to take us to school, we had to be picked up by lorry and taken to the main road in Langley to catch a bus for the rest of our journey.

Anne Diamond (née McCallum)

Yattendon, Berkshire, The Royal Oak and the Old Well c1965 Y32026

Datchet, Berkshire, High Street c1945 D9056

Datchet, Berkshire, The Thames c1950 D9045

Sudden Death

The Oak is the only pub and hotel in Yattendon. In the 1950s our next-door neighbour was the cleaner there. She would cycle to the village from the farm on a heavy green bicycle in a slow and ponderous manner. I must have been about nine when there was an awful event that haunted me for years.

One day police came to the village school to ask our neighbour's daughter where her mum was that morning, as she had not come to work. The doors in the porch of the pub had been sticking for some months, presumably because the floor beneath the doors was warping. Our neighbour had complained but to no avail. While cleaning that day, the floor opened up beneath her, and she fell into a well that had been unused for decades and not properly capped. She was not found for several days having died more or less instantly, crushed by falling cookers, fridges and masonry.

Her family and the whole village went into shock. It fell to my father and other farm workers to spend much of the next six months locating and filling in every well on the land around the village. The village is high and the wells deep, reaching down to a seam of sand that forms an underground riverbed. The seam is thought to run all the way under London, presumably roughly following the route of the Thames.

Maggi Stamp-Loshak

Where everyone knew everyone else

MEMORIES OF VILLAGE AND COUNTRY LIFE

Ghosts at the Mill

My father bought the mill at Felsted in the 1960s. We all have plenty of memories of the time we spent living there at the mill. The most memorable occasion was the first time we encountered the ghost of the mill. My mother called my two brothers, my sister and I into the hall, and demanded to know who had been playing the grand piano in the main lounge. We were not allowed in there. We looked at each other in amazement. Suddenly we heard piano music again. Mother, armed with a brass poker, went with all of us into the main lounge. To our surprise no one was in there. It was a bit creepy at first, but after a while we got used to hearing the music. The ghost was a woman who used to play on the grand piano, and beautiful, soothing music came from the room.

Christina Bryan

> ❛ It was a bit creepy at first, but after a while we got used to hearing the music. The ghost was a woman who used to play on the grand piano ❜

Felsted, Essex, The Mill c1960   F76015

I lived in the mill from 1978 to 1982 with my parents, brother and sister. I was only five when we left, but I have memories of seeing a lady and man, both dressed in very old-fashioned clothes, beside the mill pond – and nobody ever saw them except me. I'm sure they were looking after me and making sure that I didn't fall in the water.

It was a very creepy house, and our dog Polly would go mad in the hall at night. When we left the mill, my mum went back one day and saw builders inside doing the house up. My mum asked to look around, but they told her to hurry as they wouldn't stay there in the dark. My mum asked why, and they said because they had heard children screaming and a huge bang as if someone had fallen down the stairs in the hall. They went outside, thinking some children might be in the drive, but there was nobody around. I'm pretty sure that my dog knew something had happened in the hall.

Victoria Brook

Summers in the River

I have many happy memories of my childhood at New Rossington in Yorkshire. Spending the long hot summers in the river at Stringy Billies and walking to Waddy Lane to the river there and fishing for sticklebacks with my little net. When the water was frozen in the winter, skating on the ice. Going on bike rides to Tickhill with a bottle of water and jam sandwiches to share between five of us, which were always dry, and how crumbs always found their way into the bottle. Watching the majestic steam trains passing through the village *en route* to London and Scotland, waving from the bridge at the passengers and them waving back at us.

Games played in the street were skipping, with the rope turned by our mums, while we counted in and skipped; marbles, whip and top, sometimes using the stone bottle

stoppers as a top, and decorating them with a chalk design; roller skating with metal skates, adjusted with a nut in the middle to fit all sizes, and you could share and have one each; 'hopscotch'; and in the autumn great conker fights.

Sandra Faulkner

Trips to the Blacksmith's

In the 1950s I rode my pony from the Leatherhead Road in Great Bookham through Fetcham to Leatherhead to get to the blacksmith's. There was a proper big old forge at Prewetts Dairy off Randals Road. I used to have to lead my pony over this rickety little bridge. It had wobbly planks, with one missing one time I crossed it. It was probably a 9-mile round trip just to get the pony re-shod. It didn't cost much – I think it was about 7s 6d. The blacksmiths were father and son. The old man used to work the bellows and would shoe the quieter horses like my old pony. It was a lovely sight with the fire going and the smoke.

Paula Clements

Fetcham, Surrey, The River Mole 1928 80801

> ‘ These days can never be recaptured, but will remain with me forever ’

Everyone Knew You

When I was a young teenager, you could roam around the village of Watton-at-Stone in Hertfordshire and just about everyone knew you.

I loved to wander down to Mill Stream Lane with my jam jar and fishing net and walk along the stream searching for sticklebacks. The fields behind us whispered in the breeze and the sunlight filtered through the trees and glistened on the water below. You knew that you were nestled in a village that looked after its own.

I remember old 'Snowy', who worked for years in the local butcher's shop. I also remember Mr Warner, one of our primary school teachers, a steady influence in our lives, who rarely raised his voice to his students.

There was a post office and a general store, and dear old Mr and Mrs Camp ran the bakery and grocery store, where I worked on Saturdays. It was great there, and most of the villagers called in, as we were several miles from Hertford. You could take a basket and collect off the shelf, or if you were old and tired, we young ones behind the counter would run back and forth collecting your items as you sat and talked to Drue Camp or Harry Camp. We would cut and weigh the cheese by hand, the bacon too. Harry made the best cream cakes, and if at the end of Saturday there were some left, Harry kindly let us take them home.

When I was of primary school age we lived on Bardolf's Farm. We would go scrumping apples in the farmer's old orchard and get collywobbles afterwards, as they were so bitter. We ran past the pigsties so the pigs could not see us eating the apples they were fed. There was a duck pond half way up the driveway. We rode our bikes and sometimes we fell off and landed in the nettle patch, but there was always a dock leaf to rub on the skin and stop the stinging.

There were church fetes each May in the front church field, and sometimes on the common. There were raffles and cake competitions, fancy dress parades, and the coconut shy. The field was mowed, and the smell of fresh cut grass and bumpy ground are all part of my memory.

Joy Abbato

> 6 *We would go scrumping apples in the farmer's old orchard and get collywobbles* 9

Our Village

In our primary school playground, there was an old air raid shelter underground in the girls' playground. We managed just one look there, as it was out of bounds and deemed not safe. There were gooseberry bushes off to the side of the playground, and we sometimes ate some and had tummy ache later. Stone steps led up to the grassed area near the back of the playground and we spent nearly all break time jumping up and down them. We sang a little song, something about the quartermaster's stores, and someone would call out 'butter', 'sugar', or 'tea', and that determined how many steps we would jump. French skipping was the other pastime in our little playground. The boys had the front playground, and in season played conkers and marbles.

I still remember the atmosphere of the church and its smell of wood and musty books and damp air, and happy days when we sang in the choir. We celebrated our last primary days by going to church, and were given a Bible to commemorate the occasion.

In the village hall babies would be weighed in the mornings and the women's country institute would meet in the afternoons. Sometimes they showed films, and all the children would wander down to watch. If any of the boys came from the nearby town, our lads would look after us local girls and see us home to make sure we were safe. In those days good manners and polite kindness were the norm. Village life was a close community. But even though you might have lived there many years, if you were not born and bred there you were quietly called 'an outsider'.

Joy Abbato

Down the Woods

I was born in Slaugham at No1 Carpenters Arms in 1961. It was the very last house on the right-hand side before the white gate. What a great time all of us kids had, I hope they share fond memories like I do – the Talmans, the Shoplands and the Bottings. There were five girls, four older and one younger, and five boys, two older and three younger.

My fondest memories are of playing in the woods. We spent hours and hours down there, and parents had to take it in turns to give us all a call for dinner in the evening. We played Cowboys and Indians, and one time we got hold of a piece of thick rope to swing from a tree, and boy did we swing! I can't remember who put the rope up, but I reckon it was 15 feet high, and then someone made a big knot down at the bottom. What was so incredible was that this large tree was growing on the side of a stream and the limb spread out long and wide across it. What we did was to grab as high up on the rope as possible, swing out from one side of the tree and over the brook, and then leap back onto the other side of the tree and see who could go the furthest. We spent hours and hours swinging and thrusting out our legs right at the last moment to see who could land furthest away.

Lena Schriever

Slaugham, West Sussex, The Village c1960 S476018

A Peaceful Welsh Village

Glanamman, Dyfed, Bryn Seion Chapel 1956 G249017

I remember this street well – opposite and to the right (out of shot) was the local dairy, where the dairyman delivered milk from the back of a dog cart. Further behind the chapel was the Workmen's & Mechanics' Institute.

Grandfather's name was Evan Nathaniel Jones. He was a miner from Gelliceidrim Drift mine and had also farmed at Llwyncelyn Farm, Heol Grenig.

Miners coming off shift would squat or sit down in front of the gates, smoking and talking, waiting for the bus to take them to Bettws and Ammanford.

The village was peaceful and quiet in those days, and so was the forest in the distance. My grandfather took me there to shoot pigeons. He was an avid collector of foxes, and would nail up the pelt on his barn door to dry. Dealers would pay a shilling for every 'brush' – but some dealers wanted the whole pelt, and paid much more for it.

David Jones

No Mod Cons

My mam and dad, Lizzie and Edwin Ridley, moved into Slaghill (to the cottage on the right of the picture) in 1948 when I was three years old, with me and my sisters Margaret and Yvonne. My two elder brothers, Lloyd and Norman, had already left for the Army. Maurice came along in 1950.

There was no water or electricity in the house until 1961. Water came in a bucket from the iron spring on the other side of the road, and the light from a paraffin lamp, and later a Tilley lamp. We had a coal fire in the living room which Dad lit every morning before setting off to the limestone quarry behind the house where he worked as a shot-blaster. We also had a fireplace in the big bedroom upstairs which was lit only in deepest winter. The coalhouse was part of the outhouses, which consisted of a loft where logs were stored, the coalhouse, and the goat house beneath it. The lavatory was around the corner from there ... not a place you'd want to go to on a winter's night.

There was a boiler in the far back kitchen. On washdays Mam would travel backwards and forwards to the well for buckets of water to fill the boiler. Then she would light the fire underneath the boiler to heat the water. The clothes were washed in a 'poss-tub' with a poss stick, rinsed, and then mangled through the wringer before the advent of electricity!

As well as a garden full of potatoes, carrots and sweet juicy white turnips, Dad kept two goats, a billy and a nanny. We were all brought up on goat's milk and plenty of fresh eggs from our Rhode Island Red hens. We kept a pig for slaughter each year. Aunt Mary came down from Chapel Cottages to help with the pig-killing, cutting the hams and making the sausages. I used to hide under the bed on those days – I didn't want any part of it.

Mam took us picking mushrooms in the early mornings in the field by the limekiln. She taught us how to 'tickle' trout in the burn behind the house, taking them home to fry up for tea. She showed us how to dye Easter eggs by wrapping them in onion peel and making them into parcels with newspaper before boiling them. We'd pick different coloured flowers

Allenheads, Northumberland, Slaghill Cottages c1965 A221020

to tuck under the peel to make them pretty. She took us carol-singing down the village at Christmas, and walking up the Slaghill on dark nights taught us the constellations – the Plough, Orion's Belt and the Milky Way stretching over the whole sky.

There may not have been much money around the house, no mod cons and very few of life's little luxuries, but I spent a very happy childhood at Slaghill.

Evelyn Jones

Wartime in the Country

I moved to Hatfield Peverel, Essex, in late 1941, after my family was bombed out in London. My father took over the Duke of Wellington pub where we lived until 1949. My Cockney accent was a bit different, and got me into a lot of trouble at school.

At school we had air raid shelters in the playground. When the siren went we sat in the shelter until it was over, but to me they didn't feel safe as they were above the ground and had only one way in, and a little hole at the other end where you would have to crawl out. My school friends were Janet Cleave from the bakery, Edith Brown from Peverel Lodge (a beautiful house opposite the Swan Hotel), the Smith girls from the Street Farm café and Janet Weaver from New Road.

My grandmother lived in one of the blacksmith cottages. She moved down from London at the same time and for the same reason as us. The fire station was in front of these cottages, and when the engine went out to a fire all the local children followed on their pushbikes.

My brother and I delivered beer and spirits to the May family in the old Tudor house in Maldon Road, and their kitchen always had a lovely smell of home cooking. They also let people get water from the well in their garden when the pipes were frozen and you couldn't get water. We also took spirits to the vicarage in a wheelbarrow.

We had a German POW camp in the area, and most of the men worked at the dairy off Station Road. My father had two young German boys, Hans and Fritz, working as gardeners. There was also one called Herbert who worked at the bakery. My father was not allowed to sell beer to them so they would come around the back of the pub to a small room where he gave them beer and crisps.

At night when the air raids were on and we were under the kitchen table and the house was shaking, that was frightening, as big bombers flew overhead. We left the village in 1949 to go to Australia, but I have been back many times. Yes, it has changed very much, but I have fond memories of it as it was at the time.

Sylvia Cox Gromer

Not Always Idyllic

Growing up in the 1930s in Elsham, Lincolnshire, staying healthy was very important. The National Health Service just didn't exist. All we had as medicine was orange juice and cod liver oil. Our cottage was very damp, and one of my sisters died from pneumonia when she was just four years old. Many older residents also died from pneumonia – it was known as the old man's friend.

The people of Elsham were extremely poor. Everybody grew their own vegetables as that was the only way you could survive. The men worked on farms for just a few shillings a week. Their cottages belonged to the farmers. Every May Day Thursday they had to cycle to Brigg, report to the Angel Hotel, and ask the farmer who owned their cottage if he would employ them for another year. Very often the farmer wouldn't, and they had to get out of the house, which was known as 'flitting'.

Rex Whitehead

Fire at the Rose and Crown

I was four when my family moved from London in 1940 to manage the Rose and Crown at Ashbury. The pub was then about 450 years old. Six months later there was a devastating fire which destroyed the whole of the thatched part of the hotel and part of the building in Church Lane. The cottage immediately opposite was also burnt down. Fourteen fire engines attended and as it was wartime, it was important to put the fire out as soon as possible as it could have been seen for miles around.

I was in bed and my mother came upstairs with a drink. We could hear a crackling noise above the ceiling. She ran downstairs to tell my father, who got a ladder and climbed up to inspect the thatch by the chimney. He called to say that the thatch was alight. My mother rushed into my bedroom and grabbed me from the bed, and as she reached the door the ceiling fell onto the bed in flames. It was a very narrow escape.

No one was injured, and my sister and I were cared for by people in the village until we were able to return to live in the remaining part of the Rose and Crown. The bar could still be opened, and we lived in the patched-up ruins for eight years until the re-building started. My father was paid £5 per week as manager by the People's Refreshment House Association (PRHA).

It was thought that the fire was caused by wooden beam ends in the chimney smouldering, probably for a long time, before they eventually burst into flame.

Anthony Stayne

Ashbury, Oxfordshire, The Rose and Crown 1930 A98003

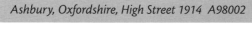

Ashbury, Oxfordshire, High Street 1914 A98002

Witches

I have visited Manningtree in Essex only once, but I have an interest in the area as my father Donald Turner is tracing our family tree. He has discovered that one of our ancestors, Elizabeth Goodwin, was tried and hung as one of the witches of Manningtree by Matthew Hopkins.

She was accused of casting a spell on a grocer's horse and making it die after he refused to give her credit to buy cheese.

Ann Martin

Denham, Middlesex, The Village c1965 D183019

My Favourite Bridge

I knew this bridge (left) when I was little and living in Higher Denham. We often walked into the village this way, past the lovely brick wall and the hut where we got free orange juice after the war. My grandmother ran the pub, the Plough, up the road straight ahead in the photo. Once my brother fell in the river near the bridge. We were in the newsagent's shop, and he went out the back door and fell into the river. It wasn't deep, and he was soon fished out, but we still tease him about it!

I took my children back to Denham a few years ago, and the same lady was running that tiny newsagent's shop. She had seemed old when I was a child, and must have been well into her 80s by the time we went back. I had been telling my children about her before we entered, and how she always told us to 'shut that door behind you' before we had got through it. Imagine my surprise when I opened the door and heard that same voice tell me to 'shut that door behind you'! How we all laughed when we left!

Nothing much has changed in the village. Seeing the photo reminds me of the wonderful times we spent in Denham as children. I went to school there, to Brownies with Miss Gilby as my Brown Owl, to the Plough for Nanny's chips and lemonade, and to our cousins' houses.

Jennifer Schinkel

The Village Policeman

In the late 1950s I was the village policeman at Great Waltham. The police house was the last two-storied house at the Barrack Lane end of Cherry Garden Road. My 'office' was the kitchen and the table was my desk. Next door to us was a lovely old lady, Mrs Woods, and on the other side the Hornsby family and their daughter Jenny.

My duties in those days were not onerous, consisting mainly of attending motor accidents, moving on camping Gypsies, and paying occasional visits to the local pubs in Great and Little Walthams, Howe Street and Mashbury. I got around on a bicycle, although once a month a police car from Chelmsford would come to Great Waltham and I would act as observer for a couple of hours.

My immediate superior officer was Sergeant Leslie Pye from Broomfield. He was always very keen for the village policemen (including Tom Mitchell at Ford End and Les Smith at Great Leighs) to catch a local poacher who styled himself as the King of the Poachers.

The squire J J Tufnell lived in the big house on the Langley estate, and had a well polished Rolls Royce in his garage.

Some Saturday afternoons I played cricket with the local team, but never managed to make a name for myself in either batting or bowling.

In 1959 I resigned from the Essex Police and left Great Waltham to go to New Zealand, where I was a policeman until my retirement in 1985, when I retired. I have had three trips back to 'the old country', and each time paid a nostalgic visit to Great Waltham.

John Butcher

Great Waltham, Essex c1965 G101008

Running Free

My parents, David and Valerie Angus, myself and my younger brother Roger lived at Rosevine in Combpyne opposite the Rectory.

It was a wonderful place to live your childhood, with a close-knit local community and little traffic, pollution or crime. You truly learnt how to live in and with the countryside, able to run free for hours in a completely safe and healthy environment.

Local farmer Frank Webber provided much-sought-after weekend and holiday employment lifting potatoes, swedes and turnips. With the Rectory children, my brother and I would would scrump apples from the neighbouring gardens. I remember turning off the village water supply and throwing away the key one sunny afternoon. This was quickly followed by a visit from a rather angry farmer, Guy Moore, who was attempting to milk his cows and I had to recover the key so that supplies could be restored. We also spent many happy hours beside the harbour, wondering at the enormity of the trout.

The church was our focal point every Sunday morning. My mother was a sidesman, and my brother or myself took the collection during service. Bored with the proceedings, I would spend most of my time looking at the ceiling trying to count the number of boards that clad it.

Simon Angus

‘ My brother and I would scrump apples from the neighbouring gardens ’

The Journey Back to Hurley

From the age of 48 hours until I was 18 I lived in Hurley.

Of all the places I've lived, and there have been a few, Hurley takes some beating. I now visit regularly to spend time with Mum and Dad and walk my dog, taking wonderful trips down memory lane as I clamber over stiles into the fields I played in as a child, enjoying them all over again.

As I leave Cheshire where I now live, I drive that last little bit of the M42, exiting along the lane telling me I'm heading for Kingsbury. I pass the vet's at Dunton Island where Tiggy the cat got the snip. I go past the Dug Outs, now known as Kingsbury water park, where I had a whale of a time with my best pals. I like to think that's what happens when you grow up in a tightly knit community.

I'm now passing Greenie's house and heading for the bridge. This brings memories of walking to the High School in protest that the school bus fares were either going to be introduced or going up. I really don't remember which, but it meant a day off school. Now I'm passing the firing range. It was a place on my doorstep, but a million miles from my experience. Guns were not part of my childhood.

Now I'm turning the corner that last stretch and past Miss Whitworth's place, and remembering crashing backwards into her enormous breasts as she bellowed netball instructions at us in the Hurley school playground. Now I'm passing the rolling rapeseed fields, I've well and truly arrived.

There she is, Mum at the kitchen sink, washing up yet another set of mugs from the never-ending flow of PG Tips. This sight always makes me think of the time our Wend was preparing to enter the world. I was not an athletic child, but those last few days before Wend was born I ran like the clappers all the way down the hill from school in the hope that she had finally arrived, but Mum would still be at that kitchen sink. When she finally made her entrance into the world, Sheila and I knew Mum had gone into labour in the early morning, and were praying that she could hold off until lunchtime so we would get the day off school. No such luck. By 8 o'clock Wend was there, and we were packed off to school. By the time I got to school I was so overcome with excitement at having a new baby sister that I burst into tears in the playground, blubbing 'Me mum's had a baby'.

As a child I don't think you are aware of what other people in the community think of your family. I imagine that some

people thought my Dad was somewhat eccentric, what with the boat, its tall mast constantly erect so he could hear the guide ropes whirring in the wind, set beneath Mum and Dad's bedroom window looking over the back garden.

We had the best ever tree house, apart from a nail that always caught your knickers as you swooshed down the slide. Dad was always in the garage repairing the latest second-hand green Mini, or constructing the old Bedford van we went to France in – what a sight that thing was. I cannot think of a better place to have grown up in than Hurley.

Mandy Simpson

Part of a Large Village Family

I was born and grew up in Turnford, a happy, peaceful village where everyone knew everyone else. My memories include long walks in beautiful countryside which could have been a million miles from London instead of just an hour on a Green Line bus; of thick fogs in November when traffic crawled at walking pace. One night my grandfather was leading the crocodile of vehicles and they all followed him up his drive, and everyone had great difficulty turning around and getting back onto the road.

One morning my father went mushrooming, as he had seen some beauties at the end of the field which would be just ready at daybreak. The mushrooms grew just below the railway, and when my father arrived at 6am a train had stopped, and the driver was picking the mushrooms!

I remember many happy Saturday and Sunday afternoons watching cricket, and the excitement of being allowed to score for the Rochford's 2nd XI and going to the away games in the back of an old lorry. Other great memories are: fishing in the stream for sticklebacks. Climbing the banks of the New River and walking for miles along the footpaths. Watching Prince and Jolly, the two huge carthorses who worked for Rochford's and

tramped backwards and forwards pulling cartloads of tomato waste. Watching the barge horses pulling barges along the River Lea. Crossing over the river on the lock gates – I go cold thinking about that one. Racing up and down the hills on the islands created in the gravel works. The village shop, and being relieved when Mrs Newbury retired as we were scared stiff of her.

More memories: growing our own vegetables and eating our own fruit. The AA man who parked in front of the New River Arms and saluted members of the AA as they drove past. Climbing onto our gate and onto the public telephone box roof when someone was in it. The time a pony got loose and was leading a convoy of traffic along the arterial road.

I lived there until I got married, and felt happy, safe and part of a large village family. I thank the people I grew up among for helping to make the first 20 years of my life so happy.

Geraldine Atkinson

Turnford, Hertfordshire, High Road c1965   T158001

Barham, Kent, The Mill c1955 B592023

Through the Kitchen Window

I was born in my grandparents' house in the valley below the mill. I spent many pleasant hours sitting in the kitchen with my grandmother shelling peas that my grandad had grown in the garden. The mill could be seen from the kitchen window high on the downs. When travelling through Bridge on the Canterbury Road, we would all try to see who could spot the mill first, a sure sign that we were home again!

Mark Whitaker

An Almondsbury Lad

What a rush of memories return with this view of the vale of Almondsbury. I grew up in the lower village (then known as Marshwell Crescent). My father's family hailed from Patchway Common, where my grandfather was the local cobbler. He was always making ready the boots of the local Gypsies as they prepared to make their yearly trek to Kent for the hop picking season, paying him on their return from picking.

I have wonderful memories of running, hiding, and enjoying family picnics on the tumps, and enjoying a glass of cool lemonade from the local pub, the Swan on the hill, while my parents had a glass of a more portly brew. Every weekend, we would go down to the marshes to catch elvers. They were always there in abundance, living in the myriad of rhines (ditches) that criss-cross that marsh area. I was and am blessed to be called an Almondsbury lad.

Alan Jarman

> ❝ I have wonderful memories of running, hiding, and enjoying family picnics on the tumps ❞

Almondsbury, Avon, General View c1955 A103015

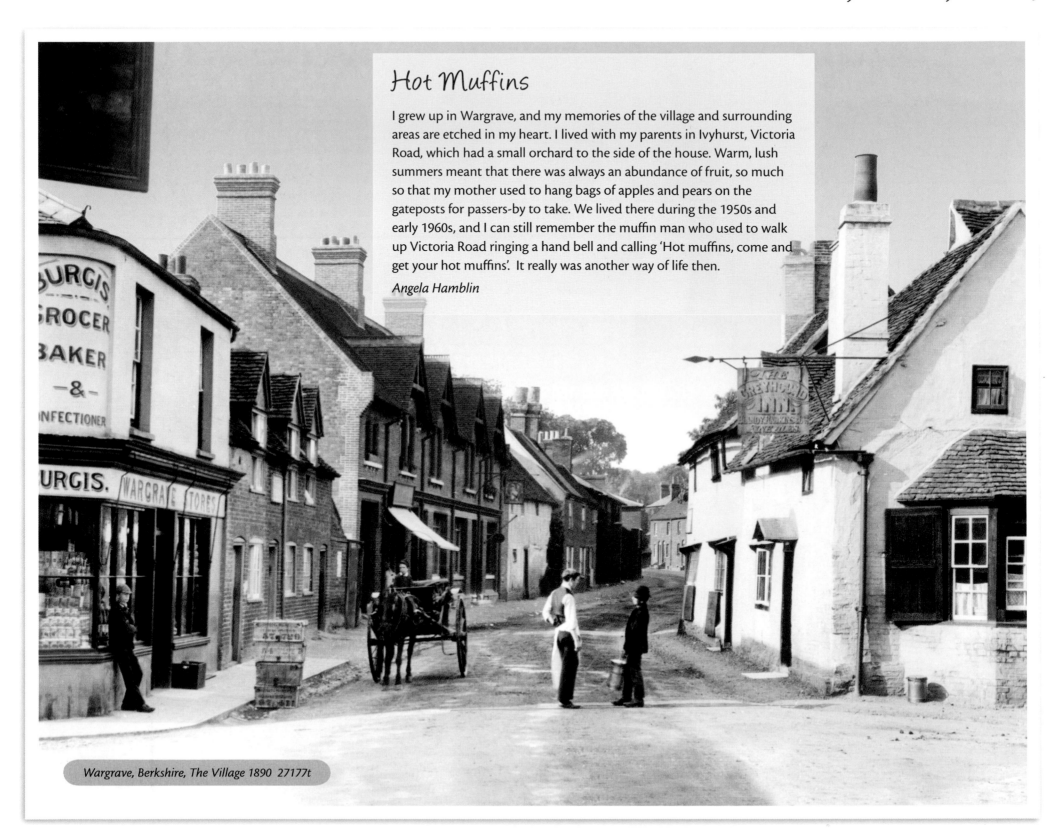

Hot Muffins

I grew up in Wargrave, and my memories of the village and surrounding areas are etched in my heart. I lived with my parents in Ivyhurst, Victoria Road, which had a small orchard to the side of the house. Warm, lush summers meant that there was always an abundance of fruit, so much so that my mother used to hang bags of apples and pears on the gateposts for passers-by to take. We lived there during the 1950s and early 1960s, and I can still remember the muffin man who used to walk up Victoria Road ringing a hand bell and calling 'Hot muffins, come and get your hot muffins'. It really was another way of life then.

Angela Hamblin

Wargrave, Berkshire, The Village 1890 27177t

The Wonderful Hill

Runcorn Hill was a wild place in the early 1960s. I remember even now the smell of the trees and the shade they brought on hot summer days. As a child I loved going 'up the hill' to play, even on my own. We didn't worry about what might happen to us; we believed if anything did go wrong we could call on a nearby adult for help. But I loved the hill ... with its birdsong, away from the hustle and bustle.

Rosemary Probert

> **" I loved the hill ... with its birdsong, away from the hustle and bustle "**

Bersham, Clwyd, The Cottages 1952 B459009

Runcorn, Cheshire, Runcorn Hill 1923 73911

Fresh Veg, Milk and Eggs

As a young child, I lived at my grandparents' house, 5 Mill Terrace in Bersham. Their names were Stanley and Alice Timberlake, and they were able to rent the house because my grandad had worked for a local landowner by the name of Fitzhugh. My mother, Jeanette, was born there. Although we moved to the Midlands when I was five years old, we continued to visit until the mid-70s, when Nan and Grandad moved to nearby Rhostyllen.

There was no bathroom there for many years, and I remember taking a bath in front of the fire with water heated up on the stove. The rooms were icy cold in winter, and I stayed in bed waiting for my grandad to light the fire before daring to go downstairs. We did the washing in the backyard in a metal tub, using a dolly pin and a hand mangle. The toilet was also outside, and we used chamber pots until a bathroom was added to the house but I never liked it much.

My grandparents called the kitchen the back kitchen, and there was a long cold scullery alongside it where milk, butter and eggs were kept. I used to collect the milk from the shippon (cowhouse) across the road. I was great friends with the Thomas family who let me 'help' on the farm whenever I wanted to. I also collected eggs from the yard at the side of the farmhouse. Milk churns were left on a bench across the road, and I loved watching the cows go back and forth from shippon to field twice a day.

We planted some apple pips and over the years watched that apple tree grow. There was a gate at the end of the garden, so you could get out and cross the river over to the fields at the back of the house. It was an idyllic place to spend your childhood.

Jane Hann

Saving the Clock

The clock tower has two dates on it – one from the original building, and one from when it was restored. Apparently the village council sold the clock to a visiting Australian who wanted to take it back to his country. The villagers were outraged, dismantled the clock overnight, and hid it in a local field for twenty years until they were sure it was safe. I lived in the house in the photo, so the clock is very dear to my heart.

Amanda Pickering

Tregony, Cornwall, The Town Clock c1955 T208308

No Fridge, Washer or Telly

I was brought up in the white cottage at mid-left, by the roadside, by my grandparents. They had a lodger called Sidney Elijah Durrant, who had lost his wife and all four of his children during the 1918 flu epidemic. He himself died in the early 1960s aged over 90.

The Crown Inn at the middle of the picture in the distance was run by Jim and Winnie Tuer, and I was friends with their daughter Ruth. The white cottage on the right was the shop, and later became the post office. The original post office was in the white cottage

to the left, and was run by Mrs Rowlands until her death.

The village school was on the right past the pub, and when I attended, pupils were taught by Mrs Glaister and later by Miss Jopson too, who taught the younger children.

At the side of my grandparents' cottage there was a tap where some villagers had to collect their water in buckets as they had no water in their houses. The old well was situated on the village green to the right. Until water was piped in, everyone had to use that.

The school has been a house for years, and the playground is a garden. There is no pub now, no shop, no post office, but when I lived there nearly 60 years ago, there was no electricity and no bathrooms, except at the pub! We had no washer, fridge, telly, or computer games, but we always found

Ainstable, Cumbria, The Roads End c1955 A287016

something to do and lovely walks to take, and there was no vandalism because the policeman lived down the road, and would give you a clip round the ear if you got up to mischief.

Kate Walker

Malborough, Devon, Lower Town 1927 79903

The Young Water Carrier

My father, Sydney Wood, was born in Malborough in 1914. He moved away to get married in 1940, but considered Malborough as home. He maintained that he was the young water carrier in this picture, and had a copy of the original postcard. It is believed that the gentleman with the beard was 'Datcher' Shepherd ('datcher' is Devon dialect for 'thatcher'). Some of my relatives still live in Malborough, and I have traced our ancestors there to 1712.

Tony Wood

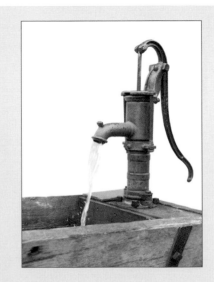

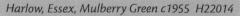

Harlow, Essex, Mulberry Green c1955 H22014

The Blacksmith

This is where my dad used to take our horse Kitty for her new shoes. One day I was riding her, and Dad was leading her, when she trod on his foot and broke it. He had to ride her back to see Dr Busby, who had a surgery near the blacksmith's. To the right of the blacksmith's there was a big field where they put on fairs, circuses and rodeos. Down Old Road was the Royal British Legion Club where we went every year for the children's Christmas party. The pub is called the Green Man and was one of my dad's favourite pubs.

Eddie Tait

Fish, Game and Ducks

Shere, Surrey, The Village 1903 50268

I lived in the house on the left with my parents until I was nearly 13. The long narrow upstairs window was my bedroom. My mother's mother and brother lived in the house with us. My uncle, John Grover, had a shop to the left of the porch, where he sold fresh fish, fruit and vegetables, some of which he grew himself. During the war people came from Dorking and Guildford to buy fish from him. Fish came from Harlow's of Grimsby in wooden boxes, and when the empty boxes were returned to Grimsby, my uncle filled them with rabbits and other game because food was scarce as a result of food rationing. My uncle smoked kippers in a shed near the stream and kept white ducks which swam in the stream. Virginia Pawlyn

The Broads, Norfolk, Hunsett Mill on the River Ant at Stalham c1925 T213064p

Uncle John

My grandparents lived in Hunsett Mill House around 1920-1930. They had the house as a tied cottage as part of Grandad's job on the farm. He had to keep the dykes clear. The child in the rowing boat is my Uncle John. He used to stop cabin cruisers and offer them a cup of tea, so Granny had to stop what she was doing and make a brew for his new friends.
Eileen Austin

Kingsley Green, Sussex, The Farm 1910 63049

Twopence for a New Suit

I started work at this farm in 1946 when I was 14 – it was my first job. On the left-hand side of the house was a garage. The farm was owned by Mr Suthered and his son-in-law, while Sid Dibbin had the garage. Sid had one other man working there, a chap called Perce Quinnell, with me as the grease monkey. There was a man who came from London and stayed in a sort of caravan out in the farmyard. One of my jobs was to carry buckets of water in the morning for him to wash in, and to make tea. He would give me two pennies and tell me to buy a new suit. That twopence came in handy – my pay was just £1 per week.

George Larbey

Felling the Elms

During the Dutch elm disease crisis that cleared so many beautiful trees I was employed to fell the elm trees lining the walk. My only consolation was the glorious view up to Oliver's Castle, which is now sadly blocked by housing estates.

Tim Evans

Devizes, Wiltshire, Quakers Walk 1898 42315

Chinese Coins and Horseradish

When I was five or six my dad worked at the mill, and we lived in one of the mill cottages in Mill Lane. I played around the mill, and one day in the old pond across from the blacksmith's I found strange washers with square holes in them. I later discovered that they were Chinese coins – they had been used as ballast for the grain barges.

Martin Bradley

When I was five my parents took us kids for a Sunday walk to Stambridge mill. Back then the roads leading to the mill were just country tracks. On the way to the mill Dad would dig up horseradish to take home and mince up in Mum's mincer. I can still smell the aroma of the place now: cornfields and wild flowers. When we got to the mill, the wonderful smell of grinding corn hit you. We would walk through the mill and on to a place called Broom Hills. After a good ramble around the place, Dad took us to the Cherry Tree pub. He and Mum would go inside, while we were outside with our lemonade and crisps.

Mary Jones

Rochford, Essex, Stambridge Mill c1955 R226016

Rochford, Essex, Stambridge Mill c1955 R226011

The Harp and Crown

This pub is the original Harp and Crown, which burnt down a few years after this picture was taken. It was rebuilt further back from the road. There are still people in the village who remember their parents and even grandparents going to the local for their usual.

Lucy Treby

Gastard, Wiltshire, The Village 1907 57826

Past, Present, and Future

I was born on 3 July 1959 and spent the first few months of my life in Ramsbury, until our house burnt down and we moved to Crabtree Close, Chilton Foliat. Crabtree Close has four houses; we lived next to Mr and Mrs Pett. There was also the Ford family and Mr and Mrs Fox. The lane goes up past Crabtree, where you can walk for miles and have uninterrupted views across the fields.

I attended the 'old' Chilton Foliat Village School. The headmaster was Mr Hassel. Mr and Mrs Dobson had the village shop and post office. I can still smell the scents from the ham that Mr Dobson used to slice up at the back of the shop. There was also Bunce's garage and the Wheatsheaf, where I used to work as a barmaid in the evenings.

Dean was my brother. The day Dean died I was playing in the barns. He was born at Crabtree Close and died at Crabtree Close. He was 9 years old when he was knocked off his bike as he was turning up the lane on his way home. We could see the flashing lights from the barns, but we were totally unaware why they were there. He is buried at St Mary's Church in the new part of the graveyard in the company of lots of fellow village people.

It's a lovely view from Dad's kitchen window where the River Kennet runs; there's nothing to block the view, and you can almost see right through to Littlecote. And then there is Fairyland. Fairyland used to give me the creeps, and even after all these years it still makes me sweat. As you go through there is a bridge where we used to pick watercress from the fresh clear running water. Then there is a good 5- to 10-minute walk through sullen trees until the next bridge. But it's well worth the effort, for it's the most beautiful sight. I always thought I was in another world, a world of bliss. If you happen to pass through Chilton Foliat, don't hesitate in going to Fairyland.

Now in 2008, a hundred years on from these photographs, there maybe a few extra houses in the village, but the only thing that has changed in Chilton Foliat are certain faces.

Mandy Chaverou

Chilton Foliat, Berkshire, The Village 1908 60954

> ‘ It's the most beautiful sight. I always thought I was in another world, a world of bliss … Fairyland ’

Chilton Foliat, Berkshire, The Village 1908 60955

We Lived in our Wellies

As I was a small child growing up in the 1940s, the village green at Bearsted seemed gigantic. We used to paddle in the pond up to the top of our wellies, hoping that the water wouldn't run over the top and give us wet feet.

The green was a favourite gathering place for a lot of children. One particular place was the village pump. In fact, there was no pump, only a shelter which looked like a church lych gate with seats around the inside. As kids we had a lot of freedom to wander the local fields and the golf course. We even went as far as the hills where there was a ruined castle although we didn't appreciate its archaeological value.

Another of my favourite places was a pond just inside the fringe of the golf course. During the summer holidays, we'd go to the pond and catch a newt in a jar or get some frogspawn. From there we'd wander through the woods and into long grass looking for snakes, lizards or slow worms. On other occasions we'd walk along a lane called Malling Lane, through the railway bridge, and along the railway bank to a stream. Sometimes we'd walk all the way along Malling Lane to the manor at the top near the Pilgrims Way. It had been destroyed by fire, so only the outer walls of the house remained. As a child, it seemed strange to look into the house and see three fireplaces at different heights on a chimneystack, with no floors between.

Just after the war when food was still rationed, we would somehow obtain a loaf, a bottle of water and pinch a couple of fags and a few matches and make off to the hills. The bottle would be passed around for each to have a drink. Eventually there would be loads of breadcrumbs in the bottom of the bottle. Most of us carried a knife in our pocket, which we used to cut a stick and carve a pattern in the bark. We never thought of hurting anyone with the knife. Most of the time we wore wellies, so we would have red rings round our legs where they rubbed.

Bearsted, Kent, The Green 1898 41565

One of the big attractions of the village was the yearly fair held on August Monday. Attractions included a rolling horse, archery, a coconut shy, swings, and 'pin the tail on the donkey', and a big tent for tea and beer. Since our garden backed on the village green, we were asked to supply the water. A hosepipe was frequently fixed to our tap on the day of the fair.

It seems hard to believe that the lads I knew then are now over 60 years old, some over 70. I suspect that many of the fields we roamed across are now housing estates, and there is now a car or two in each drive.

Beverley Simmons

> It seemed that most of the time we'd wear wellies, so we would have red rings round our legs where they had rubbed

Days Out on a Tandem

My story starts on 1 March 1950, the day I was born at Doncaster Royal Infirmary. My parents, Jack and Mary Flather, lived with relatives in Old Rossington at 65 Haigh Crescent, until a house was available for them. They moved to 57 Gattison Lane, one of the houses built for mining families in this area. My father worked as a miner and then as a deputy at the pit. My mother had many jobs, including working in the fields picking vegetables. As children we used to pick peas and beans to supplement our pocket money in the summer holidays. We competed with the older women for the best rows, which yielded more produce and heavier sacks – these were weighed, and a ticket was given you to exchange for cash at the end of the day.

I attended Rossington church school with my two brothers Stephen and Jack. As it was a church school, we got all of the holy days off after attendance for registration and a short church service. On Ascension Day we climbed to the top of the church tower for a service before going home. The church had cast iron fencing which my younger brother Jack occasionally got his head stuck in. It took some effort to release him!

Sunday mornings meant a circular walk from the village to the Great North Road, and back. In the afternoon we used to go to church and were given money for the collection. Half of it we spent at Billy Bonza's garage on the way, and the other half we put in the collection plate.

Gattison Lane was in the new village, but we went to the little open market in the old village on Fridays and Saturdays to buy produce and spend our pocket money. The cinema was opposite the market and had a 'tanner matinee' on Saturday mornings. The films featured Zorro, the Cisco Kid, the Lone Ranger and Tonto, and lots of cowboy films for the boys, with the goody always winning the day.

Days out were to places such as Finningley to see the Vulcans, Spitfires and Lancasters flying low over the airfield. We got there on a tandem, an old racing bike which my father used for work and a bicycle borrowed from a neighbour. Or we went to the races at Doncaster (the St Leger), where they had an enormous fair and lots of things to do, and a little flutter on the horses.

Sandra Faulkner

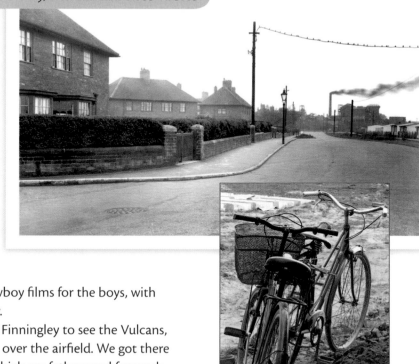

New Rossington, South Yorkshire, The Colliery, West End Lane c1955 N73005

Daisy, Buttercup and Bluebell

I knew the row of houses on the left in the 1940s. The house on the right was a farm, and I recall where they housed and milked the cows. It was in the days of hand milking. Each cow had its own little stall and above was the name of the cow beautifully engraved. I can even remember some of the names – Daisy, Buttercup and Bluebell.

Brenda Burton

Pickmere, Cheshire, The Pond c1955 P272001

Mangling, Churning, Milking, Shearing

We moved to Park Farm at Kettlethorpe in Lincolnshire in the 1950s, when I was seven. When Dad was promoted to Farm Foreman, we moved down to the main farmhouse. This had a small kitchen added on to the main house. In it was a copper over a brick fireplace for washing. Mum had a mangle with large wooden rollers. The washing was washed in boiling water and lifted out with a large stick. It was then put through the mangle to get the water out, rinsed and put through the mangle again. We helped with turning the mangle. The clothes were carried outside into the garden and hung on a long clothesline strung between four posts. Sheets were put through the mangle again to straighten them before they were folded away. The hot water from the copper had to be emptied using a bucket and the mangle dried, the rollers loosened and then stored with a cloth between them to let them dry. The mangle was folded down to become a tabletop.

We got the milk from the three cows used for milking. Each morning and night the milk was put through the separator to extract the cream. Once a week the cream was put into a butter churn. This was a wooden barrel on a stand, and it had to be turned by the handle on the side. You knew the cream had turned to butter when you heard a liquid swishing around. Mum then weighed it into one-pound lots and it was patted into an oblong shape with wooden butter patts.

We watched everything that happened on the farm. The milking, the shearing of sheep by hand clippers, the killing of the pigs. Well, not the actual killing, but we were allowed to watch the pig being cut up by the

butcher. It was put into a large wooden tub of hot water and the hair was scraped off. Then the carcass was cut up, and we had to carry the bits into the house for Mum to deal with. Washing out the intestines to make sausage skins was never a favourite job. We helped to make sausages, and would help to deliver the pig's fry. This was a plate with a bit of each part: liver, meat, sausage, etc, which was traditionally given to each farm worker. The plate had to be returned unwashed, I'm not sure why, but that was how it was.

The cows were kept in crewyards in the winter. Each week a new layer of straw was added to the floor, so by the end of winter it was about six feet thick. This was then taken out and put into a muck heap to be spread over the land. Dad always used to have some to plant his

potatoes on. There was nothing better for vegetables. I can remember growing the following in the Park Farm garden: potatoes, brussels sprouts, cabbage, cauliflower, beans (runner and broad), strawberries, raspberries, gooseberries, blackcurrants, onions, carrots and beetroot.

Gillian Emerton

Pymore, Dorset, The Village 1909 61650

Burton Bradstock, Dorset, The Beach c1955 B255026

Feather Bed in the Attic

We were clearing the last furniture from my mother's bungalow a few weeks ago. Behind the last set of drawers, on the floor, I found an old sepia photograph. It showed a group of children with some adults, outside a building which must have been a chapel or a school. From the clothes they wore, the photo would have been taken in the early 1920s.

Later, I searched the internet for clues and found the Francis Frith site. There were no clues for Salway Ash, but I found Pymore. One photo. Surely it couldn't be! Yet it was – the cottage my grandparents lived in when we were young! The memories flooded back.

We lived in the Midlands for some years, although I was born in Walditch. We returned to Dorset for holidays, staying with relations, many of whom lived in the Bridport area. We often stayed in that cottage with my grandparents. I remember the feather bed in the attic and the views across the fields. A little stream ran by the cottage, and there was always the sound of trickling water. I remember the outhouse across the little yard, how cold it was at night, and to this day the smell of Palmolive soap reminds me of that outhouse.

One of my uncles, his wife and three children lived just down the lane, so we were well supplied with playmates. We played in the old factory, and I remember the big mill water wheel, and the swans that nested in the reeds of the mill pool. Yellow irises too. How lucky we were,

wandering free as little birds, coming in to be fed, and finally collapsing into bed when the light was going, safe and so aware of the love that surrounded us.

We spent other holidays with another aunt and uncle and more cousins in Burton Bradstock. Joined by yet more family, there were some very big family gatherings on the beach at Burton Bradstock and West Bay – so many happy memories. Thankfully, we moved back home to Dorset in 1958. Eventually Nan and Grandad had to leave the little cottage behind, but their hearts were always there. I have not been back – except so often in my mind. Now I look at the picture my mother painted of the cottage, and the album photo from Francis Frith, and I know our time there will never be forgotten.

Veronica White

Hascombe, Surrey, The White Horse 1906 53577

Hascombe, Surrey, Mare Lane 1908 61127

Changeless Hascombe

I was born in 2 Pound Cottages at Hascombe in 1940. It was the home of my maternal grandparents Arthur John and Katie May Street. He was a gardener who worked for Colonel Harper at Lamberts.

Ron and Molly Hoare ran the White Horse pub and later I played with Rosemary, their daughter. My aunt, Vi Street, did domestic work at the pub. Nurse Caines exercising her goats on their leads was a frequent sight if one were walking around the village. She ministered to me when my grandfather's terrier bit my wrist.

The scenes in these photos have changed little. The village is a popular eating place and a magnet for walkers and horseriders.

Hilda Jean Waddington

Turners Hill, Sussex, The Village 1895 35225

Turners Hill, Sussex, The Corner Shop and the Chapel c1960 T248044

Carefree Hours

I lived in Turners Hill from 1941 on Tulleys Farm just down the road from the village. On a Sunday evening my family went to St Leonard's Church and then we all sat on the wall looking over the village green to listen to Copthorne Brass Band. Some weeks my grandfather Charlie Covey played in the band, and other weeks he was on point duty directing the traffic that trundled up North Street (to the right of the photo). He also went around with a wooden collection box for the band.

Timothy Franks

As children we spent many carefree hours playing and making camps in the woods and fields around Turners Hill. We had to keep a watchful eye for the keepers. I'm sure they knew we were about but most of the time they turned a blind eye. I was fascinated by their traps. The estate owned much of the village then. Carpenters, woodsmen, decorators were all needed to maintain the many properties that the estate owned, while the farms needed

labourers, stockmen, cowmen, and carters for the horses. I worked on a farm and one of my jobs was removing mayweed from the rows of parsley so that it was clean and ready to be cut by the converted forage harvester. I once found a pair of leverets (young hares) in the sixteen-acre field behind Worth Hall farm – mother hare had carefully hidden them.

Tim Fieldwick

Fishing with Billy

SOME UNFORGETTABLE CHARACTERS

No Ordinary Cat

Two elderly women lived at the top end of the village of Llangattock in Powys, and devoted their time to looking after injured animals. I was in awe of their knowledge of animals and their habitats and their ability to mend injured animals. If someone found an injured animal they would take it to the ladies to be cared for. This also seemed to make them drop their reserve and one would be invited into their home and rewarded with a lemonade and a cake. One time my friend and I found a wounded buzzard. It had been shot and it had an enormous hole in its chest. We took it to the women and this time we were shown around the property. It was an amazing place, given over to some weird and wonderful animals.

While we were being shown around, I heard a peculiar sound. It seemed to be a mixture of mewing and snarling and it scared me. At this point a large and very ferocious looking cat appeared, the like of which I had never seen before. I knew instantly this was no ordinary cat and it looked dangerous. The ladies assured us that it was a Scottish wild cat which they had tamed. It did not look very tame to me and I was glad to get out of there. It came as no surprise to find out later that it had attacked the ladies and injured them quite badly and the evil looking creature was shot.

David Palfrey

Great-Grandfather, the Town Crier

Marlborough, Wiltshire, The Town Crier c1900 M34501p

This is one of the two portraits that hung in my grandparents' hallway. My great-grandfather Isaac Waylen was born in 1837 in Berwick Bassett, Wiltshire. He taught himself to read and write whilst working as an agricultural labourer, and joined the Wiltshire Constabulary in 1874. In the winter of 1881-82 he was pensioned out of the police from injuries sustained in the line of duty. Apparently he was set upon by poachers in Savernake Forest when he was local constable at Froxfield, and nearly lost the sight in his left eye. He also lost his first wife, the mother of three children, at around the same time.

He subsequently moved to Marlborough to become Town Crier, Beadle and Bill Poster. In 1888 he married again, to Elizabeth Simms from Barbury Castle, and had another three children with her – the youngest was my grandfather, Albert Reginald, born in 1894. Isaac remained in his position until his death, aged 73, in 1911.

Little remains in the family that belonged to Isaac. There is a large kitchen chair, Isaac's copy of Waylen's (no immediate relation) 'History of Marlborough', and a pocket watch as well as the two photos. Isaac also left a legacy of family sayings, amongst which this is one of the most memorable, reflecting his dealings with local personages and the law: 'Bell-ringers, psalm-singers and band players are amongst the biggest rogues in the parish.'

Peter Waylen

Fishing with Billy

Billy was a hero to us boys. In the daytime you could go crabbing with him; at night, out drifting. He drove an old open US-army jeep and at times you would see five, six or even seven boys clinging to parts of the vehicle as it bounced its way up the slipway, or tore through the Cornish lanes on the way to Looe, where he kept his bigger boat, the 'Ella'.

I remember a shake, or an alarm clock, at 5.00am. I'd pull on my boots and a thick woollen jumper. It would be pitch dark. As I made my way 500 yards to the centre of the village, my heart would be in my mouth; every shadow a threat, every noise a danger. Then, through the night, the clumping of heavy sea boots: 'That you, D'Arcy?' The comforting sound of Billy.

As we launched the boat off the beach, using his jeep and a clever device that lifted and lowered his open boat into the water, the sea spray would sometimes dribble down my neck and a cold, pre-dawn wind cut beneath the several layers of clothes to make me shiver. But we would never let Billy know we were suffering: he might not invite us again. As the little engine chugged us clear through the rocks, dawn would be slowly lighting the eastern sky. Billy stood in the stern, tiller between his legs, the yellow of his oilskins reflecting the slightest glimmer of light.

Four or five hours later, loaded with crabs and an occasional lobster, we surfed up the beach to be met by boys who hadn't done that dark, pre-dawn walk and, perhaps, by curious holidaymakers. The boat was pulled up the beach by the jeep and then we all jumped in, scrabbling to get a handhold on the cold green rusty metal as it swayed its way up the slip, round the corner, down past Jean Thom's shop, the boys hooting and hollering with glee and Billy shouting orders to hang on. If we were lucky, he would take us to Looe. If not, we would buy a bottle of Corona, perhaps, and make our way down to the beach, sit by the boats and listen to the old men telling sea stories.

D'Arcy Blank

Downderry, Cornwall, From the Sands 1930   83310

Looe, Cornwall, The River c1955 L102029

Looe, Cornwall, The Pier 1906 56390t

Looe, Cornwall, Fishermen 1906 56413

> ❛ My heart would be in my mouth; every shadow a threat, every noise a danger. Then, through the night, the clumping of heavy sea boots: 'That you, D'Arcy?' ❜

Sheringham, Norfolk, The Fishermen 1906 56880p

Sheringham, Norfolk, The Beach 1893 33311

Sheringham, Norfolk, Fishermen's Cottages 1901 46545

Iron Men in Wooden Boats

The gentleman lying on the ground in the front of the photograph opposite is my great-grandfather John 'Teapot' West. He was a fisherman and a lifeboatman. He was also well known for being a 'fisherman evangelist'. Together with William Craske and William Long he was a Methodist preacher for over 50 years. They travelled throughout the county preaching, and later appeared at rallies in such places as London, Birmingham and Liverpool.

These fishermen/ lifeboatmen were strong, brave and somewhat exceptional men. There is a phrase describing them which I think fits them beautifully – 'Iron Men in Wooden Boats'. From the left, they are: Henry 'Joyful' West; Wilson Able (with pipe); Grice (in the background – I'm unsure of his Christian name); 'Brighams' Bishop; 'Joyful' West (father of Henry); John 'Sparrow' Hardingham (the young lad); John 'Rook' Reynolds; 'Potter' Hardingham (leaning on the boat – father of John); 'Fiddy' West (seated); and John 'Teapot' West (lying on the ground).

The fishermen nearly all had nicknames. When this photograph was taken, the fishing community here was huge – hundreds of fishermen on the beach and scores of boats. Fishing was a family tradition and sons followed fathers and grandfathers for generations in going to sea. Families were large and a lot of the community was related in some way. As a result many men shared the same names, both surnames and Christian names. For example my great-grandfather John had a son, my grandfather, also called John, and he in turn named one of his sons, my uncle, John! This led to some confusion when all of the men were working together on an overcrowded beach. Fishing was a dangerous occupation, and it was important that when you called to someone the person you were talking to responded – not half the beach. So they all had nicknames to differentiate them from other men with the same name.

I do not know the history of all the individual nicknames. Some are obvious, such as 'Squinter' or 'Red Eye'. I do know why my great-grandfather was called 'Teapot'. He rescued a pilot who had been wrecked in the North Sea and brought him home in his fishing boat. In return for saving his life, the pilot and his wife gave my great-grandfather a silver teapot.   *Barbara West*

Farnham, Surrey, The Colonnade 1936 87793p

Buy my lily of the valley!

On one day of the year, through the 40s and probably the 50s, my grandmother Ethel Glazier would pick all the lily of the valley she had in a bed about three foot square in her back garden in Rowledge. She would bind them into small bunches, with leaves around, and tie them carefully with thread.

They would sit in a bowl of water on the flagged floor of her larder overnight. She got on the first bus to Farnham from the village in the morning, and sat in the Castle Street end of this Colonnade, selling the bunches from a basket. She would be home in time for the midday meal, with a pocket full of cash, and a treat of fish heads for the cat (patriotically called Monty after the general).

My grandmother was a most respectable woman, and this was totally out of character, but I think she just liked to disprove my grandfather's maxim that 'you can't eat flowers!'.

Raela Croft

The Fish Seller

The lady on the left in the white apron
is Miss Douch selling fish.

The Frith Memory Archivist

Mevagissey, Cornwall, Fore Street 1890 27558

Polperro, Cornwall, The Pilchards Inn 1907 59269

Famous Meetings

My great-grandfather and great-grandmother lived and worked at the Pilchards Inn. They had three children. My grandmother used to tell me about how they kept chickens and ducks in the garden, and how she met Daphne du Maurier and Alfred Hitchcock whilst he was in Cornwall making a film – that's not bad for passing trade! I can't wait to visit Polperro and sit a while in the Pilchards Inn to remember my wonderful grandmother in a place that was very close to her heart.

Jane MacCallum

The Fishermen's Parliament

Mevagissey, Cornwall, Parliament 1924 76299

The old men in Mevagissey (mostly retired fishermen) would sit on the bench seat and discuss the weather, fishing and local politics. Their keen eyes never missed anything that happened on the harbour. So the seat was known as 'Mevagissey Parliament'.

My grandfather, Claud Hunkin, owned the house the old men are leaning against in the photo. In 1954 he wanted motorcycle access to the doorway, so he cut a hinged flap in the seat. Outraged, the Mevagissey Harbour Trust sought to renew the bench at Grandfather's expense. The case went to court, and was defended by the Harbour Clerk, Miss Effie Hunkin (a distant relation!). Judge P L E Rawlins at the Liskeard County Court found that Grandfather had a right of access to his property and that the seat could indeed be adapted for this purpose.

Judge Rawlins then went on to say that the 'Members of Parliament' were not a limited ascertainable class, and he could not say how they were elected: whether it was by right, age, force of arms or verbosity. 'All I can find is that if anyone not a member sits on the seat, it is likely to lead to dire consequences', he commented. Judge Rawlins pointed out that he had not 'dissolved Parliament' for it never to be recalled. 'Parliament continues, but like so many ancient institutions it must adapt itself to changed circumstances'.

Incidentally, the washing in the background (probably belonging to my aunty, May Clark) reminds me that on poor drying days the old women in the village would comment: 'There id'n no dryth in the air today'!

Roland Deighton

The names of the 'MPs' from left to right are Siah Longmade, Tommy Cloak, Bill Mills, Wilbur Hunkin, Harold Barber, Dick Nicholls, B Over, Bill Joe Robbins, Jimmy Dunn, and lastly Jim Bullen. Bill (or Will) Hunkin is standing holding the little girl's hand. She is his daughter, Katheen. By the wall, the man with the pipe is Willie Dyer and Cliff Nicholls is behind him.

The Frith Memory Archivist

Jack and Jill

My parents, Alan and Jennifer Ross, moved to Clayton in 1954 when I was a year old and lived there for the next 25 years. For most of that period the Jack and Jill windmills were owned by Henry Longhurst, a celebrated golf journalist of his time. My father was writing about cricket in those days, so they knew each other as fellow sports journalists. I visited the windmills as a child, and later, when I drove

Clayton, Sussex, Jack and Jill Windmills c1955 C419021e

down to Clayton for the weekend, the sight of Jack and Jill on top of the Downs always made my heart lift as I approached the end of the journey. The Longhursts lived in Jack, the black mill, and in an attached cottage, as far as I remember, while Jill was pretty much in its original working condition.

As you can see from the photograph, Jack did not have sails in those days, but in the 1970s a movie called 'The Black Windmill', starring Michael Caine, was filmed there and the film company paid for sails to be added.

When I was about six or seven my father wrote a children's book called 'The Onion Man' for which the setting was Clayton. The story featured a little boy called Jonathan and his best friend Percy Boyd (in reality based on my childhood friend Jon Lloyd) and was illustrated by an artist who lived down the lane – Raymond Briggs. He later became famous as the author of 'The Snowman' and 'Fungus the Bogeyman' etc.

Jonathan Ross

The Man with the Barrel Organ

Dewsbury, Yorkshire, The Town Centre c1960 D100006

The island in the middle of Market Place had a unique feature. Between the two zebra crossings on the island each Saturday was a man with a barrel organ. The music could be heard all over the town centre. You had to walk past it when you wanted to cross the road, so it was the perfect position for the man with the organ to collect money for charities.

I used to like listening to the music and was fascinated by the organ. The people who shook the collecting cans scared me though. I probably thought they would take my pocket money (one shilling), although they never did.

I used to spend my pocket money in Caddy's ice cream parlour on two scoops of ice cream with fizzy pop in a tall glass. This was a real part of Dewsbury's history and my childhood recollections.

Janet Hagger

Ipswich, Suffolk, Major's Corner c1955 I18034

Burgh-By-Sands, Cumbria, The Greyhound Inn c1955 B709011

Crafty Stumpy

To the front of this picture, the Tudor-style building is the Beehive pub. This pub was frequented by a fellow called Stumpy. He had one leg, and he would prop himself up against the downpipe of the pub. He would challenge any passer-by to put his money down on the path and try and kick Stumpy's remaining leg from beneath him to win the pot. But Stumpy would then give the passer-by a beating with his crutch … so you couldn't get near enough to kick his leg!

Tami Cross-Halls

An Illustrious Visitor

My grandmother, Margaret Flint, was landlady of the Greyhound from some time during the Second World War until 1954. I lived there from 1944 until she retired. As a publican, Grandmother was entitled to more than the normal rations in the immediate post-war era, since she was required to provide food to any traveller. Travellers were few and far between; but one day George Bernard Shaw and his companion appeared on the doorstep in the afternoon requiring tea, so she had to fulfil her duty.

Bryan Flint

Meeting 'Romany'

I was evacuated to Chester during the Second World War and met 'Romany' and his dog Raq on a number of occasions when he visited our school. He talked to us about the countryside, did beautiful simple charcoal drawings of the creatures he was discussing, told us what to wear to become 'nature detectives', and even played tunes for us on the piano. He was a lovely man.

Frances Stewart

Wilmslow, Cheshire, Romany's Caravan c1955 W103001

During the Second World War, 'Romany', the Rev George Bramwell Evens, was a great favourite on the radio programme 'Children's Hour' with his nature talks, often accompanied by his dog, Raq. Evens restored this traditional caravan in the 1920s, and Raq is buried beside it.

The Frith Memory Archivist

My Beloved Village

At the age of 30 I finally left Binfield but the memories of growing up there have never left me, nor the love of the countryside which living there instilled in me. I have listed just a few of the people who lived in the village during my time there:

Pop Rapley was a small round man who lived in Red Rose Hill opposite the White Horse pub. He was always dressed in corduroy trousers, highly polished leather gaiters and brown boots. I think he earned a living by hedging and ditching and gardening jobs. One day, roughly 1949, Bill (Blocker) Sergeant, who lived next door to my family, discovered that his chickens were disappearing one by one. A fox wasn't believed to be the culprit so Pop was summoned and diagnosed the problem as the work of a badger. They traced the old badger to the drains that ran down the length of Rose Hill. With some hard pushing they rodded out the drains from Blocker's house to ours and after lifting the manhole cover outside our gates, Pop stood there with his twelve bore shotgun and duly dispatched the badger. Imagine that happening today!

The Misses Woods were a strange pair. They were sisters and lived in a house in Terrace Road next door to Timms Garage. I think their names were Freda and Vera. They both had short hair, wore very masculine clothes and rode around on big sturdy bicycles. On one occasion they showed me around their house. It was full of artefacts, mainly African, for their father was a missionary.

Binfield, Berkshire, The Stag 1892 B97301p

Norman Munday was the village barber; his shop was really the front room of his mother's house opposite Timms Garage in Terrace Road. There was only one barber chair when I was a boy but this increased to two later on. The problem was that Norman had learnt his barbering skills in the Navy, so when it came to styling he had no idea! Consequently, after about the age of 12 you tended to go into Bracknell or Wokingham for a haircut.

PC Bob Hope was a true village copper. He lived in the police house with his family. You had the impression that he knew exactly what was going on, but all you ever got was a warning. He always varied his nightly patrols so that you never knew when he'd turn up. On one occasion, a friend of mine, Ken Tugwell, and myself had fallen out with Mr Price, the butcher, who ran a small youth club. Outside Mr Price's shop was a bubble gum machine on a stand. Ken and I thought it would be a good idea to put said machine in the pond in the field opposite, with just the perspex top full of bubble gum showing. This we did and the following night PC Hope appeared, but all he said to us was 'I know you two b*ggers did it'. I don't think he was too fond of Mr Price either!

Mr Burnham was the epitome of the English gentleman, always immaculately dressed, complete with a brown trilby hat. He lived in a beautiful house in Monks Alley. At the time of the Coronation in 1953 not many people had television sets, but Mr Burnham did, so all the Scouts, Cubs, Guides and Brownies, all in uniform, marched round to Mr Burnham's house to watch the Coronation on his small black and white television. His wife, who was a very graceful lady, served us with cakes and lemonade. We thought this was marvellous.

In later years Mr Burnham moved to a bungalow nearly opposite my cottage in Terrace Road. Although my partner and I were unmarried and 'living in sin' at the time, whenever he met her in the street he would always raise his hat and say 'Good morning, Mrs Richardson', like a true gentleman.

I will always be grateful for my childhood spent in Binfield.

Terry Richardson

The Francis Frith Collection

Over 150 years ago the pioneering Victorian photographer Francis Frith set up his company with the intention of photographing all the cities, towns and villages of Britain; his two sons, and later his grandson, continued Frith's massive task.

The Francis Frith Collection now contains over 360,000 images of 7,000 cities, towns and villages taken between 1860 and 1970. Over 120,000 Frith images are available to view online, and prints of the photographs as well as a wide range of other products and local history books featuring these vintage images are available from the Frith website.

www.francisfrith.com

With Grateful Thanks to All our Contributors

All the Memories featured in this book have been contributed by visitors to the Frith website, and we are very grateful for these contributions. We are delighted to be able to continue Francis Frith's ambition of making his photographs available to as wide an audience as possible and now, by collecting the memories contributed by our website visitors, we are, together, building an archive of living history that will be valued by generations to come.

An Invitation from The Francis Frith Collection to Share Your Memories

The 'Share Your Memories' feature of our website allows members of the public to add personal memories relating to the places featured in our photographs, or comment on others already added. Seeing a place from your past can rekindle forgotten or long held memories. Why not visit the website, find photographs of places you know well and add YOUR story for others to read and enjoy? We would love to hear from you!

www.francisfrith.com/memories

For further information, trade, or enquiries please contact us at the address below:
The Francis Frith Collection, Frith's Barn, Teffont, Salisbury, Wiltshire, England SP3 5QP.
Tel: +44 (0)1722 716 376 Fax: +44 (0)1722 716 881   Email: sales@francisfrith.co.uk

www.francisfrith.com

FREE PRINT OF YOUR CHOICE

Choose any Frith photograph in this book.

Simply complete the voucher opposite and return it with your remittance for £3.50 (to cover postage and handling) and we will print the photograph of your choice in sepia and supply it in a cream mount with a burgundy rule line (overall size approx 14 x 11 inches). (The picture ref. no. can be found at the end of the photograph title in the book).

Offer valid for delivery to UK addresses only.

PLUS: **Order additional Mounted Prints**
at HALF PRICE £9.50 each (normally £19.00)

If you would like to order more Frith prints from this book, possibly as gifts for friends and family, you can buy them at half price (with no additional postage and handling costs).

PLUS: **Have your Mounted Prints framed**

For an extra £18.00 per print you can have your mounted print(s) framed in an elegant polished wood and gilt moulding, overall size approx 16 x 13 inches (no additional postage and handling required).

Mounted Print
Overall size 14 x 11 inches (355 x 280mm)

IMPORTANT!

These special prices are only available if you use this form to order.

You must use the ORIGINAL VOUCHER on this page (no copies permitted).

We can only despatch to one address.

This offer cannot be combined with any other offer.

Send completed voucher to:
The Francis Frith Collection, Frith's Barn, Teffont, Salisbury, Wiltshire SP3 5QP

I Remember When
MEMORIES OF BRITAIN

First published in the United Kingdom in 2009 by The Francis Frith Collection ISBN: 978-84589-381-1
Front cover: Caister-on-Sea, Norfolk, The Holiday Camp c1955 C450025p

and for Readers Digest in 2009 ISBN: 978-0-276-44531-6
Front cover: The Broads, Norfolk, Hunsett Mill on the River Ant at Stalham c1925 T213064t

Frontispiece: Appledore, Devon, Meeting Street 1906 55968p

The Francis Frith Collection
Frith's Barn, Teffont, Salisbury, Wiltshire, S₁ ₃
Tel: +44 (0) 1722 716 376
Email: info@francisfrith.co.uk
www.francisfrith.com